Simply Difficult
*Field Notes on Knotty
Questions of the Spiritual Life*

Susanne Folkers

Copyright © 2023 Susanne Folkers

Print: 978-1-7376718-2-4
EPub: 978-1-7376718-3-1

All rights reserved.

Unless otherwise noted, Scripture quotes taken from Holy Bible, New International Version®, NIV® Copyright ©1973, 1978, 1984, 2011 by Biblica, Inc.® Used by permission. All rights reserved worldwide.
Additional citations from The Holy Bible, English Standard Version. ESV® Text Edition: 2016. Copyright © 2001 by Crossway Bibles, a publishing ministry of Good News Publishers.
Some citations from The Lutherbibel, revised 1984. Lutherbible Standardausgabe mit Apokryphen © 1985 Deutsche Bibelgesellschaft Stuttgart indicated as LU84. Translation into English for *Simply Difficult* provided by the author.

Cover Design: Dena Taherianfar | DenaDesigns

Published by Solano Sun.
Printed in the U. S.

To make public what had been personal had not been the plan.

Throughout the years many times I said, "No,"

A few times ,"Perhaps"

And only very lately finally, "Yes."

From the bottom of my heart, *Thank you*, to all who contributed to this "Yes" in terms of content or technical realization.

A few words about this edition:

I keep my diary in German, and the first version of this book was in German. Translation into English made it necessary to edit the entries here and there, but still as little as possible. A handful entries were left out, as they are too specifically related to German context. The original entries had no titles, but they were added here as a rough guideline for what the reader can expect.

Special thanks to my friend Susan Martins Miller. Having professional experience as an editor is one thing; to work on a German book like this and with me being on the other side of the ocean still another one. With faithful stubbornness, patience, helpful critique, creative suggestions, e.g. for all the headlines, and organizational experience, she kept me on the track, checked my translation and made possible what I had not been able to imagine.

This English version is also a way of saying thanks to St. Luke's Lutheran Church in Colorado Springs, Colorado, our loving American church family during many months.

CONTENTS

Preface
1 Relating to the One Who Is Different ... 9
2 Communicating with the Different One ... 57
3 Existing in a Search for Meaning ... 72
4 Wondering as a Response to Realism ... 111
5 Doubting as Training for Reassurance ... 125
6 Teaming Up to Believe, Hope and Love Together ... 186
7 Trusting as Guidance on Tough Roads ... 227
Parting Perspectives ... 321
Footnotes ... 322

PREFACE

There are people who seem to be blessed by nature with a sunny disposition and an unshakable basic confidence. They radiate something refreshingly cheerful, infectious. And when they become Christians, it often shapes their faith life accordingly; they can tackle life without being slowed down by tedious musings. That is something very beautiful.

With me it is different. I have been living consciously as a Christian for over 50 years and am very happy and grateful for many precious experiences along the way. But I have always been a rather thoughtful melancholy kind of person. And that also shapes my life of faith; what I perceive, how I question, how intensively I have to get to the bottom of things. The extent to which I have nevertheless had to spell everything out anew over the past few years was, however, surprising even for myself—and sometimes led to sheer despair. Yet it was ultimately reassuring, strengthening, encouraging. A great help for sorting my thoughts has always been writing them down. I have written a lot of diary accordingly. And finally—prompted and encouraged by other companions—I have compiled some excerpts here in the hope that what has moved me, and still moves me, might also be helpful for others.

So in the foreground it is about thoughts mainly from a period of about nine years, often fragmentary perspectives, prayers, experiences, minimally revised or anonymized and without claim to complete coverage of the respective topic. Thought-prompts in the form of mostly rather short notes (possibly several on one day), but sometimes also longer trains of thought. Brainstormings. Attempts to simply honestly record, perceive and sort out what I believe or don't believe and to find out what that could be. It is therefore not a general reference book for Protestant Christianity! It is also possible that one or the other reader will first encounter questions and problems that he or she did not have before. But maybe someone in the reader's environment has them.

At a deeper level, it is also about sharing a lifelong experience: Discipleship does not usually follow a panoramic high road. There are easier stretches of road, but also very arduous ones; there are confirmations that we are on the right path, but also phases of uncertainty or disorientation. There are stretches of path with a good overview, but also jungle-like paths where you fight your way forward step-by-step and question whether you are still on the right path at all.

Therefore, I consciously kept the diary character of my notes and also included undeveloped, open or similar questions. Sometimes I interacted with the "daily watchword" from the annual edition of the Moravian Textbook. This all reflects the experience of how much our faith develops from a chain of snapshots. And no one remains always aware of all insights, once they have come to mind. This is true even for what one thinks one has "finally understood." Leafing through a diary can reveal the weaknesses of our memory in a disillusionary way.

I suspect that not a few Christians will find themselves in the ups and downs of the life of faith. Opening up and sharing with one another, even and especially in the lean times of our lives, does indeed also mean making ourselves vulnerable; but this is precisely the chance to deepen our relationships with one another and with our Lord, to weld us together. And I hope, therefore, that I can encourage others to confidently question what seems to be self-evident and also to deal with what is bulky and painful instead of avoiding it. It is a healing path. Jesus endures it, endures us; I have no doubt about that.

Putting together a few larger thematic complexes seemed to make sense for me, even if this inevitably creates moody pages that do not always do justice to the actual variety in daily life. Not only to read along, but to also to browse a bit through the chapters can serve as a good counterweight.

This book is not a devotional—and yet it is, in some ways.
All in all, then, simply no more and no less than:
Observations. Encounters. Experiences. Thoughtfulness.
To think about …

1
RELATING TO THE ONE WHO IS DIFFERENT

To live in a relationship—even among humans—is challenging in many ways. How much more so in a relationship between beings so different as humans and God. And still more as love is to be the essential mark of this relationship. A unique love relation. Really.

~

An Unexpected Heavenly Nudge
May 27, 2013

I have been thinking a lot about an everyday occurrence in church that made a deep impression on me. We (the choir) were sitting in the gallery. A young mother had her little baby with her, a few months old. The little one slept most of the time. But sometimes he would open his eyes and look for his mother's eyes. When their eyes met, he was content. His mother smiled, rocked his seat a little, and he fell back asleep.

Immediately I understood Jesus's message to me at that moment, "See, this is how I am toward you!" An unexpected heavenly nudge in a difficult phase of life.

This loving eye contact is what we absolutely need in our relationship with Jesus. Knowledge, understanding (my natural focus by nature) is very important, but not the most important thing of all. If we try to find our peace there, we will not succeed. Certainty that loving eyes have us in view is the most important thing. Why? We are needy and limited beings who long to be safe and not alone. Individual loving contacts and touches are signs that point to the constant love behind them, which remains present even if the touch is not felt at a particular moment.

The question is: What does eye contact mean with regard to the risen and invisible Lord? How is it possible? Where can it take place?

It is not something we can force by any kind of technique or behavior.

It can happen during prayer.

It can happen when suddenly a word from him not only comes to our mind, but touches our heart.

It can happen when we celebrate the Lord's Supper and recognize him at that moment as the true Host.

It can happen in daily life (as in the beginning with the choir).

And when it happens, it is an indication of the highest reality.

A Touching Vision and the Certainty of Nearness
May 27, 2013

As I was looking through my journal, I came across a note from a few years ago (why are we such forgetful people?). We were together in a short evening service at that time, reflecting on Jesus's journey to the cross. The scripture reading was from John 13; Jesus washing his disciples' feet. Suddenly I had a very intense inner "vision" (extremely extraordinary for me) of Jesus respectfully and tenderly taking my feet in his hands. He, who deserves all the respect of all humanity, is so close to me, an individual woman. He, who is the Lord of all creation, is so focused on the one person in front of him—indescribable impression.

The task remains not to fix on his absence, when such touching experiences are missing (because they are rather the big exception). Instead, it is necessary to trust in the subsurface reality to which these exceptional experiences refer: He is near and remains near—only in a way that is hidden from my senses, yet he effectively protects me and ensures that I do not collapse under my burden. He will not let me out of his sight. He has sealed this with his life and death: He, who in prayer (John 17) testifies to his heavenly Father that he has not lost any of those entrusted to him, as promised—and as befits the Good Shepherd. He who even in the last minutes of his life was concerned about the future of his mother (John 19:6). And the day will come when he will wipe away my last tears.

We do not live only from experiences nor only from the Word—we need both, and both interact with each other.

Paul's experience of the shipwreck (Acts 27:22) fits here. He gets the promise of being rescued from the shipwreck, but that does not correspond to the human ideal that God would rather just prevent the shipwreck right away and all the panic and pain that comes with it.

I am still often tempted to think that I need more knowledge. But often certainty actually is much more important (without simply playing off knowledge against it); certainty about Jesus's character, presence, promises, ways of acting—because this certainty leads to serenity and flexibility and a way out of false fixations. And it grows from his Word, time with him, listening to other witnesses, and seeing his traces of faithfulness and care in their lives.

"But I have calmed and quietened myself, I am like a weaned child with its mother; like a weaned child I am content." (Psalm 131:2)

A Faithful Love
June 29, 2013

I am still very much haunted by an encounter. I met a very dear old couple from our church community in front of a supermarket, pushing their shopping cart together very slowly. Their only son had died of cancer at the age of 40. They had held his hand until the end. Now they themselves are facing their last stage of life, drawing strength from prayer. But of course this does not stop the process of increasing weakness. Very likely they will not leave this world together at the same time. And they ask themselves, "If *I* am the last, who will hold *my* hand?"

Facing the ultimate loneliness deserves respect; it is completely realistic, but also gets very under the skin. How blessed is the one who knows from experience that Jesus will always be able to keep his promise of faithful love and stay by our side; that he will find ways to make us sense his presence even where human love reaches its limits. He has been through it himself; he knows what dying feels like.

Yes, that is what counts in the end. Psalm 131 came to my mind again. This love counts: "My heart is not proud, Lord, my eyes are not haughty; I do not concern myself with great matters or things too wonderful for me. But I have calmed and quietened myself, I am like a weaned child with its mother; like a weaned child I am content. Israel, put your hope in the Lord both now and for evermore."

On Forsaking First Love—Or Not
August 22, 2013

On the keyword "to forsake the first love," I read Revelation 2:1 and following.

Frightening. One can do so many right things—and still lose the center: the first love. This is the heart of everything.

And also: "This is what the Lord says: 'I remember the devotion of your youth, how as a bride you loved me and followed me through the wilderness, through a land not sown.'" (Jeremiah 2:2)

Jeremiah 2:8 adds to this with a profound description: "The priests did not ask, Where is the Lord ... ?" They probably know already—the unquestioning matter-of-factness with which they live is evaluated as "they do not live the relationship." Routine is the death of every relationship.

Consider John 21: Peter is not asked whether he has finally understood and accepted the scriptural evidence of Jesus as Messiah, but whether he loves his Lord.

Again and again it is about the heart, about love, relationship, passion. Everything else only serves this or should be an expression of it or arises from it. Actually. Do we realize that enough? And our congregation? There is a lot of talk about trust, and sure, there can be love in it. But who would spontaneously answer to the question: "What is being a Christian about?" with an answer: "About the restoration and living of a love relationship with our invisible, but present Creator and Lord!"? Perhaps, however, the frequent conscious formulation of this center could lead to a change of consciousness among us, to a search for spiritual life that is more than guarding traditions and values; if we would kind of try to hammer this in as a learning goal! Surely learning to live as a Christian means learning to hear and understand the language of Jesus more and more, and trying to help one another to do so! To ask: "What makes Jesus lovable?" would incidentally also direct our gaze away from our presumed or real needs first of all to the person of Jesus and thus take faith out of the trap of being purpose-oriented ("What does that get me?"). Love needs amazement.

Many years ago, I once tried to change the big bill "Love of God" into small coins to get things more concrete. This resulted in a memo for the refrigerator. To fill up the overview again and again with suitable Bible passages is a good exercise, from which joy and amazement can grow:

God's love is a reason for celebration, for worship. It is expressed:
- in his *thoughts* about us:
  - thoughts of peace
  - like a mother, he never forgets us
- in his *feeling* for us
- in his *deeds*:
  - redemption, forgiveness
  - on this basis every day is a new beginning
  - protection
  - care
  - carrying through
  - guidance
  - consolation
  - hope
  - ethical orientation
  - meaningful tasks
  - healing

If the relationship with Jesus is to be our most important concern, is to occupy the most important place in our thinking, feeling, willing, doing—what are the possibilities for shaping it?

Relationships are cultivated by:

With people	*With God*
talking with each other	praying
listening to each other	church, Bible reading, etc.
pursuing the same values, the same goals	pursuing the same values, the same goals

working together, working for each other, being committed	shaping everyday life in his Spirit, with him and for him
eating together	communion
celebrating, rejoicing, mourning together	music, worship

The Heavenly Counterweights of Everyday Life
August 24, 2013

Learning to love Jesus (again)—what can that look like? John Eldredge[1] points into the direction: To connect every experience with Jesus; I take up the thread. Everything beautiful (now on vacation, for example: from Italian bed linen to houses decorated with flowers to a pretty butterfly) ultimately comes from him.

Everything that I rejoice in comes from him.

All friendship among people, all love, all understanding, all reconciliation, all tenderness, all romance comes from him.

Everything I marvel at comes from him, is his invention, reflects his glory and imagination.

All work that succeeds, all toil that leads to a good result, ultimately comes from him.

All small and great victories over evil come from him.

He has given me senses to perceive all this and a mind that can understand all this as a reference to him.

And should.

But does not do that automatically.

And has to practice it consciously exactly for that reason.

And then "must" take the step from (rather distanced) reflection to (heartfelt) expression in prayer.

The little things of everyday life often seem so inconspicuous, so self-evident—and thus they escape us as given counterweights, loving heavenly indications against what pushes itself as oppressively negative into the foreground or even tries to present itself as the actual reality.

So learning to love is actually very simple: Learning to pray in everyday life. To *ex*press *im*pressions again, in joy, amazement, petitions, etc. To supplement "thinking about" with "talking to."

Nothing new, of course. I just have to do it instead of just thinking about it—without the thought of telling myself something with it, but with the thought of expressing something true and thus acknowledging it (and hoping that this expressing has an assuring effect)

Theology of Night Wonderings
January 14, 2014

Night thoughts, written down in an unsorted way, starting from the question what happiness means.

Feeling of happiness:

Where I am oblivious of myself, at one with myself, living in the present, absorbed in something greater, where I "am" amazement—there I feel a touch of eternity. (Goethe's Faust: "Moment, bide awhile, you are so beautiful!")

Is this perhaps a characteristic of life that has prospects—the "actual"? Life with a sense of both reality and transcendence?

Happiness of being close to God (motto of the year):

In dogmatic theology and church history, there are always these steep theses that one must love God for his own sake. At first, this sounds very noble, but in the next moment also frustrating, because the possibility of implementation is obviously missing. This lack is then seen as an indication of the sin in us. But I ask myself: Isn't there perhaps a faulty reasoning involved?

It's about love, and love is about relationship—how can God mean anything to us apart from relationship with us? Isn't that completely abstract? He is our creator, savior, and so on. How are we to think that away? (Even if we could, what would remain?) There is always something selfish in it. But does selfish really hit the mark?

The moment I expect something from somebody, I also honor him with it, take his care seriously, recognize his gifts, prove my trust.

Otherwise, love takes place in a vacuum, doesn't it?

Another thought on God's kind of love:

Human love rejoices in the joy of the other one, suffers with his sadness, grieves over his indifference or rejection, longs for being together. If it were not so, one would be indifferent to the other. So love is actually always connected with need, with longing, with potential deficits. Should this be different with God, who is the inventor of love and relationship and whom we should reflect in any case? The philosophers and old theologians do not get tired of emphasizing that we have not earned God's love and that he gives gifts out of absolute freedom. Sure, it also sounds kind of wrong to say that God lacks something, God who is the epitome of fullness and happiness and perfection in person. But somehow it sounds just as wrong to emphasize that he is happy independently of us. One wants to preserve his sovereignty and prevent God from becoming a caricature, a helpless grandpa or something like that, and that concern is certainly valid. But isn't that going to the wrong extreme? Is it not precisely a sign of strength, for example, to bear rejection passively without oppressing or forcing the other person? The Calvinist theologians try to keep the reasons of election by God for salvation pure from everything that has a point of reference in us, out of concern for pride, fear of belittling our sinfulness, etc.; but doesn't this actually—contrary to the positive intentions here—make the Creator look bad? Appropriate language is a difficult thing.

Jesus's Eyes of Love to Help
February 6, 2014

I started reading John 13 and following.

Jesus's love, until the end, reflects the heavenly Father. If he looked with eyes of love, respect, mercy at people in the shadow, in need, then this is still true today. This is his nature.

Why then does he not help more clearly?

He helps through closeness, guarding, strengthening, whether we perceive it or not; he is with us, his gaze rests on us. Like that of parents at the crib, who cannot yet explain or spare the little ones many things.

From such realization, love in return can grow from us. And hope that it will come true: "Those who look to him are radiant; their faces are never covered with shame." (Psalm 34:5)

The Big Story Behind the Little Stories
March 3, 2014

To get to the bottom of what is elementary, fundamentally important, it is worth asking: What does change when someone becomes a Christian?

Attempt at a catchy answer:

There is a new relationship in life and one begins to sense the big story behind the many little life stories, one begins to see things in a new light.

The ordinariness becomes transparent with respect to the author.

Or said with another image: There is a tour guide; a meaning, a future.

Learning to Live in the Greater Truth
April 2, 2014

There is a greater truth that encompasses all our little lives.

We should and can learn to live in it. Experience him, in whom the immeasurably great truth becomes humanly illustrative.

Jesus speaks. He wants the relationship with us.

To experience Jesus—what can be meant by this?

If he appeared to me alive as he did to the disciples, it would be about: Seeing, hearing, feeling; making experiences together; witnessing his reactions to what is happening.

Now that he is invisible:

Seeing does not apply.

Hearing is on the different "channels" (biblical word, also mediated by people, dreams etc.).

Feeling is ambiguous, but happens occasionally (but different from back then in Israel, of course).

Making experiences together—this is a question of how aware I am of his word. He assures me of his presence.

The inventor of joy rejoices with me.

He has compassion with me.

He shares my sadness over unbelief, incomprehension, indifference, hard-heartedness. He knows this from his own experience. In this respect, we share in his suffering at such moments.

He does not abandon me when the attitudes just described come through in myself.

He shares my pain when I am ill. He came as a physician in a comprehensive sense. As a savior.

The Invitation of Love
April 8, 2014

"The Son of Man has nowhere to lay his head." (Luke 9:57ff)

Jesus offers—at least here—nothing to these who are willing to become followers except himself, his nearness. No bribe. Even if this is only one way of his invitation (he invites also the thirsty, etc., who feel their need and get presented with the prospect of satisfaction by him):

He does not lead to a goal (in the first place), he is the goal—or the communion with him; in his closeness then to experience and to suffer the variety of life and to go through it. Only if the concrete things of life are subordinated under the relationship with him and arranged in his larger script, will they have their right place (which, seen from the creator's perspective, they should anyway have in principle, without question). It is (first of all) not about having things or people or dreams, not about getting "something," keeping it, but about being something or becoming something again, being transformed into his image. Therefore, always let go. He gave everything for us (Philippians 2:5ff), for us the same applies. The Greatest Commandment is to love God and love others.

We tend, however, to base his love for us more on our well-being (and thus to assure ourselves of it) than on the events of the cross, on his giving himself for us.

Another important thought in this context: Concentration on the essential feature of God's love—which in itself is correct—can tempt us to overlook the lasting strangeness in it. But the world does not revolve around us, although we are so important to him that he lives and dies with us and for us. This seems contradictory; but consciously thinking ourselves into this tension helps us to find the larger framework we need, so that we do not build up expectations like little babies whose thinking revolves only around their need fulfillment.

Missing God because of Missing the Map
April 10, 2014

I was reviewing a pastor's meeting with a professor of systematic theology giving a talk about the meaning of the cross. It feels like having been in a wrong movie. In short:

Hell: does not exist.

Devil: In a way not really either.

Atonement: no.

Omnipotence of God: no.

God's love: Yes. Powerless love.

The moderator afterwards gives thanks very much for the refreshing update of times at university long ago.

Triggered by that, I looked up what official church websites say about some of the topics today, with similarly frustrating results.

More and more I see:

- If our Volkskirche* presents being a Christian differently from the way life in discipleship is biblically seen (and from the way it is still predominantly seen and lived in worldwide Christianity),
- if it withholds important elements, reduces them, reinterprets them, empties them,
- then this practically amounts to the fact that people are deprived of the possibility of experiencing the reality of God for no other reason than lack of information or thanks to misinformation.

For they lack the map, the equipment, the training of perception or whatever images one wants to take. Approaching the truth about our reality is a dynamical process for which we need Scripture plus other Christians plus practice in daily life plus communication with our Lord regarding all of that. It is a holistic concept. But most pastors hardly talk about that on the few occasions where nominal Christians still show up. Instead, people are simply told that they are accepted and loved by God, by baptism. But they don't notice anything of it in their everyday life. When something bad happens, they naturally ask themselves: "Why does God allow this, if he supposedly loves me?" The promise of God's love without binding discipleship is cheap grace. Liberalism may intend love, but produces disappointment in this way.

*Volkskirche refers to churches made up of members who largely belong by cultural tradition, such as the Lutheran and Reformed churches and the Catholic Church. For centuries in Germany, it was a duty of the citizen to belong to the church. Even in the last century, more than 90 percent of the population belonged to the Volkskirchen, though membership was nominal and separated from personal conviction. Now, with increasing secularization, for the first time in German history, membership in the Volkskirchen has decreased to less than half the population.

The Persistence of Love
April 19, 2014

Jesus's loneliness on the cross is reflected in the everyday reality of our Volkskirche. Good Friday services are attended by only a few, a downward trend since years (I remember full churches at least on this occasion 30 years ago).

But Jesus knew this from the beginning and did not let it stop him from doing what had to be done. And what would benefit even those who, for whatever reason, would remain ignorant of the whole event (benefit: At least in the sense that Jesus in an objective sense weakened the powers of evil). Selfless, giving love. Without reservations. Utter devotion, not: "service by the book," because most would not appreciate or understand it after all.

And: When we say goodbye to a dying person, we try to reassure the person that we will take care of those who are left behind. On Golgotha it is the other way around: Jesus takes care of his mother while still in the throes of death and entrusts her to John. Lord of the event until the end. And love in person. Once again, how far away are we humans from this?

Longing for Communion
October 6, 2014

Observations on how Jesus's love is expressed and how it is not.

"And he said to them, 'I have eagerly desired to eat this Passover with you before I suffer.'" (Luke 22:15)

Jesus longs for communion with his people; the fact that so far they have hardly more than a clue what it is really all about and of all that is still to come, is not an obstacle, and neither is all their human and spiritual weakness. They are his people. He loves them. That is why he longs for being together with them.

This statement is a pledge that the Lord's love is something real, even if it has become more obscure for us again after the resurrection. But the nature of our Lord does not change.

Luke 22:31 and following: "Simon, Simon, Satan has asked to sift all of you as wheat. But I have prayed for you, Simon, that your faith may not fail."

Jesus did not pray that the process of sifting would cease, but that Peter would be able to go through. Paul has the corresponding experience at the shipwreck. (Acts 27:22)

What Makes Our Value?
November 5, 2014

What makes our value? We are original children of the Creator; he died for us. That's how much we mean to him. But for our confirmation students, for example, this usually remains bloodless, much too far away. Now I thought of an example, even if it is still bumpy. A big Hollywood star (e.g., George Clooney) is on a boat with teenagers on the occasion of an advertising campaign; a teenager falls into the water, Clooney jumps into the water and saves him. What would that mean for the teenager: "He did that for me!?" What Jesus did was much more, but much less vivid. If we somehow managed to convey that for us this is just as real as the Clooney story could be, then we would be one step further!

Finding on the topic "Becoming a Christian means learning to rethink": "Spiritual vision is a practiced preference for biblical views."[2]

Freedom Is Too Big
November 15, 2014

Yesterday, the question of election and freedom of will came up briefly in a group.

On the one hand, it is said ultimately, God does everything. On the other hand, we also do something. That is paradox.

Paradox does not mean one is appearance and the other reality, but both are reality. This is true even if we cannot really imagine this in view of the hierarchical gradient between God and humans.

God's action does not switch off our person, our individuality, but switches it on. We may then spontaneously immediately think of foreign control; the comparison with robots comes to mind, or as if we are being hijacked (as in the novel *The Host*, where aliens invade human bodies and take over the controls); but that does not hit the mark. That would be devilish kind of domination, because it wants to reduce us to mere tools. Divine dominion, on the other hand, wants to develop us into personalities of our own. We lack the appropriate words and concepts for it; freedom is too big, unfreedom somehow too small.

A Paradigm for Times of Darkness
April 13, 2015

Last night I woke up and John 13:1 came to my mind, and spontaneously stations of the Passion story passed by me in parallel, in such an impressive way that I still could write that down after I had got up.

"He loved them to the end" (according to John 13:1).

They would not yet understand the deep meanings of the washing of the feet. But *he* loved them to the end.

They would not yet understand his willingness to die (despite years of close fellowship and instruction). But *he* loved them to the end.

They would not be able to stay awake and pray with him in his final battle. But *he* loved them to the end.

They sank into despair, disregarding his words and perspective of hope. But *he* loved them to the end.

In what does his love toward them show itself? Doesn't it seem to be a kind of empty word?

He did not give them deeper insight and understanding. He did not overcome their weariness. He did not cast out their cowardice. He did not prove to be a comforter. He did not shorten their time of anguish, despair, and grief. He left them in their agonizing illusion of frustration and loss, feeling trapped in a dead end.

He simply went his way, did his work. He did what he did for their sake.

This is the factual, objective solid part of his love.

Did he act in it like an unfeeling robot? Certainly not.

He, who cited the double commandment of love as the highest commandment, was the first and only one to fulfill it with a pure and passionate heart. This is the emotional part of his love, though often hidden from our eyes.

Yes, for sure there is an element of strangeness in his relationship with us. We must not forget: He is human, but not only human.

But he knew: The time would come when the tears of sadness would turn to tears of joy, when the inner eyes and ears of his followers would finally open and grasp the truth about his steadfast intense love.

And he was determined to carry them to that point whether they knew it or not—until they would realize it.

The Greek word for "end" also means "goal."

I think this can be seen as a kind of paradigm for times of darkness in our lives.

God's Doing Cannot Be Grasped
June 17, 2015

The theme of election and predestination came up again, in thinking together about the question of how responsible or "capable of faith" are the people who request pastoral services (baptism, confirmation, wedding, funeral) that include promises or confessions, even though they otherwise don't want to have anything to do with the church.

On the one hand, I rely on the fact that Jesus is not lying when he says that the hairs on our head are numbered and there is no coincidence; on the other hand, this cannot mean that it is God who instills in people cruel thoughts, desire to destroy and torment—or that God has made the devil evil. In God there is no darkness (1 John 1:5). Things must be more complex than we can grasp; the image of the two sides of a coin does not fit. Nor does Luther's talk of the hidden God—for that amounts to something like concluding that the revealed God is only a mask, a sham reality. We slip again and again into the trap of a mechanistic worldview, where everything can ultimately be traced back to a simple relationship of cause and reality; but the God-human relationship is not comparable, for instance, with the programmer-computer relationship. The distinction between God's *doing* and God's *allowing* may seem like splitting hairs, but it is not. It keeps alive the knowledge that God's doing cannot be grasped with our categories. We need such linguistic devices. One of them is to say what is *not* meant by God's omnipotence. Even if logical problems arise, this is closer to reality than a logic that is only at first sight coherent. For such a logic exceeds its range and competence at the moment when it makes the epitome of good ultimately the cause of evil and thus the devil—and thus ends in a meaningless statement, an emptying of the terms *good* and *evil*.

Freedom beyond Our Knowledge
June 19, 2015

And again predestination, triggered by John 15:22–24: "If I had not come and spoken to them, they would not be guilty of sin; but now they have no excuse for their sin. ... If I had not done among them the works no-one else did, they would not be guilty of sin. As it is, they have seen, and yet they have hated both me and my Father."

According to the Reformers, it is enough that one has received the right information, that the physical ears and eyes have been confronted with it—even if God at the same time keeps the decisive ears and eyes of the heart closed and thus actively prevents a positive reaction, while he leaves humans in his illusion of the self-determined possibility of choice. If Jesus's words would be construed in such a way, then one would have to unmask the offer of God as a sham. His real and literally effective will stands in contradiction to the outwardly testified one (just as well one could preach to a rock). In the human realm, such behavior would be called deceitful, lying, pretending, fake, duplicitous, speaking with a forked tongue. This is absurd in light of a God who is the embodiment of truthfulness, sincerity, and love. And Jesus himself explicitly says that lip service is not what counts, but deeds—which again would be a self-contradiction, because God would fall short of his own moral claim.

If the Reformers' interpretation of Jesus's words in John 15 is to be excluded, this can only mean that Jesus here points to a relative freedom which is opened in the encounter with him; how and how big or small is beyond our knowledge. But to assume in principle the existence of such a scope of decision makes sense.

Loves Beams Joy
June 19, 2015

"As the Father has loved me, so have I loved you. Now remain in my love. If you keep my commands, you will remain in my love, just as I have kept my Father's commands and remain in his love. I have told you this so that my joy may be in you and that your joy may be complete." (John 15:9–11)

Reflecting on the last verse, Andreas told of the baptismal conversation in the morning. The father had just come back from work, and his wife handed him his three-month-old baby girl. The father beamed all over his face at his little one, but she could not return it—not yet. When the moment comes when she smiles back, his joy will become complete, the joy of both of them—an impressive picture!

Why Be a Christian?
July 15, 2015

Why should a person become a Christian?

We owe our life to our Creator.

Our life also runs towards him.

According to his will, we should live in this world and shape it.

Either people face reality or reality will catch up with them at the latest in death.

Becoming a Christian means becoming a realist.

To witness means:

Using God's information to subordinate our lives to our Creator, to make them understandable, to help us cope and to shape them.

Living in discipleship is "useful" because it is appropriate to reality, because it is right, because it corresponds to the truth. The "usefulness" cannot be evaluated independently of the primary! question of truth.

Divine Feelings
October 8, 2015

Further thought that it makes quite a certain sense to speak of divine "feelings": Jesus, for example, also took only three disciples to his prayer in Gethsemane. It's striking that he does not ask all of them! Likewise: "he longed for" the common Passover; admittedly, this can also be understood as conditioned by his human nature, but on the other hand, human nature is created in the image of God. In other words, the desire to share things is anchored in the essence of the Trinity.

As If Abiding Would Be So Simple
February 26, 2016

On the expression "abide in Jesus" (e.g. John 15):

I realize I often have a hard time feeling and expecting the kind of closeness that the word *abide* suggests.

It seems to me more accurate how C. S. Lewis describes the experience of the inhabitants of Narnia: they see their king Aslan occasionally and then live again more or less for a long time on his words and memory. This reflects the dynamics of the relationship, which cannot remain without effect.

It is one of the basic human experiences that encounters "freeze" into snapshots, pictures, and possibly also fade with time. The temporal and spatial distance causes something like a loss of reality of the distant person. A living person is always more than we can perceive, take in, hold onto. This is already true *in* the encounter, and distance adds to it, even with people we love and know well. How much more is this true for encounters with God!

Of course, all this is described from the human, subjective perspective. But the objectively constant presence of God remains rather abstract. Or better: It's not constant subjectively perceptible truth. But in order to counteract, to prevent false expectations and disappointments, it is helpful—for me in any case—to describe the subjective way of experience in a very consciously *differentiated* way and not to sugar-coat it boastfully, as if all this were so simple.

"Do You Love Me?"
March 3, 2016

Yesterday I was still thinking in vain about an approach to address a friend about her tendency to be afraid of God. This morning, when I woke up, I suddenly had the scene before my eyes where Jesus asks Peter, "Do you love me?" (John 21:15ff) And I could imagine using this scene to simply ask her two questions: a) how she would answer, b) whether she thinks Jesus loves her.

Based on this, I thought how I myself would respond if Jesus stepped in front of me now. And my spontaneous reaction was a yes, a deep sigh of relief—all the fascination, joy, hope, longing, which has been connected with his person over all the years, suddenly stood before my eyes and the idea that he would suddenly turn out to be "unmistakably" true and real in such a situation was overwhelming even now in half-sleep. (It all passed by me in a few seconds).

What a feeling it must be when the day is really here …

After-thought: In the literal sense *noteworthy*, what gifts shared burdens can contain! Without vicarious reflection for the friend, this probably wouldn't have crossed my mind right now.

Being Small in a Gigantic Place
April 21, 2016

As a small human being, I need a space of security. I can hardly live with the gigantic size of the universe.

That's why I try to create an emotionally effective counterweight to the overwhelming impression of the universe.

The problem is: The emotional and mental change of view away from the uncanny size of the universe and the even greater Creator to his nearness succeeds, depends on concentrating on the metaphors of the shepherd, father, mother, friend, etc. But then these images, because they are shaped by human experiences and expectations, can in turn become a stumbling block in the sense of the theodicy question (God and his relationship to evil). The balancing act between the awareness of God's greatness, holiness and strangeness on the one hand and goodness and closeness on the other hand is and remains difficult. Both are concentrated in the cross.

A Path Back to First Love
May 7, 2016

How much does longing reveal about the measure of love?

If I painfully miss the sense of God's nearness, I should consider this thought before I see my condition blacker than justified? On the question of what a path "back to first love" might look like:

Love lives from wonder.

What do I admire about God?

What can I infer from the world and nature, despite brokenness?

What do I admire about Jesus?

"Remember"—not without reason we are challenged to do this again and again in the Bible.

God's Compassion in Our Despair
August 12, 2016

Jesus says, "I am moved within"; "I have compassion for these people;" literally, "my bowels turn" (Mark 8:1–9). This is a vivid description of how the body is involved in the pain of the soul. According to my study Bible, this is always used when talking about God's or Jesus's mercy, when Jesus feels compassion, sees the misery of people. Our God is a passionate, compassionate God, not a cold and distant principle. He who created our capacity to love and to mourn, to rejoice and to weep, knows it himself. Our feeling is a small echo of his great love.

Someone asked for intercession for a family affected by suicide.

Thereupon all this went through my mind again, together with the critical question: Isn't the reference to God's compassionate being in such a situation of despair just hollow talk that can't really help?

No. Error in thought.

First, when people express their sympathy, such as in a letter, and this comes across as sincere, then this also comforts us, even if they can do nothing else. We know that we are not alone. And that feels good. That in itself is a certain relief and precious.

Then second, God, after all, surpasses this experience. He not only informs us of his compassion, but he also promises to get us through. He has the resources that no human being has, even though Hollywood heroes in disaster movies, of course, always promise that they will surely save their people (which regularly throws me out of the movie emotionally because it is such obvious nonsense). The road may be terribly difficult and often is, for whatever reason, and that can make us rebel or weary of life, but *he* cannot lie nor overestimate himself. Even if we give up on ourselves, God will not give up. No one can snatch us from his caring hands, not even we ourselves.

The Perplexity of God's Wrath
September 14, 2016

In Bible study, we try to think our way into John's Revelation.

"Talk to God about the positive aspects of His wrath."

This phrase from the workbook we are using is a successful impulse. We become aware:

Anger is an expression of passionate love that does not watch indifferently as beloved creatures perish in the captivity of evil. The God who is angry and calls injustice by its name and ultimately puts it out of action has given his life as Savior. We must never lose sight of that.

Another train of thought that I wrote down some time ago and found again: Is hell a concept unworthy of a God of love and should be abandoned as obsolete?

1. It all depends on whether hell is a concept based on revelation or originates from human ideas.

2. We must also consider that this hell exists only if this God exists —who is absolutely good and just and love in person. If he exists, then the existence of hell must be compatible with this absolutely good being, or everything else would be nonsense. But that would logically mean, we can assume that everyone will recognize his judgment when the time has come for that, due to total insight into connections, which we may still lack now.

The God, who is not stingy now will not be then.

The God who now likes nothing better than to give, will do so also then.

But also:

The God who does not call evil good now will not do it then either.

The God who does not let evil be inconsequential now will not do it then either.

3. Why does God punish if he wants voluntary obedience? Possible answer: Under sinful behavior the whole creation suffers. If God would let everything run without comment and consequence, the weakest would have no protection, no lawyer, who stands up for their right. All the corresponding words in the Bible to the contrary would remain empty words, would give the lie to God.

4. We very easily lose sight of what God is *fighting for*: Love, mercy, honesty, humility, modesty, goodness, justice.

5. We also very easily lose sight of the fact that for us, responsibility is part of human dignity, which we hold so dear in other contexts. Only when it comes to the negative consequences of our own responsibility do we prefer to retreat into self-pity. Like the young adult who says: "I'm experienced enough to be able to drive my dad's car," and who, after the accident following a visit to the disco, says: "I don't have that much experience yet ..."

6. Of course, it would be best if we did the good out of conviction and refrained from the evil out of conviction; but the second best is still, the good happens and the evil does not, even if the motivation behind it leaves much to be desired. For the one who was not murdered because the gangster hesitated at the last moment for fear of punishment, it is not the motivation that is important, but that he lives.

Words from the Eternal Home
September 29, 2016

Someone commented on the high demand of the Sermon on the Mount (Matthew 5–7) and how he felt the oppressive weight of his "lagging behind." I became aware of the following while reflecting on it.

It is always an enriching experience to see how the same words of the Bible can trigger different thoughts, depending on where we are on our personal journey through life.

I can very well relate to the feeling of not being able to live up to the Sermon on the Mount. Nevertheless, something else is in the foreground for me at the moment. For several months now, I have been struggling again and again with the impression that God seems to be somehow far away, even somehow unreal. One morning I "accidentally" read Matthew 5. And it felt a bit like coming home and hearing Jesus's voice again, to which I could just say "Amen." Yes, the way Jesus describes things—that's how they should be. More specifically, *we* should be like *that*. Then the whole world would look *very* different—and better, of course. God did not keep his life-giving and protecting truth as a secret, but he raised his voice clearly.

Spontaneously, these thoughts downright warmed my heart, and they are doing so again now. I can understand the joy in God's good commandments that Psalm 119 reflects. And in the Sermon on the Mount, it is especially the Beatitudes, "words from the eternal home," values which deserve to be named values.

Recognizing Character
October 22, 2016

How do you recognize the character of a person? It is not directly visible. But: It shows itself in the words plus in the deeds plus in the harmony between both. That lead me to the next question.

How was God's moral nature recognized in the Old Testament? We see it in Jesus, but where did it become "tangible" for the Jews? Answer: In the law, in which God expresses his values, his will; also in the passionate struggle of the prophets, who fight for the implementation of God's will and impressively describe God's suffering under this disregard. I have often kept in mind that in our love God's love is reflected and imaged, in our joy, God's joy. I have to extend this further also to truthfulness, faithfulness, justice. Psalm 119 is a good example of how the prayerful comes to such a high "opinion" of God that triggers his worship (assuming that it comes from within and not from a sense of duty). The existence and content of the law allow us to infer God's character and therefore inspire hope in the ultimate victory of good.

Love that Allows Rebellion
November 2, 2016

From Bible reading today: "Brother will betray brother to death, and a father his child; children will rebel against their parents and have them put to death." (Matthew 10:21)

This reminded me of Isaiah 49:15: "Can a mother forget the baby at her breast and have no compassion on the child she has borne? Though she may forget, I will not forget you!"

The same God, who created and knows parental love has nevertheless arranged this world in such a way that children can fight parents (and vice versa), for evil and against good. What a scenario. However: The parents, who mourn over their rebellious children, can rely on God's compassion (see Isaiah's word above, as well as Luke 15), on his strengthening closeness and care. He knows what it means when selfless love is rejected on the deepest possible level, beyond our imagination. Because he *is* love. His love is not limited to the parents, but remains in force also towards the children. Otherwise his love would be less than human love, since already parental love does not end when children turn their backs on it. Again, however, this divine love consciously allows the freedom of rebellion and accepts the price of own suffering and pain, where we as humans would sometimes rather try to hinder our children with all possible and also actually impossible means because of our need of protection.

Eternal Traces
November 3, 2016

"Do not suppose that I have come to bring peace to the earth ... a man's enemies will be the members of his own household ... Whoever does not take up their cross and follow me is not worthy of me. Whoever finds their life will lose it, and whoever loses their life for my sake will find it. Anyone who welcomes you welcomes me, and anyone who welcomes me welcomes the one who sent me. ... If anyone gives even a cup of cold water to one of these little ones who is my disciple, truly I tell you, that person will certainly not lose their reward." (Matthew 10:34–42)

God is not a God of false promises and illusions. We are born into a war between good and evil. We must not be surprised by the difficult sides of reality. We know little of the full picture. Very little. Just enough to have reliable reasons to hold onto faith, love, hope; just enough to know God's trustworthy and lovable character; just enough to choose the right side in the battle, to accept and live our calling. Every deed, however inconspicuous it may seem, will leave eternal traces.

Alternatives beyond Our Imagination
November 18, 2016

At the funeral of a young mother who died suddenly, here at the grave, so obviously without control over our lives, comes the test of what foundation we have built our lives on—sand or rock, as Jesus says in the story that begins in Matthew 7:24. Is Easter a fairy tale or truth? If truth, then what Jesus promised is also true—that he has gone to prepare eternal dwellings for us. Then there is hope also for the way to this goal. Then we are not alone, but have our Creator and Savior with us, going before us and being by our side, although we may certainly still often feel alone. As I watched the young teenager walk away from the grave, scenes of her future life flashed through my mind. First love, without mom to share it with; steps into her own independent life or job without mom; marriage without mom, children without mom, to name just the major stages of life. And surely the daily "little" versions of "without" are equally painful, at least for a long time.

Can anyone face such a prospect without complete despair, or at least becoming bitter?

I think it is most possible when one knows there is a loving Lord who never loses control and by whose hand I can walk safely, no matter how weak and shaky my legs may feel. The great challenge of life is to answer this question: Is there a living and loving God whom I can trust, and how can I live with him? Finding a positive answer is not easy. I know how fragile my faith often is, how severely attacked, over and over again. It is good to know that God remains faithful even when we fail.

An image came back to my mind that has accompanied me for many years: A man sits in a small boat on a canal, and the finger of God creates before him, piece by piece, the continuation of the canal. *There* is hope for the teenager, the little sister, the husband, the family— for everyone. We only know what will be impossible from now on, the things listed above, for example. But he will find alternatives beyond our imagination.

In a way, we must live as if the next hour is our last. What were the last words we said to those with whom we live? Have we really done everything to seek peace with everyone? Have we been faithful to the people and tasks for which we are responsible?

And on the other hand, we can't really do that at all. It exceeds our limitations, and we have to live as if we have enough time to fulfill our responsibilities and obligations. Difficult balance … challenging balance … maybe impossible balance!

It felt very surreal at the cemetery today—both death and the message of life.

Is Genuine Faith Still There?
November 21, 2016

What can it look like to get back to the "first love"?

All I know at the moment is: I wish that everything is true, and I am extremely happy when everything is true. Is this something similar to "I believe, help my unbelief?" Should I interpret it as a sign that at least something of genuine faith is still there? And is it enough that the anticipatory living on "as if" is not to be evaluated as hypocrisy, but as faithfulness in times of much attacked and challenged faith? My confirmation verse comes to mind more often. "I no longer live, but Christ lives in me." (Galatians 2:20) Perhaps Jesus's quiet voice?

Knots in the Head
January 3, 2017

The Trinity.

Christians profess the triune nature of God, but most of them prefer to give thinking about it a wide berth and leave it to the theologians. One simply gets knots in the head! However, one book on the subject unexpectedly captivated and kept moving me: Michael Reeves, *Delighting in the Trinity*.[3] For example, Reeves asks questions that at first glance seem simply outlandish, but then open up surprising approaches to the subject. (What did God do before creation? If there is a God, why something else?) Of course, even Reeves cannot make the incomprehensible comprehensible; but he awakens a sense of the beauty and the deep and realistic meaning of this mystery, wonder, joy. Therefore, a few impulses here.

Very important is the reference to the experience that we usually have a pre-understanding of "God" and try to accommodate the Trinity in this more badly than rightly (try to stuff 3 in 1) instead of pushing all the pre-understandings aside as far as possible and instead to trace the self-revelation of God in the Bible—an unexpected "kind of God."[4] Staying in the biblical word choice, tracing the descriptions more than dissolving them into abstract terms (and thus losing more than gaining) makes sense.

Impression: What love is ignited by within the Trinity and in which it is expressed before the creation remains a divine secret, that remains literally unimaginable. The repeated emphasis on mutual love is on the one hand impressive, on the other hand not really to be filled with content (especially since in the visible world little or nothing unambiguous of it seems to arrive). Is the whole thing therefore basically just a game with empty words? No. This thought overlooks the fact that information has several levels. On the emotional level, words trigger something that guides our hunches and longings into the right direction (especially since experiences from our interpersonal relationships can certainly serve as a viable mnemonic), even if on the factual level things remain obscure or foreign to us. In the natural science it is similar; our models of the atom are conscious to us as provisional and limited and nevertheless true enough to be able to work with it.

So don't push it aside, but take it up constructively.

I think we can only think starting from the fact of creation. We need concreteness; love cannot be lived and expressed or believed in a vacuum and depends on give-and-take. Our admiration and love can be ignited

- in nature (greatness, diversity, beauty, inventiveness, humor, music, harmony, wisdom)
- and by the justice and wisdom of the commandments
- and above all by Jesus (his devotion, mercy, care, will to heal, selflessness, philanthropy, humility).

In Jesus's being and activity, God's life-giving fatherhood becomes visible to us—if we can believe that Jesus is God in person.

And the "contemplating of his image" (2 Corinthians 3:18), which the Holy Spirit "dwelling" in us makes shine in us, is a transforming, dynamic force; it draws us into the loving community of God. Therefore: His personal presence is the content of grace; grace is not a portion of energy that is somehow instilled into us.

Prayer: Image or Reality?
February 10, 2017

In those cases where my praying is only one intense cry for help, when I *am* more pray-er than "say a prayer," the tense ideas about the one to whom the cry for help is addressed usually disappear into the underground. "If you are there, Lord, howsoever, then make yourself noticeable, then intervene!" But outside of such impulsive outbursts, these ideas intrude into the picture or even into the foreground in a disruptive, distracting, obstructive way.

Whether we like it or not, we always have some kind of image in mind when we talk to God. None of them quite meets reality, so I would actually have to constantly correct the respective focus in order not to succumb to false expectations and produce disappointments. When I focus on the Creator and King of kings, his greatness and mysterious nature make me marvel, but somehow also put me at a great distance. When I focus on the Father, the Shepherd, the Friend, the Savior, it tends to produce feelings of familiarity, security. But at the same time I actually have to protect myself from some too short-sighted human fillings of these words (a human father who would have the power to free his child from the hands of an SS-man or to influence his brain would do it and would not refrain from possible help—the question of theodicy pushes itself immediately into the picture).

How do I get back from these knots in the head and ambiguities in the heart to unbiased simplicity in the good sense of the word?

Jesus prayed to the Father and instructed us to do the same. (Again: If Jesus is risen, this also seals his teaching in this point!) From this I can deduce that the Father-image, despite the justified and necessary safeguards against all-too-human misunderstandings, is the one which evokes the most appropriate ideas in us, rationally as well as emotionally. We have, so to speak, divine authorization for this narrowing, for this focus, through Jesus's own example and through his teaching. Our Creator knows how we are wired, what we need, and gives us what will bring us closest to him. Daily life, which provides the flanking protective measures against an absolutization of this image, and above all God's Word, ensures that our image of the Father does not become fossilized and we then break as a result. In any case, from the Creator's point of view, the Father-image is the best idea on which we should focus in prayer with a clear conscience.

Our Faith, God's Instrument
March 12, 2017

I am working on the lecture about the Trinity. In parallel, the usual horror news (the worst famine since 1945 threatens in Africa due to drought and civil wars and corrupt governments that take their peoples hostage; once again mass graves are discovered in Mosul; Erdogan is secretly flattening the southeast of his country; attack in Essen here was at least prevented), and in the near vicinity the misery does not stop. The evil is inescapable devastating reality, the love of God and the joy of Michael Reeves, who describes it with enthusiasm in his book *Delighting in the Trinity*, appears against it like a dream on paper.

What good is the overflowing love of the Trinity if it does not reach the people—in the prisons, in the areas of famine and civil war, and so on? But: I must not forget what is part of this love (even if Reeves does not mention this because of the focus of his book). This love includes compassion for those whom God has not (yet!) delivered from the hands of evil. He, who created time and knows himself how minutes and hours can become eternities, longs for redemption as we do. Consider the images of the disappointed and struggling husband in the Old Testament, which God uses for his relationship with his people, such as in Hosea 2:4 and following. But he holds back—still—because he obviously considers a certain freedom of humans (also for evil) as a higher good than simply enforcing his love. This remains for us—still—difficult to understand; he wants to fight the war between good and evil essentially through people. But is it possible that our faith, as God's instrument, can achieve anything at all in these hardships? Isn't it often not even a drop in the bucket, simply because we don't even get to many buckets? A) We stand on the side of truth and hold it high, which will have the last word. B) What would it change if we abandon faith? Would things get better? Could any other worldview accomplish more? Hardly. No one can escape the dimension of time. But Christians can at least get through it as a transitory phase to eternity. They can offer hope in the face of sheer despair. At least if this hope survives all the attacks from outside and inside.

The Son Who Suffered
April 4, 2017

During Bible reading, I noticed again: "I have eagerly desired to eat this Passover with you before I suffer." (Luke 22:15) Fellowship means a lot to Jesus. And verse 28 struck me for the first time: "You are those who have stood by me in my trials." That Jesus himself speaks of such temptations, *before* the coming prayer struggle in Gethsemane, I have not noticed before. Hebrews 5:7 and following thus has a basis in Jesus own words: "During the days of Jesus's life on earth, he offered up prayers and petitions with fervent cries and tears to the one who could save him from death, and he was heard because of his reverent submission. Son though he was, he learned obedience from what he suffered and, once made perfect, he became the source of eternal salvation for all who obey him."

Choosing a Side for Today
January 26, 2018

I think about how Jesus demonstrated God's love to the people on two legs, with two hands, eyes and ears, tangibly, readably. In the process, I also think of scenes where he is frustrated with people: with disciples as well as the people and individuals who still have not understood anything, are slow on the uptake, run after him on the one hand and yet on the other hand do so partly with very questionable expectations, "lost sheep without a shepherd." He, who created this world in such a way that all this is possible, lives through the resulting frustration, the tiredness, the powerlessness in his own body, exposes himself to this experience. And sighs, sometimes gives vent to it in front of people, but especially certainly in prayer—and goes on.

On which side do I want to stand? Perhaps it helps to consciously ask myself this question anew at the beginning of each new day, in order to approach things more resolutely and not be so easily knocked down. Just as to pray aloud can enforce concentration, be helpful, I put a piece of paper on my desk, in front of the keyboard: "Which side do you want to be on today?"

Meditations for Assurance
February 4, 2018

For assurance, it helps to meditate thoroughly on God's character again and again; to internalize:
- commandments
- Sermon on the Mount
- how Jesus lives
- how he deals with people

To ignore all this would be an escape from reality. Alternative explanation attempts are unsatisfactory in my opinion, have not been able to convince me so far despite all occasional doubts.

But if this God exists, he cannot lie.

That would be a senseless assumption.

Whatever may be the reasons for the many tormenting riddles of our life, it is not his lack of love, not his unreliability, not his deaf ears. And thus it makes sense to wait for the day when everything will be redeemed and solved.

And until then, to resist all diabolical subjunctives. ("Should God …")

And to concentrate on the very elementary things, which are more or less clear.

The basic elements of the gospel.

And: "He has shown you, O mortal, what is good. And what does the Lord require of you? To act justly and to love mercy and to walk humbly (or: prudently) with your God?" (Micah 6:8)

Longing for a Heavenly Shoulder
February 10, 2018

There is so much longing in me to be able to lean my head on a strong heavenly shoulder, like a baby with the daddy, like a sheep with the shepherd. To feel: *He* will do everything well, I am safe, even if I understand so little or nothing. To be able to hand over responsibility. To be a child instead of a mother.

While thinking and praying, I increasingly slipped into intense inner images of how people must have felt with Jesus at that time. He must have radiated something like that kindness, loving compassion, gentleness, credible attention, especially to those who were otherwise in the shadows. Of course, under no circumstances would a woman have been able to cry on his shoulder—at best at his feet. But what he felt towards the people probably came across anyway and awakened hope and confidence: The one who created eyes sees; the one who created ears hears; the one who created sensitivity understands what we long for. And he cares about all of this. Which is why he often helped in a tangible way. And also approached people on his own initiative (the Samaritan woman at Jacob's well in John 4:1ff, the sick man at the pool of Bethesda in John 5, and so on). He sent them back to everyday life, but nevertheless this everyday life must have been transformed from then on by this knowledge, this experience of having seen God's loving eyes in Jesus, of having heard healing words.

My inner restlessness slowly calmed down a bit. The change of perspective did me good; it was a bit like refueling.

Another image also came up in the meantime, that of a marathon runner who, at the last when he is about to hit rock bottom and is almost only stumbling forward, is surprised at the next bend by the trainer who has been watching him via drone and knows when it is time to hand him a fresh water bottle.

Worthiness Has Two Directions
March 29, 2018

Various thoughts on the background of the Passion story.

Jesus asked his followers to live rightly and wisely, according to God's values and guidelines; he also healed, took care of their concrete need. Both correspond to God's will; but priority is given to doing what is right, if necessary at the expense of one's own well-being. The reverse order of priority, preferring to remain silent in the interest of one's own well-being, would be unthinkable for Jesus. We should also be aware of this if we want to be followers or invite people to follow us: Do we also want to accept this basic sequence of values? More precisely: Do we want to submit ourselves to this God who is a being so different from humans yet wants genuine relationship? Or do we seek God only to get an easier life, a great protector?

Moving: Jesus abstains from wine until the reunion with his disciples. He is looking forward to the celebration together with them, with us. The Lord's Supper reminds us: Jesus is looking forward to us! It is a meal of anticipation.

But it can also become a problematic meal. I remember a conversation about this and found my notes again: From Paul's comments on the Lord's Supper in 1 Corinthians, the question of who is worthy to go to the Lord's Supper has arisen in church history.

Worthiness has two directions.

Vertical:

I know that I keep failing at God's good rules of life.

I know about my guilt, about my half-heartedness, about my limitations.

But I cannot cope with this alone. And I don't want to cope with it alone. I seek forgiveness.

I want God's love to become more and more the driving force of my daily life.

If that is my goal in life, then I am worthy no matter how miserable I feel, even just when I feel miserable.

And in it also rings the second direction, horizontal:

Jesus does not call me into a purely private relationship with him. "This is my body given for you" (plural). Jesus calls me into his family, the community of Christians. Jesus and the community belong inseparably together.

For love cannot be learned and lived alone. Therefore, church is the training community of love.

Who is still training has not yet reached the goal, but is on the way to the goal. That's why church is not just fun, but often also exhausting.

So if living with Jesus in his family is my goal in life, then I am worthy no matter how miserable I feel, even especially when I seem miserable.

Conversely, this also means that if this is not my goal in life, perhaps indeed if it is *not yet* my goal, then I should not go to communion. Because then by deed I express allegiance to the Lord of a community of which I do not want to be a part, and that would be dishonest. No one has anything to gain from that.

Jesus's mercy and patience was and is for all who honestly seek and doubt, but harsh words he chose for those who wanted to seem more pious than they wanted to be.

Turning Sadness to Joy
April 21, 2018

In the evening in bed, spontaneous thoughts on the words that suddenly came to my mind from somewhere:

"You will grieve, but your grief will turn to joy." (John 16:20)

No reproach, no attempt to gloss over or play down, that is, it is "acceptable" in the sense of appropriate to the weight of reality.

And, it is also in need of being overcome, from Jesus's point of view. Jesus knows about the pain of being limited and of having to let go again and again. He has lived through it himself. This cannot and should not be the end.

Obviously he considers this mortal life nevertheless worth to be lived. Otherwise he would not have set it in motion and shaped it that way. The price is high, but not too high in view of where this life leads.

Is *he*, who is so realistic and empathetic and does not shy away from his own commitment, not worth to be loved? If not he, then who?

Humanity and Otherness
April 17, 2019

We need the reference to God's humanity.

On the one hand, because it is the truth; on the other hand, because it is an essential basis for our ability to trust.

We also need the reference to God's otherness.

On the one hand, because it is the truth; on the other hand, because it is a protection of our trust against (self-produced) disappointments.

We tend to think in either-or categories.

But reality is too complex and our understanding too limited for us to get by with tension-free descriptions and conceptualizations. Tensions and paradoxes tend to be closer to reality than a system that would try to get along without them.

Mixed Christmas Feelings
December 24, 2019

During the Christmas days, when the focus is actually on the joy of Jesus's first coming into our world, someone wrote in haunting words on Facebook of his longing for Jesus to come again. My response:

I can understand it. Even if it has become very rare to think and openly express such thoughts. (We are much more trained these days to be careful that Christians love this world enough in light of some other tendencies in church history in the past.)

Because:

- if we love our Lord and at the same time feel how inadequately we do so and therefore long for healing,
- if we feel at least a little of the pain of this world, so beautiful and yet so broken, and long for its healing and the restoration of its full beauty,
- if we feel solidarity with the enormous number of persecuted Christians in other parts of the world, for whom perseverance involves terrible suffering,
- if we truly believe that such a new world is not utopia but will become reality,
- then the longing for Jesus's return is the logical consequence.

One more thought on this: Jesus, too, has a longing for unbroken communion with his people and expressed it, underscored by his determination to drink no more wine until the heavenly reunion (Luke 22:15–18).

We express this longing consciously or unconsciously every time we pray the Lord's Prayer ("Thy kingdom come") or in parts of the Communion liturgy such as "Maranatha. Our Lord is coming!" "Yes, come, Lord Jesus!" (according to 1 Corinthians 16:22 and Revelation 22:20). Certainly, there are two levels of his coming, not only the definitive one in the future, but also the more hidden one in the present that does not diminish the weight and reality of the final return.

Do we take seriously what we pray? Then sooner or later we will end up with the mixed Christmas feelings.

Questionable Safeguards
February 22, 2020

While leafing through a book on the subject of conversion, I keep coming across—as I have often done in other books and sermons—a concern that now seems almost neurotic to me: Faith must under no circumstances become a "work." That is, it must be 100 percent God's gift, and human lostness and inability to believe cannot be thought of comprehensively enough. Otherwise this amounts to a disregard for the work of redemption.

I have my question marks there.

Which shipwrecked man, who was searched and found and then a rescue ring was thrown to him, proudly says: I have saved myself? And even if someone showed up—the appropriate reaction then should be to get him out of his weird thinking and pride.

By the way: When Jesus says to healed people—"Your faith has healed you!"—he nowhere adds a securing additional comment that this is a gift, and of course a completely undeserved one; possibly this is namely simply not necessary in such a situation.

God's Enduring Nature
May 22, 2020

"Is not Ephraim my dear son, the child in whom I delight? Though I often speak against him, I still remember him. Therefore my heart yearns for him; I have great compassion for him,' declares the Lord." (Jeremiah 31:20)

God's very nature, the same in both testaments. For the same words Jesus also chose when his stomach literally "turned" with regard to people who had lost themselves and God.

The One Who Carries Through
July 31, 2020

A friend is under enormous pressure, and some others from her project team probably are too. If only I could alleviate or solve at least part of these problems.

At some point I end up with the thought: The compassion we feel, like all good things, comes from above and is only a reflection of Jesus's even greater and more enduring love and faithfulness.

He lives in us. (Galatians 2:20) That is what we need to hold on to.

Also, 2 Corinthians 1:4 comes to mind: Paul passes on the comfort with which he is comforted. What does that look like? Remembrance of that which carries through. *The One* who carries through. Sometimes through deliverance from crisis. Sometimes through strengths to persevere. It doesn't automatically just finally come easy. But he does not abandon us.

More Important than It Seems
August 22, 2020

Old note rediscovered.

It is often pointed out that today Luther's question about a gracious God no longer plays a role; instead, the question today is about the existence and knowability of God and how suffering and evil in the world can be reconciled with him. And the meaningful response to this observation is controversial.

I share this observation. But I'm just realizing it's actually only a partial truth. People don't think far enough; that would have to be made clear to them.

1. The fact is that we urgently need someone to help us out of our miseries, selfishness, greed, and so on. Appeals alone will not make it. Obviously, we can rely very little on "the good in people." Good intentions do not last long ("The road to hell is paved with good intentions.")

2. The fact is that according to biblical statement, God's "offer" stands.

3. The fact is that only self-experimentation will bring you further.

4. At the entrance gate, however, readiness is necessary for self-knowledge and surrender, submission under his rule.

Justice Will Win
August 23, 2020

Another rediscovery from old notes:

God loves—and judges.

Why does God punish when he actually wants voluntary obedience? Isn't that blackmail?

Consideration: The whole creation suffers from sinful behavior. If God would let everything run without comment and consequence, the weakest would have no protection, and his announcement that at the end of all days justice would win would be an empty promise.

Guardrails for Self-talk
October 2, 2020

Clear goals can be helpful guardrails to avoid going down useless or harmful wrong paths in inner self-talk.

What kind of person do I want to become? What kind of person do I want to die as? My answers:

As someone who is aware of the love of my Lord.

As someone who trusts the Lord and can confidently testify to him as trustworthy.

As someone who has a firm yet soft heart because I am secure in Jesus.

As someone who lives by grace and passes on grace—without succumbing to cheap grace.

As a grateful person, in whose response to the question "How are you?" sincere gratitude is greater than any kind of "But" or "even if …"

Longing in the Right Direction
December 12, 2020

There are many people who are not able to conceive of God being their good father, because they themselves have experienced no fathers or only bad ones. So far, I have been able to understand this statement only in part, because even in a bad role model, one notices what one lacks, what one longs for: for arms that are strong and at the same time tender, so that one finds security in them; for reliable care, instruction, protection.

But it finally dawns on me now, as I reflect back on a pastoral conversation, what lies behind the difficulty. The longing points into the right direction, yes; but it is less than the holistic experience of how it really is. A mountain farmer who has spent his entire life in a small village and on the alpine pasture can read descriptions of a great city and, with the help of his imagination, develop ideas that certainly engage his feelings. But what life there really feels like, he must experience holistically. Or, what it means to be married, to have children, and so on, one can only guess beforehand. And some people cannot fall back on such holistic positive father-experiences, so that talking and thinking about it seems to be more like walking around the city wall, behind which some outstanding towers give a hint of the beauty, but the gates are closed, one remains outside, caught in the imagination. Therefore, not knowing reality gives the idea of it something emotionally unreal (what our diabolical adversary knows how to exploit). This is already the case in the realm of normal life, and it is reinforced with regard to an invisible God.

Is there a solution to the problem?

In this world probably only to a limited extent; most likely through experiences in prayer, which gradually change the entire attitude to life somewhat. And maybe this is also such a problem, which one cannot get rid of directly, but which one has to pack into a kind of inner handcart like so many other burdens and pull along! To fixate on it, probably only narrows the horizon, especially since all human images in relation to God fall short. I cannot simply transfer an image from human experience 100 percent to God, but must openly approach what that can mean in relation to God.

My attempt to lead my dialogue partner away from thinking about the experience to have missed the father towards observing Jesus, how he deals with people, probably went intuitively in a meaningful direction.

God's Song of Joy
December 24, 2020

"On that day they will say to Jerusalem, 'Do not fear, Zion; do not let your hands hang limp. The Lord your God is with you, the Mighty Warrior who saves. He will take great delight in you; in his love he will no longer rebuke you, but will rejoice over you with singing." (Zephaniah 3:16–17)

God sings—and sings a song of joy over his saved ones, over us! New Testament parallel: He himself joins in the rejoicing of the angels in heaven over a sinner who repents. (Luke 15:7)

The Fatherhood of God
January 24, 2021

What does the fatherhood of God mean? A collection.

Fatherhood applies first in relation to his Son, that is, intra-Trinitarian.

An image that almost always comes to mind when I address God in prayer is Rembrandt's painting, Return of the Prodigal Son.

Mary must watch the pain of her son. Waiting. Until the end. She *cannot* intervene. It is "forced" powerlessness.

The heavenly Father also knows how it feels to watch the pain of the Son. He does *not want* to intervene. It is "voluntary" powerlessness, out of an inner *must* that is mysterious to us, conscious sacrifice.

The compassion of a father with his children is somehow still different than that of a brother with his siblings.

But is it transferable to Trinity?

The Spirit points to the Son, and the Son to the Father (John 14:8–9!), who is ultimately the origin of everything in a way that the others are not—whatever that may mean concretely. Origin of life, of care, of education, of orientation.

"A father to the fatherless, a defender of widows, is God in his holy dwelling." (Psalm 68:5)

And: "Religion that God our Father accepts as pure and faultless is this: to look after orphans and widows in their distress and to keep oneself from being polluted by the world." (James 1:27)

As well as the accusations of the prophets that widows and orphans are not cared for, these are all examples of how God proves and implements his fatherly care by showing the way and ultimately does not want to tolerate injustice to the weak. This is not the only way of his care, but it is an essential one.

Other important passages: Psalm 27:10; Isaiah 9:5; Isaiah 63:16; Isaiah 64:7; Jeremiah 3:19; Jeremiah 31:9; Malachi 1:6.

Fathers let go of children so they can have their own experiences. They have the strength to bear weaknesses. To accompany developments, to wait, to support. To stay within calling distance.

1 John 3:1, our wedding verse, comes to mind: "See what great love the Father has lavished on us, that we should be called children of God! And that is what we are!" (based on: John 1:12)

Continuation of 1 John 3:1, by the way: "The reason the world does not know us is that it did not know him."

There it is again. Closeness on the one hand leads to strangeness on the other. There is a loneliness that is natural.

Interpreting God's Seeking Love
March 24, 2021

God testifies that he stretched out his hands to his people all day long (Isaiah 65:2). How did this express itself to the people, by what could they have perceived this pursuing, seeking love of God? For instance:
- by the existence of the Torah, the holy scripture (which, however, could also be understood as a one-time gift in the past, which therefore did not necessarily have to mean that Gods closeness still continued in the present)
- by the priesthood
- by the prophets

In each of these cases God revealed himself through his Word (by which also all experience had to be interpreted).

A Praying Mantis Surprise
June 10, 2021

The day before yesterday we arrived in Crete (a very spontaneously booked short vacation). Today we went hiking.

I was quite frustrated yesterday and today, to say the least, about my still strong inner tension. Then pretty soon after we started hiking I saw a praying mantis (German name: "worshipper of God") on the trail. An interesting surprise, after all, but it only snapped me out of my gloomy mood for a very brief moment. Shortly thereafter, someone asked me via text message if I already was relaxing well. I answered hesitantly and cautiously, "Rather still mixed, but will get there ..." This was answered by the comment that this trip was a gift from God and that I should enjoy every palm tree, every grain of sand, every wave. And then, finally, everything suddenly puzzled together. The

SMS was a *very* fitting timing, because it finally reminded me again of the homework I had been given for the vacation, but which I had faded out in the meantime: To prayerfully bring everything into connection with Jesus.

Mantis—of all things, this quite rare creature with this name had crossed my path right at the beginning. There was divine humor in the encounter with it. The name was appropriate in the situation. Nevertheless, with it the switch was not yet simply turned, yet from there the perspective changed, slowly, but surely. "Heavenly network" was once again in action.

Further addition and encouragement to this through the prayer under the watchword of the following day:

"To the lost Jesus comes as way, to the ignorant as truth,

To the dead as life, to the blind as light,

To the sick as physician,

To the comfort deprived as comforter,

To the condemned as liberator, to the deceived as counselor,

To the despairing as savior." (after Thomas à Kempis)

God's Honor, Our Weakness
June 13, 2021

In sermons and books, it is often pointed out that success on our part is connected with a certain danger, namely that we take the honor for ourselves, which is due to God alone, who, by the way, is also anxious to receive it and not to leave it to anyone else. Most of the time, I spontaneously have rather grumpy feelings, and I wish that something like this would not be put into the room strikingly, as if it did not need any explanation.

But what exactly is God's interest that *he* is given the honor, that *his* glory is in the center? He is no emperor Nero. He has no inferiority complexes, no fears of losing prestige and power. Rather, his glory consists in his purity, holiness, love, devotion, passion to give.

And when we in contrast to that acknowledge our weakness, two things result:

- Simply acknowledging the fact of our limitations and dependence makes us realists. Illusions, on the other hand, lead to pride, to bondage, to false dependencies, sooner or later to fall.
- This leads us to the life in the sphere of influence of the one who wants to infect us with his being, who wants to share, to give gifts.

A different question: Couldn't God make life at least a little bit easier for us and at the same time still uphold his vision for us, for instance, training our character?

Useless question!

Fact: It is also a dignity to be Jesus's co-worker and light-giver in this world. Though he himself as a man is no longer among us, he cares for us beyond a supernatural, rather more direct and at the same time also hidden way. Through other people he can give us some kind of more human closeness which we often long for; as his co-workers we become his tangible representatives for one another, if we then consciously practice this perspective.

Jesus in Real Life
September 10, 2021

I have continued to watch the new Jesus television series, "The Chosen." Always moving. I was particularly struck this time because it was *not* just everything completely different and simpler back then. At least not as much as it may seem to us sometimes.

Also at that time there was a lot of insecurity, fear, confusion, difficulty with learning to trust. Today we have the events in the gospels as a summary in the absolute time-lapse before our eyes. Real life happens so much more slowly. When I catch myself with false expectations of Jesus and then try to scale them down, sometimes the question creeps in whether this is not actually self-deception, glossing over resignation or unbelief. But it is rather appropriate realism, which is in the line of the beginnings without major breaks.

The scene between John and Jesus is remarkable. John wants to go to Herod at all costs. He longs for things to come to a head, not even shying away from his own sacrifice. Because things are finally gaining reality. And he asks Jesus if he feels the same way. Jesus affirms. "But that does not make them easy." A short remark, but nevertheless a so-deep one—what incarnation also means for God.

One more point:

Matthew chafes at Jesus's frequent use of ambiguous imagery; why doesn't he say what he wants in mathematically unambiguous terms? Jesus: "These things will make sense to some, but not to others. I don't want passive followers. People who really want it, they will intensely seek truth, will dive deep."

Interesting thought that Jesus might have used Matthew, who knew how to write, as secretary to draft the Sermon on the Mount.

On the Beatitudes: Matthew asks Jesus what he means by these serving as a kind of map. "If anyone wants to find me, these are the groups where he should look for me."

First Comes Grace
January 18, 2022

John 1:14: The glory of God, which became visible with Jesus, is described as grace and truth—not justice, not holiness, not omnipotence is the first characteristic of his glory, but grace. And truth (which in the Hebrew language is connected with faithfulness, reliability). Hardly a coincidence. In Islam, this would sound different. Verse 16 reinforces this: "Out of his fullness we have all received grace in place of grace already given. For the law was given through Moses; grace and truth came through Jesus Christ."

This is the auspices under which Jesus's coming stands; his trademark, his unique feature among the gods of this world.

The Old Testament believers also knew this: "We do not make requests of you because we are righteous, but because of your great mercy." (Daniel 9:18)

Three Basic Rights
February 26, 2022

Three basic rights—whether I'll ever become aware of more is open to debate—that kind of thing is always moment-taking.

There *is one* right that we can claim towards Jesus: that he keeps his promise to be with us and to bring us through and to deepen in a mysterious way through everything the bond with him within a short, longer or long time, as long as we follow him. But he has not promised to spare us or at least reduce situations in which fear, sorrow, grief, despair, or whatever troubles us so much that this bringing us through becomes necessary at all. This world is miserably unfair, this life remains miserably unfair, in view of almost infinitely many possible or actually impossible and unbearable situations, which we will experience in our life. If already Jesus himself often enough literally turned his stomach when he saw the misery of his people, then it will be even more so for us.

And there is a *second* right. We may pour out our hearts to him, untamed, unfiltered. Alone, or also together. He can take it. But then it goes on. Because then our life belongs to him, which means in consequence: Our *third* and last "right" is only the quitting of trust and discipleship. This would only add another unfairness to the lasting unfairness of life: the unfairness towards *him*, who has laid down his life for us and thus deprived us of the reason to doubt his character and his love. Quite apart from the fact that such a dismissal would ultimately amount less to something like a liberating blow and more to something more akin to suicide.

Jesus Receives Good
March 8, 2022

John 12:1–11: Jesus allows himself to be done good, allows himself to be given love. He, for whom wellness was certainly not a top priority, definitely appreciates it. Even if this world is so needy, effectiveness is not everything that should determine our life. Love is not calculating, can be wasteful, impulsive—and that is good. A small and yet so great gesture has indelibly found its way into the Bible. Jesus does not think of shaming Mary by rebuking her. He looks at her heart. Once again, Jörg Zink's book title comes to mind: *What Abides the Loving Brings About*.[5]

How can we anoint Jesus's feet today, show him our love? In loving other people, in loving his community, but also: "Truly I tell you, whatever you did for one of the least of these brothers and sisters of mine, you did for me." (Matthew. 25:40)

I spontaneously remember the story of Rilke: "A Rose for a Beggar Woman" (Rilke probably told it in his diaries, I found it again on the Internet):

The following story about Rainer Maria Rilke (1875–1926), who is probably one of the most important German-language poets of the first half of the 20th century, is told during his stay in Paris: Together with a young French woman, he passed by a place around noon where a beggar woman was sitting, asking for money. Without ever looking up at any giver, without expressing any sign of asking or thanking other than always holding out her hand, the woman always sat in the same place. Rilke never gave anything; his companion often gave a coin. One day the French woman asked in wonder why he gave nothing, and Rilke answered her: "We must give to her heart, not to her hand." A few days later, Rilke brought a white rose that had just blossomed, placed it in the beggar woman's open, emaciated hand, and wanted to move on.

Then the unexpected happened: the beggar woman looked up, saw the giver, rose with difficulty from the ground, felt for the stranger's hand, kissed it and went away with the rose.

For a week the old woman had disappeared, the place where she had begged before remained empty. Rilke's companion searched in vain for an answer to the question of who would now give the old woman alms.

After eight days, the beggar woman suddenly sat again as before in her usual place. She was silent as before, again only showing her neediness with her outstretched hand. But what has she been living on all these days, since she received nothing? Rilke answered: "From the rose … "

The very food of love lets us experience: there is someone by my side, I am not alone, someone is interested in me, someone is aware of my fate, someone stands by me, looks at me, gives me attention. Love takes the pressure off, takes the weight off the problems and worries of life, lets us exist in a sometimes absurd and long-suffering world. Who knows himself loved and accepted, for him a window is opened into another world.

The story of the beggar woman and the rose says that our heart hungers for something and our soul thirsts for something that we cannot buy. The rose is a symbol of this; it stands for all that gives nourishment to our lives, which cannot be bought and seems superfluous from a purely economic point of view. But does anything other than this abundance do justice to the dignity of man, who does not live by bread alone?[6]

2
COMMUNICATING WITH THE DIFFERENT ONE

*Relationship is living in communication.
To think about God is one issue,
to talk with him another one.
In talking with him we leave behind
the non-binding nature of thinking.
We step into the binding nature of a
relationship.*

~

God's Incomprehensible Ways
April 16, 2012

After several weeks, I spoke to a friend on the phone and asked what had become of her compound hand fracture. She is devastated, just desperate. She had to get surgery on it again because the first surgery had gone wrong. She also has massive secondary problems due to anesthesia, nutrition, and others that make coping with everyday life extremely stressful. No help on the horizon.

I am desperate. "Lord, why this pain without end?" I ask so much for peace, without being able to imagine how that could be possible, and for help. Not a prayer of faith, rather a cry of desperation that he at least somehow might show her his nearness and if at all possible provide relief.

The friend wants to try to contact a doctor where she had received help a few years before.

A few days later I call again and ask about the state of affairs. The doctor refused the treatment in a roundabout way by the receptionist. I can't think of anything else to say. The friend asks, "Did you pray for me?" I answer in the affirmative, a little surprised by the question. She tells me that after our first conversation at the beginning of the week, a peace came into her heart that she had never experienced before; she has usually found peace in her own prayer, but never so strongly independently of it or as a result of intercession. And that's why she could now get over the frustration with the doctor and say: who knows why it shouldn't be? God's ways are so incomprehensible.

Supplication with Thanksgiving
February 9, 2014

I have rediscovered a devotion that I gave in my student days. Then, as now, to myself: "Do not be anxious about anything, but in everything by prayer and supplication with thanksgiving let your requests be made known to God." (Philippians 4:6, ESV)

Those words were kind of a pedagogical slap in the face for me last night. Supplication with thanksgiving—does that go together? Either I plead or I give thanks, but there is only one thing I can do if I am honest about my mood. When I plead, I don't feel like giving thanks, and when I'm thankful from the bottom of my heart, I've usually gotten rid of the motivation to plead, haven't I?

And I felt very much like pleading. There I found myself again; this keyword had let me become attentive.

These were the first reactions, and I could not really accept that this should be God's word on this day. I was looking for encouragement—quite desperately. At the moment I can understand very well how some psalmists cry out to God, plead for help and instruction. As I said, encouragement was what I wanted. But this encouragement to plead had a flip side, which I found to be a very uncomfortable demand. To be grateful in the midst of all the pleading? But I did not feel like it at all. What was the point? And then I remembered another word, for the second time on the same day, Psalm 50:14–15: "Sacrifice thank-offerings to God, fulfil your vows to the Most High, and call on me in the day of trouble; I will deliver you, and you will honour me."

Offer thanksgiving to God. Thank offering. Sacrifice usually hurts, otherwise it is not sacrifice. Gratitude, then, is not simply identical with joy and gladness. Gratitude also involves recognition and acknowledgment of what God is, was, and will be to me. Gratitude, then, is not just a matter of the heart, but to a large extent also a matter of consciously thinking about God. And that can sometimes take effort, does not always come spontaneously from the heart.

Why does this cost me effort? I asked myself after this excursion and made the observation: If I stop at supplication, I basically stop at myself, at my need, which I cry out to God. But if I then begin to give thanks, then I have to sober up again, to think about God's activity and intervention. That is healing. In the process, some peace can return, because I have to distance myself a bit. But there is a stumbling block in this matter: If, while thinking about reasons to give thanks, I realize how God has taken care of me so far, then the ground for my despair is taken away, because God remains faithful to himself. Then I have to give up my worries genuinely, I can no longer hide behind them, work myself up into them and thus become blind and deaf and unresponsive to God's speaking and comforting. Then I can no longer stand rooted to the spot or paralyzed, but must go further into the dark to the best of my knowledge and conscience, trusting in God, until he considers the time to grant and strengthen me to have come. And that is exactly what I would like to avoid—walking in the dark valley, taking each further step into the unknown. Trust would have to become practical by entrusting my future to God on the basis of the care I have experienced in the present and in the past. Only such practiced trust makes further experiences with God.

If I do not give thanks, it is a sign that I have not yet entrusted my worries to God except in words, but that I have stopped at myself, still looking to myself instead of to him. That is why Paul encourages such prayer, supplication with thanksgiving. Supplication is more the aspect of entrusting, of expressing oneself. Giving thanks also includes trust. In this way we gain confidence and hope, we are promised help and comfort. "To comfort someone means to put a coat of security around him." That's what God wants, but not without taking off our mantle of self-pity.

Finally, a few sentences from missionary Jim Elliot that struck me very much in this context:

> 'In His temple doth everyone say: Glory!' The Lord is
> a hard taskmaster, telling me to rejoice and sing a

praise-psalm when things oppress. Naturally, I rebel and quote Proverbs 25:20, 'As he that taketh away a garment in cold weather … so is he that singeth songs to an heavy heart!' … 'Sympathize', I cry, and He peels off my overcoat of self-pity by saying, 'Praise, child, and be warmed within!' Ever notice that? Whenever I want comfort He tells me to 'count it all joy', and then, queerly, I heed, and it all becomes sweet.[1]

Heartfelt Worship
March 2, 2014

Isaiah 58 asks the question about the kind of worship that is in God's mind—holistic, honest, from the heart, not just formally right. Going on thinking, associatively, I was once again occupied with the topic of worship. What does this mean for the design of liturgy in our services?

Three important basic thoughts in advance:

"It is the one shining jewel that has been lost to the modern church, and I believe we should look for it until we find it."[2]

"A person becomes a worshipper when he sees something great that arouses his admiration or veneration. That is the only way worshippers are made. Worship responds to greatness."[3]

"Ultimately, worship can never be a performance, something you act out or take over. It has to be an overflow of your heart. … Worship is about getting very personal with God, getting close to Him."[4]

I think there's a lot of truth in that. But it also raises a tricky question: How can a group of Christians be authentic in worship (since all of them are in different life situations and certainly do not come to worship directly out of collective wonder about God)? On the one hand, heartfelt worship cannot be prescribed; on the other hand, some form must be preset if we are to worship together.

I see how easily forms can become empty, traditional rituals, a constant temptation to hypocrisy. But what is the alternative? The Psalms, for example, are a regular element of our worship services. They are spoken by all—but prayed by few, if any.

So I sometimes think: shouldn't we stop doing that? But actually, things are not so much different with regard to songs and creeds. So should we stop doing that, too? All this cannot be a solution. Normally I end up with some more or less pragmatic approach, trying to focus on the fact that every form can be used and abused.

I always find C. S. Lewis helpful in this context, in his book on the Psalms. "When we perform our 'religious duties' we resemble people who dig canals in waterless land so that the water, when it finally comes, will find them ready. I mean, most of the time. Even now there are happy moments when a trickle seeps through the dry bed: and there are happy souls to whom this often happens."[5]

A Prayer for Every Day
September 30, 2014

An attempt to formulate a short prayer suitable for everyday use for the pocket (literally: on a little index card, for my card-box).

Help me to live *now before you*
that I may rejoice in what is beautiful with an undivided heart:
that I may do what is due with a determined heart,
that I bear what I cannot change with a trusting heart.
And that I learn to keep *you* in view in everything.

A Prayer through the Day
November 24, 2014

Once again, I am trying to formulate a prayer from my reflection to go through the day with:

Lord, you have given me my life.
It is a journey of discovery to you.
The small and great beauties of this world are a foretaste of the new world.
Thank you for allowing me to be your witness—
witness to joy, hope, love.

Help me today
to see with your eyes,
to join your joy,

to share your love,
to perceive your gifts
that you have placed in everyday events.

Help me,
to keep your human face before my eyes,
your honesty and love for the truth,
your caring,
your joy in beauty and goodness,
your longing for communion with me,
your sense of humor;
your reluctance against hate and unforgiveness,
your compassion for your battered creation,
your will to defeat evil;
but also
your unavailability,
your greatness and incomprehensibility.

Save me from imputing to you what is in truth diabolical.
Your motives are always positive.
There is light in you and no darkness.

Please remind me of this again and again
so that I can remain faithful to you. Amen.

A Prayer for Trust
December 24, 2014

I ask this very consciously:

Help me to trust that it makes sense,
to behave as if you were standing in front of me as a human being.
That this is what makes more sense than anything else,
even if the truth is much *greater*,
but just *not smaller*. Amen.

Do not forget: Truth reveals itself in obedience.

Space for Encounter
April 22, 2016

"Through Jesus, therefore, let us continually offer to God a sacrifice of praise—the fruit of lips that openly profess his name." (Hebrews 13:15)

Atonement has had its day; thank-offering has not.

Does God need our praise? Certainly not. But we do need it, as a space that allows for encounter with God. (The praise movement interprets Psalm 22:3 as: God dwells in the praise of his people).

In worship, cognitive and emotional elements, head and heart, conjoin and can lead to a more holistic perceptiveness. Whether I think about someone or express it to them makes a difference. In the first case I stay with myself, in the second I consciously open space for encounter, I consciously also "switch to reception." Our reality is too complex to be grasped only with the mind. In contrast, the heart is rather something like a sensory organ integrating all layers of our being, safely withdrawn from our analytical grasp. Nevertheless, we instinctively feel that it is real, can grasp deeper dimensions of our reality, and is more than superficial feelings that come and go.

What is worship about? In praise, I give reality the weight it deserves: Consciously recognize it, in clear awareness of my limited insight into the mysterious relationship between God, man and evil. This is actually true realism, and thereby the depressing weight can be taken away from the atheism pretending to be realistic, sober. That can be unmasked as illusion, simplification. Atheism does not know better, it knows less. God is really great, he is really glorious.

A Prayer to Abide
December 18, 2016

My wish, my prayer: To abide in him

Lord, bless my hands
    that they may become your hands.
Lord, take my feet into your service,
    that they may carry me on your ways
    to your goals.
Lord, make my eyes your eyes,

that they may see what *you* see,
that they may perceive how *you* do.

Lord, use my mouth as your mouth,
that you may speak through me.

Help me to live,
that those around me may discern a little more:
This is who Jesus is.
Transform me into your image. Amen.

Longing to Be Like Him
January 2, 2017

When we talk about faith with people who are not consciously living as followers of Jesus, we often talk about the fact that faith is about more than saying yes to the question of God's existence, that it is rather about a personal relationship. This phrase "personal relationship" does not exist literally in the Bible, but it does in content: It is based on the images of the father, the shepherd, the brother, the friend, the teacher, the Lord—images of closeness, albeit of varying degrees. Nevertheless, in reading Philip Yancey's book, *Reaching for the Invisible God*, I found it helpful to note that in the Bible, worship is at the forefront of relationship, not the image of friendship;[6] this can save us from rashly simply transferring what we know of intense human friendships to the relationship with Jesus—and then having to struggle with the fact that he sometimes behaves differently. Worship, too, has to do with relationship and closeness, but also with respect, healthy reverence; and it is therefore a counterweight against oversimplified emotional expectations of this still very special relationship of God and man. From the contemplation of his being and the growing longing to become like him, increasing and thereby healthy closeness can arise.

A Pledge of Right Feeling
January 13, 201

Worship songs often talk about "lifting up" God. What is actually meant by this?

Thomas Watson, an English theologian wrote in a sermon: "The glory we give to God is nothing else than that we exalt his name in the world and make him great in the eyes of others."[7]

The English word *magnify* "to make great" can be used for "to glorify," which seems helpful to me. Even more helpful: The remembrance triggered by it, the Hebrew word *kabod*, to give something or someone the weight that does justice to it or him, that is appropriate. ("His voice has weight," when we say that of someone, we refer to the authority of that voice).

Worship, then, practically means thinking appropriately (great) of God, speaking appropriately of him, acting appropriately as creatures accepting and respecting their place assignment in his great plan, admitting that his perspectives and judgments are right, and rejoicing in him; almost all of which can only come from contemplating God's self-revelation in his Word.

Pursuing this thought: Worship, therefore, includes elements of suffering. For example, when we share God's sadness, when it hurts us to see people deceived or thinking wrongly of him; when we stand up for him in the face of an indifferent or hostile world.

Worship in the sense of "expressing adoration, affection, praise and thanks in prayer/songs" is therefore only a part of the whole. Feeling is also only part of the whole. Certainly the first commandment clearly implicitly intended "from the whole heart," but in Luke 24:32 we also see that "Did not our hearts burn …?" is a *re*action of the disciples to the conversation with their Lord. And is not also the longing for it already a sign, a pledge of the right feeling?

And About Modern Worship?
January 13, 2017

The following are thoughts on two essays that address the modern worship scene.

Tragic Worship by Carl Trueman:[8] "The church should certainly be the most realistic of all places," in the sense of "most in line with reality."

Trueman says, with a somewhat pointed ironic undertone, that we have too little entertainment in modern worship, namely, that it lacks the tragic element that characterizes our earthly existence. He points out that in modern worship, the cross, suffering and death are usually left out. One wants to jump straight to Easter, not to endure Good Friday. I am reminded of the old terms from Luther's time "theology of the cross" versus "theology of glory." Theology of the cross strikes me as a more realistic, honest, down-to-earth perspective. It relieves one of a guilty conscience in the face of a lack of high spirits (which, after all, can often only be achieved through manipulative musical techniques). In the Psalms, as in the New Testament, it is clear that songs are also meant for remembrance, for exhortation, for rooting in the Word—ultimately, it is always the Word that is *the* meeting gate par excellence between the invisible and the visible world, not our high spirits. Ecstasy is the pagan means of choice to bring about an encounter with God. The meaning of light shows and endless repetitions in church services is therefore quite question-worthy.

Todd Pruitt, "Worship,"[9] takes a clear look at this misuse of worship. According to his observation, worship in some congregations today has virtually the status that sacrament once had in providing intimate encounter and communion with God. Referring to Vaughan Roberts's *True Worship*, Pruitt summarized four arguments and consequences:

1. God's Word is marginalized.
2. Our assurance is threatened (dependence on feelings).
3. Musicians are given priestly status.
4. Division is increased.

Worth thinking about.

A Prayer for Closeness
July 18, 2017

Lord, you have given me
ears to hear wonderful sounds and noises of animals and people
eyes to see fascinating beauty in nature in microcosm and macrocosm
a nose to smell fragrant alpine meadows, spicy autumn forest and so much more
a tongue to taste refreshing, invigorating foods

skin to feel the soothing touches of people and animals, sun, wind and rain
an ingeniously designed body
which is an aftertaste of what once was
and a foretaste of what shall once be again.
Senses that actually should never cease to amaze
and should be a bubbling source of gratitude and joy in you.
And yet: So often you seem so strange and distant to me today;
the presentiment of your greatness and incomprehensibility stands in the way of a feeling of closeness and familiarity,
that formerly used to fill and move me more than anything else.
Please, come close to me again.
Help me again to hear your quiet voice and to believe it,
to perceive your traces and to trust them.
Keep before my eyes how absurd it is to assume
such an ingenious Creator,
who endowed people with the ability to love,
who enabled them to perceive time consciously,
and who has anchored the longing for imperishability and eternal home ineradicably deep in their souls,
could have done all this without the will to fulfill this longing,
only to let it run billions of times into the void.
That makes no sense.
Help me to talk to you instead of thinking about you.
Keep your human face before my eyes. Amen.

On Space for Lament
January 31, 2019

Arne Kopfermann, a well-known musician and songwriter in the modern worship scene, lost his child in a car accident. This experience has had a strong impact on his faith, changing the language of his lyrics. His honest thoughtfulness and need to rewrite overly full-bodied song lines does good.

Kopfermann says, "I am very aware of my helplessness in the face of God's greatness. I have to learn again to live trustingly like a child, because it has become clear to me anew that I do not see through the interconnections in this world. God knows, I do not."[10]

The article goes on to say:

Kopfermann formulates more carefully than many others do. A simple 'you decide, I follow' is out of the question for him because he is aware of his limitations. 'I trust myself less. I'm not sure that nothing can throw me off track.' The ideal, 'when I see you, I no longer fear anything,' is not something he can fulfill, he says. He considers the 'self-overestimation of one's own ability to follow' as a widespread evil, hard to bear for him. …

The personal blow of fate has shaped his professional work in two ways. First, Kopfermann has become more attentive to which lyrics he sings. During a performance, he rewrote a line from Matt Redman's song '10,000 Reasons' as 'sing for him today, too,' instead of sSing like never before just for him,' because he doesn't always feel closer to God than he did the day before. Mature faith is not a linear development, he says. The songwriter has become aware that lament Psalms occupy very little space in the modern worship movement. Kopfermann explains, 'We as worship songwriters lend people prayers, but not enough lines for existential questions. This is not good. Because if you don't cry out your lament to heaven, eventually you don't cry out to heaven at all." This kind of inner distance, he said, is dangerous. For that reason, and also to give authenticity to faith, he wants to expand the area 'where there is still so much speechlessness.'

Of Constant Prayer
December 28, 2020

Thinking about the attitude of constant prayer, of attentiveness, to discover God's traces in the very ordinary everyday life and to transform them into praise (such as the Church Fathers and the 17th century Brother Lawrence).

I see very quickly the danger of consumption, vanity, and addiction to pleasure, and often quite rightly. But also, through trying to avoid one mistake, I fall into the opposite and find myself in well-disguised contempt, wanting to get rid of things, and becoming ungrateful and arrogant. Also piously disguised purism is arrogance and small-minded in addition. It is the Creator who has so equipped us that there are gourmets, up to incredible wine testers like the sommeliers (what taste buds!). Food *versatility*! It is *he* who makes gardening, housework, decor, invention, play, and so on possible for us. And yes, much of consumer goods are superfluous, but it still reflects imagination and inventiveness. If I become blind to these points of view, though the motives still be so well-intentioned, I deny God-given creativity and sense of beauty and impoverish the respect they deserve. This is not neutral, but sin. I want to be more pious than the Creator, who can and will be found in everything that makes up our world, and not only in obviously spiritual exercises. They're there to help you see the big picture, not to lose sight of it. (In eternity there will hardly be only vegan muesli). There is basically hardly anything mundane, ordinary that brings me quasi automatically out of itself in distance to God, but he is everywhere and can and wants to be found everywhere. It is a question of my thinking whether I am open or blind to it.

Brother Lawrence consciously practiced such openness. That is why he could be close to God also in the kitchen, living intensively there as well, not somehow in a room of minor quality compared to sitting in the church, not finding peeling potatoes any less transcendent than reading the Bible.

Playing through the example of peeling potatoes for myself:

- I have food. > God provides.
- Enough. More than enough. > God provides abundantly.
- Diversity. > God loves variety.
- I have taste buds for it. > God wants to share joy in diversity.
- I can prepare different things. > God loves creativity.
- Each potato is unique. > God loves originality.

And so on. Work can become worship.

Rooted Thanksgiving
April 14, 2021

" ... giving thanks to God the Father through him [Jesus]." (Colossians 3:17) " ... always giving thanks to God the Father for everything, in the name of our Lord Jesus Christ." (Ephesians 5:20)

Theme of giving thanks, once again. Fitting, where I had just resolved, because of my forgetfulness, to include at least some points of thanksgiving in evening prayer.

Give thanks for *everything*. All the time.

That is a healing perspective only possible if I see beyond the negative and evil to the one who is even greater, no matter how great the burdening is. This is not a glossing over, not a trivializing, but realism, which assigns the appropriate place to the things: Looking at *him*, who knows the bigger picture.

According to Colossians 2:7, rootedness in Jesus and solid faith is shown in "abundant thanksgiving."

In the afternoon I visited an acquaintance again, with whom intensive discussions are going on at the moment. Here, too, the topic of thanks came up—from her. She had noticed that she was staring too much only at the negative. Since this is also a current issue for me, it was of course very helpful. A hint that God still is at work in her life, also through our encounter; a loving nudge in the ribs. Agreement: That we both collect reasons to give thanks in the evening, looking back on the day.

I also realized in the process: It cannot and will not be only new reasons every day. But that's not bad; it rather makes us aware of how much positive continuity we take for granted every day.

In the evening we watched a movie about the Armenian genocide ("The Cut"), death marches, etc. Insanity once again. The main actor loses his faith. Spontaneously, I can't blame him. Would the sentences of this morning still cross my lips if I were facing him? "Looking beyond evil to *him*?" I don't know. But I hope so. It is obvious not everything turns to the good here on earth for every suffering person. But this world is not the end. If also this hope would no longer be there, how can one still find strength to live in such a madness?

Steadfast in Prayer
April 20, 2014

"Devote yourselves to prayer, being watchful and thankful." (Colossians 4:2)

The topic comes up again and again at present. Prayer and thanksgiving—are they something like guards at the entrance of the heart? The image of the bearskin soldiers at Buckingham Palace comes to mind, incessantly reliably there.

3
EXISTING IN A SEARCH FOR MEANING

Our heart longs for meaning. For finding our role in a bigger story. For being in the right place. For making a difference. A lasting difference. Yet, we don't get anything that resembles a halfway precise script. How do we get what we need?

~

A Golden Thread
May 27, 2013

In order not "to be lived but to live" we need a golden thread that connects the individual events of our daily lives in a meaningful way and that can also serve as a yardstick for us to set priorities.

What was the meaning of life in paradise? To rejoice together in the world, in each other, and first and last in the Lord who created it. To live love in all relationships.

What is the meaning today? To let oneself be taken into this still current program. Reclaiming living space, time period, where joy and love can flourish. Learning to love.

What this means in concrete terms can be seen in Jesus. Jesus is the image of the heavenly Father, in whose image humans were created, and at the same time a model for us humans.

What Abides the Loving Brings About[1]—the catchy title of Jörg's book can serve as a golden thread in our daily lives.

Called for Today
May 28, 2013

It is about *today*.

We are called ...
- to the service of the highest majesty
- to the service of all around us:
  - to love and to be loved
  - to serve and to be served

... and thus live a piece of eternity in advance. It is about learning to mirror Jesus's character, his will, in the work that lies before one's feet. A different job or different people do not change the basic challenge. It is an illusion to think that other circumstances will make everything better. For what Jesus wants from me and for me, he has equipped me. Escape is unbelief, know-it-all attitude, self-will: I want something different than he does.

In what is real today and here, he wants to be close to me, I can have fellowship with him, if I only believe it and do not depend on pious feelings. A close, deep relationship consists not only of celebration and rest, but also of boringly normal work, and this is not a second class relationship!

Everything should serve to develop in us a character suitable for eternity.

Someone once contrasted something crass and yet realistic for many places in this world:

Earth:	Caterpillar Time
Eternity:	Butterfly time
Earth:	Desert time
Eternity:	Promised Land

In Search of Answers
June 4, 2013

Attempt to summarize elementary observations.

Initial situation:

No human being has decided: I want to be born.

No human being can decide: I do not want to die.

We find ourselves in the world and the questions arise: What is this all about? What am I doing here? Are there indications of a plan? If applicable: is communication with the planner possible?

If I don't avoid the questions, the search for answers begins. They are not immediately obvious. Nature and history are ambiguous and often largely silent—themselves in need of interpretation.

But: Whatever culture I look into, everywhere people assume the existence of a higher being (or several ones). It seems to have left different traces in this world, more or less consistent with how people experience this world.

The Jews say that they know this God—that he presented himself as Creator and Lord of this world and sought fellowship with them. In the Old Testament we find testimonies of this concerning the life of individual people as well as the life of a whole people, who entered into a covenant with him. With this people, God essentially speaks through priests and prophets.

Then Jesus comes and claims to be God personally.

He testifies: Our perception that this world is under a curse (as reported in the Old Testament) is correct; since then, the whole creation is poisoned by evil. Therefore, God himself comes as a man to solve the basic problem (in an ultimately mysterious way through his death on the cross)

- and then to involve us in the reconquest of his world,
- which he had created for us
- as a space of shared joy and love.

Thus Jesus invites people into a relationship with him, which is of a new and hitherto unknown quality and intensity.

It becomes clear: this God is very human in the sense of loving, kind, wise; he is also militant; and yet, in the end, he also remains mysterious, strange.

He, who himself suffers from evil and could eliminate it, does not completely cut the Gordian knot and does not explain the reasons.

(Possible motive: You can't explain the theory of relativity to an ant either.)

His program, which he himself exemplifies, is called: overcome evil with good with the help of the Holy Spirit. Love.* Which is successful only in a limited way —at least it looks like it for us.

The world remains a theater of war, where individual battles are won and many are still lost—at least it looks like that for us.

He does not want us to be afraid of him.
He encourages childlike trust.
He shows his cards—that life with him has a high price.

God is loving, but not a kind God (in the sense of nice, harmless), is Daddy** and Lord. To see both and not be irritated by the permanent mysterious and strange in him remains our lifelong challenge. The God who is love remains the holy, incomprehensible one.

*"God is love. Whoever lives in love lives in God, and God in them." (1 John 4:16) Fittingly: Jörg Zink has given one of his books the catchy title: *What Abides the Loving Brings About.*² This life experience coincides most closely with the God of the Bible (compared with other world views).

The distinction between good and evil likewise.
**This is how Jesus prays to the heavenly Father (Matthew 14:36), and this is how we can do it as God's children (Romans 8:15, Galatians 4:6).

The Age of Meaning
August 3, 2013

Visit to the nursing home. It was kind of depressing. What does a person of that age and late state get out of life? Surely, quite obviously with the dwindling of the physical forces also the intensity of the inner perception changes; the world becomes smaller, sometimes it seems to come to an inner withdrawal; a kind of distance to the outside world, which already has somewhat apathetic features. Perhaps a person who has become so old suffers at least somewhat "less" from his condition or at least differently than we do!

However: The question of the meaning of life reappears with power. I rummage through my notes and come across the entry: What was the meaning of life in paradise? To rejoice together in the world, in each other, and in the Lord who created it. To live love in all relationships.

Thinking further about joy as the original meaning, it strikes me that feeling joy is something that actually every human being can do at any age and state of mind. A baby, an old person, a sick person, a mentally disabled person. The degree may be very different, but the basic ability is much more continuous than, for instance, efficiency or thinking ability. Life can still have something of the originally intended meaning, where it is in many respects already very limited and marked by transitoriness.

It remains a difficult way. But there is something comforting and motivating in these thoughts, for me as a companion, but also for my own growing old.

Change the Question
August 4, 2013

The past weeks have been crazy. Within three weeks we had the death of our 12-year-old-dog, wedding of our son, final leaving of one daughter for the US, and final leaving of another daughter for university. Our oldest daughter was already married in 2011. So now all four kids are out of our house, plus a lot more. We are thankful for so much during these whirlwind times. But again: The emptiness of the house and the sudden quietness now brings to the foreground again even more the wrestling with a positive spiritual perspective for our ongoing ministry. And the question whether our efforts are proportionate to the "outcome," in what sense we might be "enough" in the face of what we imagine to be necessary.

A memory came to my mind, helpful not to get lost in a negative spiral.

When we look back at what we wanted to achieve in a smaller or larger section of our lives and what has become of it, paralyzing impressions of failure and futility can sometimes assail us.

Brother Andrew once challenged a weary pastor in such a situation with a wise counter-question to change his perspective. Instead of asking, "What have I accomplished?" he should ask himself the counter question:

"Look back—what would be missing if you hadn't gone?"[3]

One of the possible traps is that we take the—possibly few—visible things for the whole and block out what is still hidden and yet real. The head knows this, but the feelings often do not play along. To get at least a little bigger picture, it can be helpful to change the questioning as Brother Andrew does.

Standing Together
August 28, 2013

Despite all the horror and chaos in this world (the Syrian crisis is currently escalating, not to mention the well-known trouble spots), there is too much beautiful, wonderful, good, loving, successful togetherness that is lived out to simply leave this world to itself and give it up. Giving up can really not be the solution, but saving what can be saved. Don't forget, every individual counts.

The experience that standing together helps *is* in itself something positive, nothing meaningless.

The experience that passed-on signs and words of God's nearness encourage and strengthen others is a sign of God's presence and participation, that he is at work in all places at once, and making connections. The birthday greeting I sent across the ocean yesterday a day early (I knew I would not have internet today) and that spoke appropriately into a situation precisely because of that, is an example. Such experiences are rather rare. All the more important to keep them in mind. They are there, after all; not only is evil real, but so is good.

Where the Essential Happens
November 30, 2013

What is everyday life about? Essentially about relations:
- being on the road with Jesus and with each other
- sharing life

From this follows:
- not to expect life "that really deserves to be called life" from a more or less undetermined future, but taking seriously that the essential happens now in this and every moment, in the inconspicuous as well as in the particular. It is both unavailable, but in every moment an expression of graciously given life.

A great danger is always to reduce the experience of faith to the spectacular, the special, the accumulation of which one then strives for. But not only where for instance a hardship is overcome, but also where it is shared, carried together, the essential happens, which is also the only possible thing (in contrast to the future, which is still pending or can also prove to be an illusion or utopia).

After all, the day-to-day-life is the space which counts, and which I should simply accept gratefully as my living space. Just as paradise did not or will not consist only of rejoicing with the harp, that is not the case now. There is nothing banal. Everything belongs to God. And everything has a double bottom, is embraced by his reality and space for encounter.

The Gospel for the First Time
January 28, 2014

A bad night for several reasons; infection adding to that. Thinking about my daily experiences, the superficiality of usual communication with other people, the impression of living in some pious parallel world shoves itself into the foreground once again. I ask myself: How communicable are the signs of God's presence which I have tried to collect through past months for my own reassurance? I do not want to give in to diffuse and misleading impressions. I want to get clearer what really might be a difficult aspect of the truth, what might be due to my insufficient communication of this truth, and what simply an aspect of people's reaction for which I am not responsible.

That leads me to writing here.

When people are confronted with the gospel for the first time (extreme example: hitherto unreached people), how would one summarize in an understandable way what the message is about? What can every simple person understand?

- You have a Lord who made you, loves you and wants fellowship with you.
- But you are also part of a cosmic drama.
- You are under the influence of an evil power from which God wants to liberate you.
- Turn to him and ask him for this liberation.
- Learn to love him and his creatures.
- You are responsible to him.
- Keep his rules, his word.
- Stick together as a community, serve one another.

- Rejoice in life.
- Make something of your life, your gifts, because you are co-authors of beauty, goodness, creativity.
- Preserve the world, but do not hang your heart on it.
- Share what you know.
- Live for eternity—it goes on.
- Trust that you are not alone.
- Prayerfully keep in touch; keep your ears and eyes open.

Sometimes your Lord wants to tell you something beyond that.

All this can be understood and practiced by ordinary people.

Is the whole thing worth it, more or less lonely against the rest of the world?

Under the aspect of eternity: Yes.

And under the aspect that already here, love is what counts in the end, too.

"See for Yourself!"
February 8, 2014

I always feel strongly how fragmentary and limited my understanding of God and this world and our life is, and somehow I am always looking to overcome that.

But: Am I not just with this fragment much closer to the reality than if I would have a more satisfying system or something that would come close to it? Because that would come only with a high price, namely that of the fading out and smoothing out of many inconsistencies of our life!

And exactly to endure this is therefore perhaps the greatest measure of wisdom which we can reach here!

And therefore it makes sense to witness to that mysterious reality despite fragmentary insight—and not only when I feel able to answer the assumed or real questions of the dialogue partner. It is simply a matter of making the other person aware of a chance to encounter Jesus himself in the first place and to start their own story with him. I am not responsible for that to happen and even less for a successful story. Jesus is. And the other person is. I am only responsible to open the chance that Jesus and another human start their own relationship.

As with Narnia's King Aslan, he only tells everyone his own story anyway; but for this it is important that the other person is invited and becomes open for the encounter with Aslan.

A trap that I become aware of in this context: I think I am instinctively still looking for a permanent inner certainty, not only for myself, but with regard to others; especially because such certainty seems almost indispensable as a precondition, a starting basis for more proactive witnessing. But the big question is whether this is really so and whether this permanent inner certainty will really exist ... No.

It is actually not a question: it is *not* a prerequisite. The woman at Jacobs well said, "See for yourself." (John 4:1ff) If I don't go to someone because I think I know in advance that I can't answer them fully enough, then there is a poverty of trust behind it; I don't give Jesus a chance to equip me in the situation when it's my turn. Devilish paralysis. Jesus's word certainly applies here: "Do not worry about how or what you should speak, for it will be given to you at that hour." (Matthew 10:19)

Inviting with Momentum
April 3, 2014

Why do I often have such a hard time inviting with momentum others who don't yet know Jesus as the living Lord to follow when they are in trouble?

Possible partial answer:

I think sometimes it's because of concerns about putting the other person on a track that may lead them into frustration because they don't have the necessary equipment. After all, it's clear to me that getting involved with Jesus doesn't just abruptly solve our problems (but which I'm sure the other person longs for). I feel like a mountain guide who sends a tourist in light summer clothing and sandals on a via ferrata. That can only go wrong. But that is hastily concluded: I do not consider the possibility that Jesus could set up additional equipment options shortly after the entry.

The truth is to be communicated simply because it is true, because there is no alternative and we are to be obedient messengers.

Paul did not receive any further information before Damascus—at least not at first—only the order, and this rather in the sense of a statement, against which contradiction was actually quite futile.

It is not for us to make ourselves dependent on whether or what or how much sense we see in it and to what extent we can make the other person understand in advance where the sense might lie for him or her and how he or she might deal with difficulties. For our part, it is a matter of inviting the other person to engage in his or her story with Jesus. We are neither in the position nor in the responsibility to make things plausible for the other person in advance, to pave the way which can only be part of the person's story with the Lord.

(Don't forget: Everyone can only work on the "jigsaw" of *his* life, *his* life themes. Piece together bit by bit, from the events of *his* life. In other words, I can do this not or in only very limited ways vicariously for others).

Praying against Evil
August 5, 2014

I quickly get frustrated by the experience of not necessarily being able to eradicate or defeat evil even as a Christian. But then to my detriment I don't think the thought: Where there is a Christian, there is not a non-Christian after all, and that is possibly part of the larger story. Possibly it is about the task to prevent certain worse things, to be a dam against certain kinds of evil, as long as one does not give room to the evil in oneself. The existence of a praying person limits the sphere of influence of the evil.

Mystery in the Larger Story
October 3, 2014

Living in the here and now, focusing on the many individual challenges in everyday life is important and necessary. But so is making yourself aware again and again that there is an underlying larger story behind the obvious, often seemingly meaningless story. Keeping that in mind helps to persevere.

One could object—as some philosophers do—that this is wishful thinking, an escape from reality, from the need to endure meaninglessness. (Job, after all, knew nothing of the background to his story of suffering.)

But: First, God's Word itself gives hints about it. (Job again—he did not know the frame story, but we are told it; the Joseph story that begins in Genesis 37 is another moving example.)

Second, they are only hints, they convey foreshadowing, nothing more—much mystery remains.

Third, the old counter-question: Where is it written that hunger is not made for satisfaction?

We should not want to be more pious than God.

Besides: wishful thinking is an insinuation, no more and no less. And this can be in play on all sides, even on the side of the skeptics and those who deny the existence of meaning.

Signs of His Nearness
November 16, 2014

Jesus says, "I am telling you now before it happens, so that when it does happen you will believe that I am who I am." (John 13:19)

(And John 14:29: "I have told you now before it happens, so that when it does happen you will believe." And John 16:4: "I have told you this, so that when their time comes you will remember that I warned you about them.")

Jesus speaks out here that he is writing history—literally; his commentary on the events brings to light hidden backgrounds of the visible processes.

"But the Advocate, the Holy Spirit, whom the Father will send in my name, will teach you all things and will remind you of everything I have said to you." (John 14:26)

This is a clear biblical basis for the view that Bible words that spring to our minds can be a form of Jesus current speaking, signs of his nearness.

What the Blind Man Sees
January 7, 2015

In John 9:1–11, Jesus heals a man born blind. What a fate! How old this man was, we do not know. In any case, he was an adult. And he has spent his life literally in the dark and in dependence on others and without the kind of perspectives that could make life worth living for other young people. How much remained closed to him, how much he remained excluded from! But now Jesus is finally coming.

My first thought: "Finally, life begins after all."

Second thought: "Why did this have to take so long? And isn't that a human being misused by God himself as a means to an end?" Grumbling arises in me.

Third thought: this second thought subliminally reflects the assumption of knowing what real life is, and to attach it to certain options with positive connotations.

But isn't that a trap? Was life before necessarily only inauthentic, actually not yet a life really worth living? Preparation that is necessary, but actually still inferior? Spontaneously it appears to me that way. But thinking further: that would be a rather depressing prospect for all those who are still permanently disabled in this life. Somehow there is some truth in seeing limitation as negative (Jesus himself sees it as needing healing), and yet it is a tightrope walk.

In any case, looking at the deficit can blind us to the fact that the relationship with God is the decisive element of life, which is basically accessible to all in all situations of life and ultimately the most reliable (and in any case the only remaining) source of happiness, hope, joy, love, life opportunities and tasks—the core of every real life. The man can indeed see now and discover completely new things in life, and yet sooner or later other limitations on this path will come, at the latest in old age. What remains is the God-relationship.

The healing, which from my initial perspective looks like a qualitative increase, a quantum leap, is from Jesus point of view rather simply a change on the path of life, on which as a whole the essential can and should be lived continuously. The actual life does not take place only in the future, but in the present and depends on whether I accept my place assignment as the only possible place of the connection with my life source and experiences of his nearness. But since this is much less visible and unspectacular (as a rule, anyway) and we are easily fixated on the visible, there is always a need for training regarding the right way of looking at things. The only real quantum leap is the one into eternity, even if there are already definitely ups and downs here. To have a longing for certain beautiful experiences is normal and allowed and is also sometimes fulfilled. But to provide these experiences with the quality seal of the somehow amoebic "actual" and thus to rebel more or less against the present, which is afflicted with shortcomings (one of my permanent construction sites), can become a nasty trap that robs me of the present.

Spontaneous metaphor: sometimes this practice to change perspective seems to me like moving our baptismal font in church. It takes several people, and it usually only works in several small pushes. A quick change of glasses I would prefer (and at least sometimes it works out that way, fortunately).

Life Belongs to the Giver
February 13, 2015

Again and again I am troubled by this overwhelming impression that there seems to be an unbridgeable gap between what I believe and live and the world around me, which leads to the equally overwhelming, paralyzing impression that the worldview of faith has something unreal, distant from life. But there is a trap hidden here. The divide is there, yes; but what does its existence say about the truth of what lies on either side of it and about the different concepts of life? Nothing. But if I continue to ask, for example, "Are the commandments good or not?" then it is clear: if everyone lived according to them, we would have the most encompassing paradise on earth imaginable, for everyone—and a much better one than that of Islam or Hinduism. We have so much chaos because so few care about God's will. This does not speak against the Christian interpretation of the world, but for it—but against the human being, who is therefore also seen quite soberly as in need of redemption.

These were helpful thoughts to get on until I could later take my bike, ride to our little lake nearby, sit down, think and pray. I slowly calmed down in prayer. I haven't given my life to me. It belongs to the Giver. To him I am responsible to accept the gift and handle it responsibly, which also includes: Not to fade out or hold in low esteem the good he gives, rather to enjoy it, and without bad conscience. Live in the moment. And this also implies—repeated for the umpteenth time—to accept my place assignment.

The Allotment Garden
May 26, 2015

A metaphor that came to my mind while reflecting on the past time and future perspectives is the allotment garden. Each of us has been entrusted by God with a little piece of "land" and is to care for and preserve it in good neighborliness and with mutual neighborly help—no more and no less; to be faithful in a small way.

Does Being Christian Change Us?
June 22, 2015

What changes when someone becomes a Christian?

The great goal: Double commandment of love. One learns

… to see the world through God's eyes

… to discover his traces in the world

… to talk with him

… to ask about his will

… to put his will into practice

… to learn to love the people around oneself.

Longing grows for fellowship with Jesus. And for fellowship with others on the way.

One becomes a witness of him who now carries and governs oneself.

These are all processes that take place with varying speed and intensity.

But they get going.

Beginning in Galatians 5:19, Paul describes how the Holy Spirit begins to transform one's character: "Incidentally, it is clearly evident what the effects are of allowing one's nature to dominate: sexual immorality, shamelessness, debauchery, idolatry, occult practices, hostilities, quarrels, jealousy, outbursts of anger, cantankerousness, dissensions, divisions, envy, drunkenness, gluttony, and many other things that are equally reprehensible. ... The fruit, on the other hand, that the Spirit of God produces is love, joy, peace, patience, kindness, goodness, faithfulness, thoughtfulness, and self-control" (translation mine).

The Service of Witnesses against Evil
June 29, 2015

Again and again the (skewed) impression assails me:

Evil manifests itself through deeds, love "only" through words. (Although this is not entirely true; but it appears like that as the effectiveness or success seems to be clearly far predominantly on the side of evil, because love does not assert itself by force.)

Islamic State (IS) terrorists, for example: Three attacks in one day, the worst in Tunisia—as it is the best functioning and democratically minded country— attacking nearly 40 tourists, simply to bring the country to its knees economically.

Evil appears so powerful, and love so weak, helpless, vulnerable, suffering.

So is it preprogrammed that evil will triumph over good, over love?

For a time: In a certain way, yes. But the day of justice is coming, even if much will be suffered until then. (Especially also by billions of people who do not have access to Christian sources of survival, a terrible and frightening fact.)

The event from Good Friday to Easter is a historical one, but also a typological one, i.e., there is a pattern behind it which also exists in other places in our lives: Life follows death, healing follows suffering. But the typologically understood three "days" can be so terribly long in our experience.

What sense does it make to nevertheless testify to the truth, even if hardly anyone wants to think about it or if it is even actively opposed?

"The blood of the martyrs is the seed of the church." This mystery still holds true. Martin Luther King Jr., Dietrich Bonhoeffer—what effect have their deaths, their steadfastness had since then!

The service of witnesses remains meaningful. The evil does not remain without objection, and some people's eyes can still open about what is really salutary for this world. Regarding the IS, for example, it is also clear that this maturing of evil shakes people up and finally makes them think about, for instance, such stupid sentences as "We all have the same God" and the like.

Equality of the sexes, human dignity, rejection of lies and violence —all of this can hardly arise from the Koran (unless factual criticism is practiced within Islam). Poisonous roots bear poisonous fruit.

Anchored in Christ
June 29, 2015

I have begun to read the Revelation of John.

"I know," Jesus says at the beginning of all the epistles. So comforting! If only I too could keep this knowledge of Jesus in mind so that it is my unshakable foundation

Revelation 3:10 literally: "Because you have kept the word of waiting on me, I also will keep you ..." Reminds me of a quote from John Ortberg:

"Sometimes faith means walking through the darkness and refusing to give up. Sometimes faith means just keeping going. Faith that makes it possible for us to be changed by suffering and darkness is not to be confused with undoubted certainty. It is only stubborn obedience."[4]

Regarding Revelation 2:13, one commentator, Schnepel, writes: "The name of the man who at that time sealed faithfulness to Jesus with death is now known in all parts of the earth by all Christians as the name of a man of whom Jesus says: my witness, my faithful one. This is the greatest thing that can be said of a disciple of Jesus."[5]

I take up the thread: This Antipas, and the nameless woman who anointed Jesus (Luke 7:36 and following), and Tabitha (Acts 9:36), all seemingly unremarkable people who made history and therefore have a place in the eternal history books, even if they play no role in the historiographies of this world.

Also important note: "Although one stood in fundamental opposition to God, one had nevertheless built the living together on forces, laws and views, which were borrowed to a good part from the church of God. The great spiritual convulsions of the end times dissolve all borrowed values. Only those who are anchored in Christ Himself still have a foothold. The rest of human society loses every common basis of life, all its connections dissolve. Every firm hold that it still thought it had is dissolving."[6]

This could already be observed in the first half of the 20th century; how much more today. Without lived faith, Christian traditions and values lose their roots and become sapless and powerless. The desperate attempts to redefine family independently of the biblical image of humans are a telling example of Schnepel's thesis.

History with a Purpose
July 10, 2015

Revelation is a mysterious book. But there are wise interpreters. Erich Schnepel's and Bishop Lilje's pastoral commentaries, for example, cut helpful paths. In his introduction, Lilje also clearly assumes that history can only have meaning if there is an end to history; if meaning is only sought in an inner-worldly way, it is in vain, and this also applies to the life of the congregation and the individual Christian. There is no interpretation of history that could satisfactorily answer the question of meaning for the individual as well as for the nations without God and without the dimension of eternity and completion. In this respect, the Christian worldview is unrivaled, without alternative (without that being a compelling proof of its truth).

The information that reaches us (just through the book of Revelation) from the eternal dimension superior to us and surrounding us sounds fairy-tale-like, yes, but this is ultimately due to the constraints such as the fundamentally human limited horizon and the diversity of cultures through the millennia. However, the impression of the fairy-tale-like can lose some of its weight when this lack of alternative is kept in mind; moreover, both interpreters succeed in conveying an inkling of what the symbolic language wants to point to.

An example of Lilje's keen powers of observation:
Every great break in the historical development startles people, because it makes visible again with one blow the backgrounds and riddles of the course of history, which the peaceful times pass be. Naivety without sense of history is the prerogative of undisturbed times, because only they can succumb to the error that history does not contain any riddles. Historical consciousness, however, is born of catastrophes, of the struggles and sufferings, hopes and afflictions of history. For only they make clear to man the limits of the course of history. They destroy the naive interpretations that want to understand the course of history only from inner-historical sources and shake people up because they suddenly become aware of the possibility of the end.[7]

One could even say: Mankind only ever asks about the course of history when it has understood that history has an end.[8]

The Eternal Walk of Fame
July 12, 2015

"But thanks be to God! He gives us the victory through our Lord Jesus Christ. Therefore, my dear brothers and sisters, stand firm. Let nothing move you. Always give yourselves fully to the work of the Lord, because you know that your labor in the Lord is not in vain." (1 Corinthians 15:57–58)

Our life may not illustrate what we most long for it to show; but we may know: it will show what Jesus intended it to show. That is what he promised, that is what he sealed with his life, and that is what counts. Because it is what the eternal "Walk of Fame" will be fashioned from, whereas the one in Hollywood fades away.

Live and Let Live? Maybe Not
August 12, 2015

While shopping, I was again strongly overcome by the impression that with my thoughts I live in a kind of pious parallel world. Even though I can't see behind people's foreheads, of course, it's obvious in many places that many people's interest is focused on simply making everyday life as pleasant as possible and distracting themselves rather than thinking more deeply. As a mental game, assuming the impression is correct (and leaving aside the eternity perspective!): Couldn't or mustn't we just give up the claim that things should be different? If people can and want to live so relatively contentedly, why not let them?

One of the problems that is lost sight of, however: The standard of living that makes this kind of life possible is earned and still maintained on the basis of other values (sense of duty, solidarity, reliability, honesty, etc.). In the long run it cannot be maintained without them, and it's even more difficult to regain once whole generations have lost or not learned basic skills; the socially weak class is getting bigger and bigger, the chances to get out of it are getting smaller; the seduction by people who take advantage of naivety is growing with decreasing own life and social competence (not to mention the whole issue of globalization and that we have to counteract the exploitation of our planet with our lifestyle). It is actually in the interest of even those people who are living more or less happily to fight against this superficiality, and even more so in the interest of society as a whole. Not to do so, to treat them like children whom one does not want to disturb in the game because the seriousness of life comes soon enough, would be an individualistic narrowing which fades out the connection with the present and future community. Of course, the question then arises what should be set against it, and at last there the Christian faith comes into play as an invitation and challenge to learn how to live, factually competing certainly with other designs. But "Let everyone live as he wants" is definitely not even an inner-worldly option and leaves things just not at a standstill, but leads to further decay. Muscles which are not trained degenerate. This applies also to mental, spiritual, and social ones.

By the way, truism actually, but attention, trap:

The fact that also people who live without asking questions must be reached does not mean that I or every Christian must be able to reach them and therefore, in conclusion, one's own faith is deficient if this does not "work." Not everyone is responsible for everyone. And also: talents are different—shepherds, teachers, evangelists etc.!

Watchword today:

"Now fear the Lord and serve him with all faithfulness. Throw away the gods your ancestors worshipped beyond the River Euphrates and in Egypt, and serve the Lord." (Joshua 24:14)

"I want you to be wise as to what is good and innocent as to what is evil." (Romans 16:19, ESV)

The Strangeness of God's Love
August 26, 2015

Supplementary thoughts to my talk on "Heaven and Hell":

I remember the story where the disciples want fire to rain down from heaven and Jesus refuses them and rebukes them, according to some manuscripts with the words, "You do not know to which Spirit you belong" (Luke 9:54f). The nature of this loving Spirit, who wants nothing more than to save, does not change. Jesus does not simply postpone the revenge with gleeful gloating, when nobody expects it anymore, according to the motto "He who laughs last laughs best."

In the presentation, I try to make clear that God is concerned with closeness, with our hearts, not with blind obedience or rite fulfillment as an end in itself. With this, however, God's being itself (not only our unfulfilled or diffuse need) triggers the question why he nevertheless hides himself over such long stretches of history without people having heard of him and without them having access to the Christian sources of strength to get through the many insanities of this world. Shouldn't his compassion for the millions of beloved seduced, beloved killed children, beloved victims of civil war, and so on drive God himself into madness? Remains mysterious.

Maybe it has to do in some way with the fact that our view of time is inadequate; that our whole world history is in God's eyes only a kind of embryo stage and afterwards still much happens which surpasses this world history and does *not* let it degenerate to a horrendous cosmic multiethnic mass grave. (Otherwise this would be a testimony that the devil would have carried off the bigger booty.) The fact is that the painful tension between God's love and our experience is an inner-Christian problem; only the statements about God's love raise expectations that do not simply coincide with our experience; we then easily jump from God's hiddenness to conclude his absence. Other religions do not have this expectation at all.

The Bigger Picture
September 17, 2015

I was thinking this morning about Revelation 1:4–8. Two aspects here.

1. We are kings. Is there any correspondence of this great statement in our so inconspicuous everyday life? Yes. Jesus's reign is characterized by loving care, by service to his people. Accordingly, where we lovingly care, faithfully serving the world around us, we are putting our (sub)kingship into practice. Thereby he will prove that love is the ultimate power that will be victorious over all destructive powers, sooner or later. Furthermore, Genesis 1:28 also belongs in this context ("subdue the earth"). This kingship signifies a return to man's original calling as ruler and keeper of creation.

2. We are priests. Once again: Something to believe against the seemingly inconspicuous daily life? No; we leave traces of it even in the visible world, where we help people into the presence of God and bring God to them, e.g., by praying, by simple witnessing. This is how we act as (sub)priests of the great High Priest. And there are powers in the invisible world that are afraid of us, not only we are afraid of them.

There is a sinful kind of pride that we must fight. No doubt about it. But the alternative is not to make ourselves small (which would basically mean not trusting God's Word regarding our true worth and calling). Rather, it is to rely on and rejoice in our renewed dignity and move forward with a bold self-confidence rooted in his redemption, expecting that we will be able to make an impact in our ordinary daily lives.

Seeing the bigger picture is a source of encouragement.

Ready at All Times
April 4, 2016

I am currently reading Timothy Keller's, *Reason for God*.

Chapter 13 on resurrection is preceded by a thought-provoking quote from the Russian writer Leo Tolstoy, which speaks of his own intense questions:

> My question—which drove me to the brink of suicide at the age of fifty*—was the simplest of all questions, which is in the soul of every human being … a question without whose answer we cannot live. It was: "What will come out of what I do today or tomorrow? What will come out of my whole life? Why should I live, why desire anything, do anything?" It can also be expressed like this: "Is there any meaning in my life that the inevitable death that awaits me will not destroy?"[9]

Important challenge for every Christian: to be able to give information about this briefly and powerfully, simply and understandably.

The apostle Peter states: "Always be prepared to give an answer to everyone who asks you to give the reason for the hope that you have. But do this with gentleness and respect." (1 Peter 3:15)

*Somehow, somewhat comforting that this can also push others to the limits like this.

The Challenge of Maturity
April 23, 2016

"Remember your leaders, who spoke the word of God to you. Consider the outcome of their way of life and imitate their faith." (Hebrews 13:7)

Is something like a strongly affiliation-based, i.e., rather dependent, faith acceptable, even wanted (different talents are no coincidence, but wanted by the Creator as a complement within the community)?

The challenge of maturity and its positive fruit are close to us due to our history and culture; however, the fact that it can also mean a positive relief when people can rely trustfully on the faith of another is seldom in view. On the contrary, when the weaker or younger in faith believe in the faith of their authority figure, for us this is rather a frightening, deterrent behavior to be overcome, almost fundamentally associated with immaturity.

Verse 7 does indeed encourage to imitate faith, that is, to already have one's own and to develop it further; but nevertheless the human example is seen as enormously positively.

So maybe there is a legitimate version of it after all; only because I myself am completely different and furthermore know and fear the uncanny danger of abuse, I did not even come up with the idea to examine it impartially. I instinctively just exclusively put everything on it and into it, to make as much as possible every church member as mature as possible. That is at least the ideal vision.

A trap can result from this:

When people are overwhelmed with our notions of spiritual lifestyle, we may begin to question (I do, anyway) whether the fault is ours or the message's, besides the very real danger of tying the authenticity of their faith to theological soundness and ability to find words for what they believe.

But maybe there is another way after all: to encourage independence if possible, but on the other hand to consciously accept it as a full-fledged possibility that it is okay if someone also or still believes in my faith and draws reassurance, assurance from it and uses his time and gifts for other tasks in God's kingdom. He must only be able to have the confidence that I do not simply make unverified assertions, parrot things; and he must also be able to have the confidence that he can ask me at any time, and I will then patiently try to trace my way of thinking. (Unfortunately, there are enough pastors who then tend to feel attacked, are afraid of losing authority, etc.) So I expressly commit myself to remain questionable, to question myself on behalf of others, and show my cards as honestly as possible.

Leading the way, like a shepherd clearing the obstacles out of the way. Not every sheep has to do the same again.

There remains a difference whether shepherds demand or allow obedience.

In this, too, genuine authority can prove itself; this can serve as a criterion of credibility.

What is decisive is the goal that everything must serve: Faith, hope, love. For help in this, the theological foundation is not always necessary to know in detail.

This can result in greater serenity with regard to preaching—not to overload it with argumentation, which is often my problem.

What Is Enough?
May 6, 2016

Being a guide—what is enough?

In witnessing to others, I do not have to have everything 100 percent clarified or secured beforehand (which is not possible anyway). I can go forward with the attitude: "Show me my thinking errors and give me something better!" This frees up serenity.

In order not to unnecessarily overload discussions with contentious systematic-theological issues, it may help to focus on Jesus and the Gospels, that is, to leave Paul and his issues rather aside for the sake of simplification for the time being. The first Christians were also full-fledged Christians and that happened without Paul. At the same time, it is good to keep Paul's about-face in mind. That in itself is an enormously strong indication of the reality of the Risen One.

Obedience. Surrender. Letting Go
June 23, 2016

When I woke up, I think already at night for the first time, and ever since, Micah 6:8 went through my mind (no idea where this suddenly came from; I can't find any conscious triggers): "He has shown you, o mortal, what is good. And what does the Lord require of you? To act justly and to love mercy and to walk humbly with your God."

Obedience. Surrender. Letting go.

And this obedience makes sense, is related to the question of meaning.

One of the main questions, perhaps even the main question, that has haunted me like a broken record these past weeks has been: "What for?"

I did not give myself my life. My life does not belong to me. Whether I see the meaning or not, consider it acceptable or sufficient or reasonable or not, is therefore first of all irrelevant, rather subordinated to the question of truth: to whom does my life belong? If the question is answered in a well-founded way, it is a quite rational conclusion to believe in meaning also there, where it sometimes (still) eludes my insight. Irrational or unreasonable, on the other hand, is to construct an ideal of sense and then to use it as a generally valid standard, possibly even as proof that sense does not exist. With it I exceed my competence, ignore my position, a part of a given whole cannot bring itself face to face to the whole.

Moreover: the existence of meaning does not equal the experience of meaning in a 1:1 ratio. The existence of meaning is the greater truth; indications of it are our need for it (usually hunger is made for satiety) and quite possibly the partial experience in our world and in our lives. But because we are part of a whole on which we cannot look from the observer's point of view from the outside, we must not conclude from occasional lack of experience of meaning a fundamental lack of meaning.

A Lighthouse in a Troubled World
September 28, 2016

Jesus wants his followers to be "salt" and "light" in their environment (Sermon on the Mount, Matthew 5–7). Experiencing resistance can be a sign of being on the right path, a lighthouse of God in a troubled world. If Christians leave this post, then it can be asked with greater justification: what then does God say to all this chaos?

The Question of Meaning
January 18, 2017

In order to regard my life as meaningful, I need:

A) the certainty of being part of a larger whole, and

B) in this place to face "solvable" challenges (otherwise motivation turns into frustration, despair, exhaustion).

What do I have to focus on in order to feel that what I am doing is meaningful and to perceive its limitations honestly and realistically, but at the same time not to be paralyzed by them? What helps not to lose sight of big goals, but not to measure everything by their achievement?

My frequent sensation of meaninglessness is mainly nourished by thinking about two different areas; on the one hand in connection with experiences of suffering, on the other hand in connection with everyday life, which is largely characterized by relative insignificance, relatively trivial things, and then by the obviously much too simplified juxtaposition of the areas—usually with frustrating results. Everyday life then seems predominantly meaningless, trivial, somehow random in any case, measured against the overwhelming needs around us. And since this conflict seems unsolvable, helplessness spreads. I now realize the error in thinking that leads to this dead end. I tie meaning too indiscriminately to whether or how far-lasting major changes to the positive in the life situation of others result from my actions. I equate meaningful action essentially with successful help, intuitively have the longer-term "benefit" in mind and measure it. And consequently I feel it inappropriate to invest my time, for instance in home improvements or cake baking or flower care instead of (somehow) "saving lives," which would be so much more necessary. (The lack of knowledge of what "somehow" could look like in concrete terms makes the matter even more depressing.)

But: If God's essence is overflowing love, to which I owe my life and which aims at shared joy (see below, John 15), then God obviously defines meaning differently or more broadly. He wants to include us into his movement of giving himself away. Then everything I do for others out of love has meaning, no matter how inconspicuous and short-lived; and that has eternal value.

If creation is an expression of God's love, then we as creatures find our identity to the extent that we allow ourselves to be taken into this dynamic, expand the domain of love, so to speak, express love, share it, give it form, help life to unfold. Basically, the double commandment of love is the answer to the question of meaning, even if the scribe at that time did not ask it so explicitly to Jesus. To get conformed to Jesus means to learn to love (he is the standard of what God understands by love), to receive love, to accept it and to pass it on selflessly, ready to sacrifice. Everything, small as well as great, that contributes to people being happy, to their lives succeeding so that they can be grateful to the Father in heaven, all such activity corresponds to our very identity, is thus an echo of divine love. Everyday life is the playing field for the competition of love. Giving oneself away leads to fulfillment, because in it I participate in God's being in a small way, reflect something of it.

Doing something good for someone "just like that," just so that someone else is happy, without looking at usefulness and effectiveness or the like—there is a different spirit than that of the "normal" world. If a Hamburg "sofa group" (witty name for "house Bible group") leaves the sofa on the weekend and cooks in the children's hospital for the parents there, just like that, then that is a contribution to "climate change," to God's reconquest of the world that has fallen into enemy hands. If someone spontaneously goes out again to get their favorite drink for their house group, that is not effective, but still meaningful.

If God is,

and if he is as Jesus reveals him,

then my life has a share in the abiding, where I give away love in and out of fellowship with him.

Then my life is full of meaning.

And it has the potential to infect others with it.

Jesus's words John 15:9 and following are central: "As the Father has loved me, so have I loved you. Now remain in my love. If you keep my commands, you will remain in my love, just as I have kept my Father's commands and remain in his love. I have told you this so that my joy may be in you and that your joy may be complete."

A Garden of Meaning
October 8, 2017

What can make ordinary everyday life meaningful and satisfying? I still feel a deep-seated aversion to revolving around the care and embellishment of one's own house and property in great detail and becoming absorbed in this small world; nevertheless, not everything about it is simply wrong. Going to the other extreme and labeling as trivial everything that isn't essential for survival can't be the solution, after all. Then the image of the allotment garden came to mind.

If I make my domestic external living area as beautiful as possible, I live according to part of my destiny, as a co-author of beauty, as someone once expressed it very beautifully; however, the joy of beauty is to be shared, and furthermore, the other allotment gardeners around me also need my help. (Consider the other metaphors in the Sermon on the Mount, Matthew 5, being salt and light.) As a rule I cannot live and experience meaning for myself alone, but togetherness belongs to the process; this is true for the outer house as well as for the house of life. In other words, the more I withdraw to myself, the less I may wonder about the sensation of meaninglessness. So go out, take good things ("garden tools") with you and give them away, and point to the inventor of all that is good and beautiful and ask for help from him. Be an ambassador in word and deed: There is a God who is good, who loves us, who has laid down his life for us. Human love as a small image of this has its origin in him.

"God Told Me ..."
October 14, 2017

A young missionary told in a report in our church:

"God told me to go to ..." In a personal follow-up interview, we asked her what that looked like in concrete terms.

She told us: Neither before nor since then has she experienced something like that. She had not really dared to tell it in her report, out of uncertainty whether this would cause a commotion. ("Others could react: 'Why do I never experience something like that?'" or the like.) Anyway: it was the weekend when the decision had to be made whether she would accept a job offer in southern Germany or go on mission. Suddenly she heard a voice behind her in the room.

The voice said: (completely surprising, unmediated, hard to describe, not like an inner thought but more objective, more almost audible):

"Don't you remember what you promised me five years ago today?"

She looked around, but there was no one in the room.

She picked out her calendar, flipped open the date to see if there was a note about the day.

It said, "For you to go off as a missionary."

Comment superfluous.

The 23:1 Trust Challenge
February 28, 2018

Watchword today is appropriate:

"Do not turn away from the Lord, but serve the Lord with all your heart. Do not turn away after useless idols. They can do you no good, nor can they rescue you, because they are useless." (1 Samuel 12:20–21)

"Therefore do not be foolish, but understand what the Lord's will is." (Ephesians 5:17)

Sounds like one-sidedness, narrowness, but it is the path to freedom.

Reminds me of the note in front of my keyboard, "Which side do you want to be on today?" For the umpteenth time, am I really practically trusting in the one I don't see as if I see him (like Moses, Hebrews 11:27)? Am I really rooted in his love, in eternity—or in other relationships, things, dreams? Without decisions, that is, also against Jesus's "competitors" (who do not have to be bad in themselves, but sometimes the good is the enemy of the better), I do not come to peace. Living in a state of waiting does not work, neither for Christians nor for non-Christians. Not deciding consciously is not simply wise deliberation, but in practicality is also a decision—to drift, or to allow others to direct me.

Under the note there is also the hint: "23:1," the reminder of C. S. Lewis's Narnia story of the Silver Armchair.[10] The prince is under the curse of the evil queen for 23 hours a day, so he lives in illusion about reality and can only see the truth for 1 hour. But the pure mass of 23-hour impressions does not change the truth. When the children come to free the prince, he has to decide with advance trust—does he trust them and the 1 hour? And when he takes the gamble and sets out with them, he realizes it was right. It makes me calmer to think of all this again.

I often think about our church experiences, retrospective phase, and often a lot of frustration comes in and wants to set the omen accordingly (devilish tunnel vision, also a version of 23:1). But, even if our dreams were nourished from right values, the values of Jesus, the Lord himself is more. Him we are to serve; then we can make peace with our place assignment. Without the exuberant use of labels like "not enough," without the paralyzing look at everything we didn't manage or didn't manage enough, at the people we didn't accompany or didn't accompany enough, and so on.

And just now, through the watchword, a perspective came to my mind that amazes me myself, but—crazily—finally noticeably helps to achieve a little more peace: If things had gone so much better as we dreamed, whether I would not have become much more dependent on it, and on top of that with less openness to recognize it—which would make it even more difficult to let go again when the time comes in old age or illness?

Blessings can be hidden in the burdensome.

Blessings Hidden in Crises
March 24, 2018

We are still in close contact with "our" refugee families and also the bigger network of the community, get concrete insights into their daily challenges; only few are Christians; and also they are struggling.

Saved yet depressed refugees in Germany: what could I say to them if they asked about the meaning of their lives?

The fact is, the world is the stage of a drama; the scene of a struggle between evil and good forces. These forces are mysterious, yes, but real.

If we want to live a meaningful life, one that is ultimately independent of the pleasant or unpleasant circumstances of our lives (whose meaning thus remains throughout), then we must choose which Lord we want to serve. What pain, what suffering the evil powers cause is unmistakable. Actually, then, Jesus is without alternative. If people are not just to look back in bitterness at their losses and somehow get through the days (waiting for death), they need a higher purpose than to strive for prosperity, for personal happiness as they have experienced it—and what has proven to be transitory.

However, this means that since the strategy of goodness involves suffering and renouncing the same methods of evil, we must learn to see and accept crises and problems as opportunities for victories in the invisible dimension. The evil one will try to tempt us to mistrust, rebellion, bitterness, resignation, etc. Every time we resist these temptations, holding fast the trust in our commander, we achieve victories, we prevent land gains of the evil one, no matter how inconspicuous it seems to us, (e.g., because these battles seem to take place mainly inside us, although this is certainly a short-sighted way of looking at things, because our charm cannot remain completely hidden). The military metaphors are very frowned upon in some ecclesiastical circles; but I think they are without alternative in their realism.

Even where we think of ourselves as ineffective soldiers, these metaphors help. Of course, not every soldier can (and should!) be an elite fighter. An army thrives on diversity of gifts. The standing guard seems to be comparatively insignificant, and boring. But where a guard is on duty, evil cannot easily invade. Where we are, an enemy soldier has no room to move. At least that is obvious. What significance the individual otherwise has in the overall picture—in the sense of the scope of his activity, for example—is ultimately known only to the senior leadership. The soldiers' task is not to act out of insight into the whole plan, but to obey. Back to the fugitives: the less they let themselves be drawn away from trust, in spite of their so laborious everyday life, the more they frustrate the power of evil. For this is about soul seduction and capture.

It may all sound theoretical and cerebral. But change begins with a renewal of the mind. And is there an alternative?

Simply hoping for better times is random.

Crises are challenges to ask oneself questions that are otherwise often suppressed; they are clear decision times. That is the blessing hidden in them.

The Potential of a Human Being
January 10, 2019

When we think about what is important to be able to make the best out of life, today we think strongly about the potential of a human being, his gifts, to be able to develop them optimally seems to us ideal—necessary, actually a right, a chance that every human being should have. Our entire education and training system is working towards this. However, seen worldwide, comparatively few have these opportunities.

But we easily overlook something. What perhaps shapes a person's character more and allows him to mature into a personality is how he deals with what he is denied. (And the more something appears to be within the realm of the attainable, the harder it is to cope with deprivation and renunciation.) This, in turn, is an experience that most people have to a greater or lesser extent, and that unites us.

Of course, this thought must not be misused to simply leave the deprived living conditions of the poor of this world unchanged. It is only a matter of perceiving that even a life that has not come to fruition can be rich, can be lived wisely.

The Impression of Triviality
July 14, 2019

What can we do to counter the impression of triviality?

Only be ourselves those who live differently and thus give tangible weight to the perspective of eternity. We must witness and live the change we want to see.

Attention: a linguistic trap. Always using the keyword *triviality* in my soliloquies in an abbreviated way as a placeholder for the phenomenon of indifference in society, lets me easily miss something important.

Triviality does describe the experience of people's lack of understanding, who shut down in the face of the message, but it says nothing about the quality of the message. However, the abbreviated way of speaking can quickly pull the objective or objectively positive meaning of faith into a negative emotional vortex and lead to questioning the objective meaning. And this paralyzes the witness service.

What Is the Story?
September 17, 2019

Knowing that a big story exists, in which our little stories have their specific place, helps our need for meaning. But therein also lies a temptation: to jump to conclusions about the possible (and desired) future course of our little stories. The trap of if-then thinking, for example: "If this door opens now, then surely that can only mean that …" But we still do not have the bird's-eye view of God. Caution before short conclusions therefore, what God could have in mind. The next step says nothing about what lies behind the next curve.

Through Jesus's Eyes
October 6, 2019

If I try to learn to see the world through Jesus's eyes, because that is essential in order to live in relationship with him, then I cannot limit that to the world as a beautiful place, but leave out his struggle for people—because it was people and their neediness that drove him to come into this world.

"The world needs non-conformist people,
who do not stand in opposition to this despairing world, but stand outside of it, calling it out to something else." (Tim Willard)[11]

An older train of thought comes to mind, observations in regard to our society:

Search and result.

People wanted tolerance—and lost the truth.

People wanted to get away from the old authorities.

People sought freedom—and often ended up in arbitrariness.

People sought love, the perfect partner—and ended up in the inability to commit.

People sought self-determination—and forgot how to integrate, how to commit, how to decide.

People looked for self-realization—and found loneliness.

People looked for fun—and ended up in boredom.

People wanted to experience more and more—and the fear of missing out on something grew and grew.

Consolation in Hopeless Times
December 15, 2019

In a book about missionary work in the slums of Manila, the author describes the deadly living conditions of these people living from garbage and in garbage. He tells how the Christians try everything to alleviate the misery at least a little bit, but that they often have to limit themselves to the proclamation of the gospel and the hope for eternity.

In such hopeless situations, what can the atheists and the militant communists still say? Aren't they left only with silence? For them, the gospel is a consolation for the hereafter, which is why they tend to work against Christians. But where there is simply no chance in this world, what a difference does it make when such a person can begin to hope that this misery is not the only and last thing he will experience in life? When he can believe that he means so much to God that this Lord will lay down his life for him so that there can be a bright future? When he can hear that evil will not win, that the day of judgment will come? This is not empty promise, but a consolation that has an effect on the present, on the self-esteem, on the strength of life, on fighting at least for the last remains of humanity in this hell instead of giving up, and many other things.

Are You Happy?
February 13, 2020

A question at the end of a crime movie is on my mind, "Are you happy?"

What does being happy actually mean?

I spontaneously associate it with being at peace with one's own life.

One thing is certain: self-centeredness does not make one happy, at least not permanently.

Devotion does.

Is that then not also—just indirectly—egocentric? No, that's not the point.

We are, after all, directed to each other; that is part of our DNA, so to speak. And this does not mean, of course, to simply satisfy the egocentricity or superficiality of others, but to help them to live well. That is our very DNA; that is what we are created to do. Otherwise it would only be a common instead of a lonely wrong way—which ends in unhappiness.

In any case, more is not possible in this world.

What can this look like in concrete terms?

A song title comes to mind: "Is there anyone there?" Christians can answer, "Yes, there is someone. Wait for him! I am waiting by your side! And pay attention to the traces he has already left! Maybe I can help you notice those, too."

This witness ministry remains meaningful and authentic, even if I still have many problems in the details of my own life. I do not have to understand everything first of all in order to authentically invite others to follow Jesus. The broad lines, the basic structures still remain correct, are not dependent on my level of knowledge and can be checked out by others.

So how can I experience my life as meaningful, "working out" (this is perhaps more accurate than "happy")?

If I do not withdraw from this witness service, but consciously practice it.

And if I learn to enjoy God's gifts in parallel—that also has its time. That is *both* preparation for eternity.

People need meaning, hope, love, help, support, acceptance.

But we can only give that to each other in a limited way.

If we ourselves know the Greater One, our Creator, who has more resources than we do, we can point others to him. This also makes our lives meaningful. We are co-workers, handmaidens, mouths of that greater One. Through this testimony, if we ourselves have experienced its truth somewhere, the world of others can also become a little brighter and healthier. If so, their gratitude for this also falls back on us. And gives us the feeling of having done something that makes sense. Giving love is satisfying.

In any case: The love of our Lord is sure for us.
And it can be the same for others.
The best way to live constructively.

Faith during Covid
March 19, 2020

Covid pandemic.

Unbelievable what we get to see and to hear.

What we cannot do anymore.

Overwhelming. Paralyzing.

What *can* we as Christians do in these surreal times?

Use your powers! How?

Give yourselves away! There are still many ways to share life.

Use your senses! How?

Draw strength and hope from the beautiful—that remains part of reality! And is a hint to the new world that still lies ahead of us. We need both to not become self-centered and develop feelings of guilt or meaninglessness.

Pray.

The Covid virus teaches us about reasonable and wholesome behavior—and about the nonsense of "I only believe what I see."

Learning to think behind things—that's what we're doing right now anyway. We don't see the virus, but we take in the info that others give us and behave accordingly, and check the info a bit afterwards with the help of the corresponding outcome of our behavior.

Admittedly, with technical means (but only nowadays!) the virus can be made visible to everyone, which is not true for statements of faith in the same way. But the view on salutary or sinister consequences is available to us also here.

Implementable Possibilities
May 30, 2020

Wise advice: You don't have any friends? Then be one.

Other variation: You don't have a home? Then be one.

Parallel to this, as a basis for it I think of the advice of the apostles for widows: they should not be "idle," (1 Timothy 5). Of course the church should also take care of them; see for example James 2:27. but that is another matter. Don't revolve around yourself as long as you can. That remains the key. It is not repression of loss, sadness and pain, but broadening horizons so as not to become paralyzed, not to sink into depression. The need for meaningful engagement is not wrong. The focus on others, on togetherness, is ingrained in our DNA. Some lonely people in my circle of acquaintances immediately come to mind. For them, too, this is an implementable possibility—they just have to consciously accept it as a task. Appropriately, I read a quote from Mother Teresa yesterday: "Not all of us can do great things. But we can do small things with great love."[12]

We *shall* go.

Some go and already have the hope in their luggage that they want to bring to others, are motivated by it.

Others have lost it or it has become small.

Nevertheless, all should go, and love, and so be realists, holding on to the truth.

This is the way of obedience. This is not hypocrisy.

The presence of hope is not a prerequisite.

New things can and will appear on the way; confirmation of the existing or new germination of what is sown in our heart on the way, without us noticing it—until it germinates.

I realize that these ideas do me good. (Visualize such core sentences in the form of puzzle pieces or index cards?)

And then, as always, in the next moment concern rises about how long it will last.

This is how it must have been for Israel in the desert. Stockpiling did not exist. Living from day to day from hand to mouth.

And thus learn to trust.

Small and Bigger Dreams
August 5, 2020

To be a Christian is to become a realist. Disillusionment.

The small and bigger dreams of our life
    sometimes come true, but often they do not.
Life means to say goodbye again and again,

to people, to plans, to dreams.
This can be very frustrating
   if there is no positive counterbalance.
Hence the question: What makes life worth living?
More helpful question: who?
"If we live, we live unto the Lord."
   Struggle with him.
   Fight for him.
   In everything we do.
   And in all that we leave undone.
It is the only relationship that remains in time and eternity.

And in this relationship, our dreams do retain their value—but they are no longer the measure of our quality of life.

Knitted for Community
March 15, 2021

I can't really grasp it yet. But I keep having to think about what it is about sharing faith and the importance of visiting and community and conversation. What is at the deepest level behind one's sense of mission, if that is what drives one? Is it necessarily just activism or a sense of duty or a search for recognition, as is sometimes insinuated? And the desire for encouragement from others on the other side? Then I thought of two stories (which, of course, have nothing to do with it): The manna story (Exodus 16) and the multiplication of bread (John 6). To save, to store manna leads to rotting. Sharing bread leads to multiplication.

Without wanting to abuse the stories and derive a general law from them, they illustrate something: Speaking hope into the life of another has a reinforcing, saturating effect on oneself; it also opens up space for shared experience. Knowledge, keeping truth to oneself, on the other hand, is somehow unhealthy. Somehow something gets lost; perhaps among other things: The practical effect, the experience of the saturating effect in the life of others remains missing and leads to a "reality shrinkage"; it becomes increasingly stale, more and more theory.

The same truth I try to tell myself has still another effect when someone else tells it to me; their conviction and experience is also in the balance and adds weight. These are all more attempts to describe something than to explain why it is so. There is something mysterious at play in this process. In any case, we are knitted for community; it is in us by creation. And Matthew 10:27, in any case, is Jesus's clear invitation to make public, to share, to spread on the rooftops what he makes clear to his disciples in private.

Fitting: watchword today. I just read: "We cannot help speaking about what we have seen and heard." (Acts 4:20).

4
WONDERING AS A RESPONSE TO REALISM

*This world is amazingly beautiful in so many ways. And it is also terribly broken in so many ways. Both are real. But our eyes can become blurred. Sometimes, in the face of brokenness, the beautiful may appear and feel surreal. Our eyes need guidance
to keep the whole truth in view.*

~

Heavenly Encouragement with a Wink
May 13, 2013

Stressful days once again, externally and internally. But we urgently needed two more gifts for the next day. So, off to the bookstore. I stood in front of the shelves, quite clueless, and had a hard time choosing. Finally I decided on the book *70 Days Under the Earth*. It was about the rescue from a mining accident. And a book on Psalm 23.

This morning I woke up with the thought of someone dying; prayed and could not get rid of the thought of passing on a certain book. Finally, I wrote a letter and brought letter and book to the flat, with a pounding heart and weak knees. The action met with an unexpectedly positive response. Relief. Later that day, Andreas told me that the birthday celebrant who had received the book on the mining accident had once worked in the mine, something neither of us knew. And at the golden wedding anniversary, it turned out that the wife had herded sheep in the past, which we hadn't known either. So we hit the jackpot. And that in a double pack. Heavenly encouragement with a wink.

The Humor of the Creator
October 4, 2013

I had to look through our photo collection of the past years. Although I'm quite familiar with it, I can't count how many times I've been spontaneously overwhelmed again and again by the beauty of nature, especially in autumn, by the colors of leaves and flowers, by the blue of the sky, the light of the sun and its seemingly endless effects on everything it shines on and through, of the colors of the rainbow against dark and threatening clouds, of the fascination of dew beads on spider webs, of snow on pine needles, of trees reflected in a still lake, of the majesty of mountains, and not to forget the wonder of animals, their diversity, their abilities, beauty, originality. And sometimes they so obviously point to the humor of their creator. *Our* creator. And it is still so little that we know of everything that exists.

Hallelujah!

Living Positively and Contagiously
April 10, 2014

After some experiences yesterday in different areas of life, but all very frustrating, I try to figure out once again very consciously how I could nevertheless learn even more to live positively in a contagious way; how a positive basic tone could come into and mark my life and—as a consequence—my conversations, so that people might get a chance to become attentive and curious. For this I try to set up a positive list for myself:

From what does joy in God feed or does joy in Jesus spring?
- Observations of nature
- Experiences of his speaking; into various life situations, i.e., essentially connected in some way with his Word
- Occasional immediate experiences (security, peace, certainty)
- Experiences of successful fellowship, grounded in common faith
- Confirmations or testimonies from all over the world that and how the gospel has healing power, where one gets involved in it.

But all this works only if one stays in the "eye school or listening school."

Let Everything that Has Breath ...
August 13, 2014

Yesterday, in a break between rain and more rain, we hiked a path along a creek in Austria's Sellrain Valley. Finally we reached a bench and sat down. All was quiet except for the constant babbling of the stream and a bird quite far away and high above us in the trees. One of those little creatures that seem to be pure energy. Its sound was incredibly clear and loud and gentle at the same time. This morning I woke up with this scene in mind. Thanks to the Lord for giving us ears (and all the other senses!) so that we can share his joy in his nature, which reflects his glory in so many ways. This bird was truly 'preaching" to its Creator!

"Let everything that has breath praise the Lord." (Psalm 150:6)

Indescribable Microcosm
October 2, 2014

While googling for electron microscope images of hair, I came across fascinating photos of the microcosm. Indescribable! God must have incredible fun to come up with quaint creatures (and probably smirks at our enthusiasm, since we can now slowly guess a little more of the greatness and ingenuity of creation thanks to technology—and how little it still is!) Total joy and enthusiasm and amazement spring up.

Opportunities for Joy
October 9, 2014

When we discover and perceive opportunities for joy, we are in that moment in fact accepting an invitation from God ("hidden" in it) to share his joy. Joy is his idea, his gift and can and should create community—shared joy is double joy, this is also true between him and us!

Faith in the Great Tomorrow
November 12, 2014

We are living in times of enormous upheaval. That is not a pessimistic perspective, but solid fact. The talk of a professor to whom we could listen yesterday regarding secularization was full of evidence, down-to-earth. It is comforting (I am realistic, can trust my senses) and overwhelming (tempting to get paralyzed) at the same time. I want to face the challenge.

How can joy and gratitude gain enough prevalence to radiate contagiously? How can I become the "sparkling (water) box" that someone recently spoke of, at which people can refresh themselves? How can I eradicate the thought that keeps coming up again and again that it would often actually ultimately be better not to be in the first place than to be in the conditions I'm in?

I remember the old note rediscovered last year:

Earth = caterpillar time, eternity = butterfly time.

(Isn't the mere fact that this comes to mind again, falls in, a pointer, a word from God?)

The positive moments now are love-signs, encouragements, confirmations of the anticipation of the one who waits at the end, will become manifest and receive us.

Everything beautiful actually has a triple weight on the scales:

1) because it is simply something beautiful in itself.
2) because it is a conscious gift.
3) because it points to the perfection that still lies ahead.

Christians know from whom it comes and what is yet to come—a double head start. This can help not to undervalue the good because of its rarity and transience, can help to invite to the creator and perfecter. Nothing releases more strength and love for today than the simple biblical faith in the great tomorrow. We do not live in the twilight that passes into the last definitive night, but into the dawn of eternity.

I have to think of the watchword yesterday, Jeremiah 18:14–15, the vivid picture of an older translation stuck with me: "The rainwater does not run as fast as my people forget me" (translation mine from LU84). I also forget him so fast, paradoxically in spite of all thinking and in the middle of it. He then often gets out of sight as a person and turns into a mental system, which I look at and examine distantly. Decisive for the possibility of positive basic mood is this: *He* must be real to me, just like everything visible.

Let Joy and Sadness Coexist
November 14, 2014

Once again I have read the Sermon on the Mount, Matthew 5–7. It just feels true, right—that's how it should be. In thinking about this spontaneous strong feeling I become aware:

Wouldn't one have to realize that "nature" actually shot itself in the foot with the production or permission of such values, when one looks at them from within the evolutionary understanding of the world? For the values of the Sermon on the Mount are in any case definitely contrary to the usual fight for survival in nature, to the prerogative of the stronger, etc.

Are there not obvious reasons for joy here?

- To know the truth
- To know Jesus
- That he still gives us time

Perhaps the challenge is simply to let joy and sadness coexist without measurements; perhaps it is diabolical seduction to think that one must feel a permanent preponderance of joy if faith is true.

When Jeremiah Comes to Mind
December 1, 2014

On so many levels the world around us is miserable, broken, on fire in so many places—how to deal with that without either going down in despair or retreating into a little idyllic world of our own? (I should have enjoyed a celebration yesterday but had not been able to find a way out of my inner rebellion against the joyful small-talks.)

Jeremiah comes to mind. And that he was given the perspective of the hopelessness of his ministry even right from the start. Maybe this is still today the mission of some individuals, of some thin-skinned people, at least at some times (Bonhoeffer, Mother Teresa and others!): To be a bearer of burdens, a fellow-sufferer, and to learn from it to become all the more a prayerful person; prayer is undoubtedly the service that is so inconspicuous and therefore so easily lost sight of. Certainly, joy is the original goal of creation, but in this world it is only possible in a broken way. And if I tied the meaning and the value of life to the amount of the joy possible here, then the life of many people would be senseless, and also conversion would not change anything. Christians in a refugee camp, for example, cannot fundamentally change the misery around them, though they certainly still even there can experience moments of joy, auspices of the perfect joy. Type and frequency may decrease more or less significantly, but to exclude the possibility in principle would give a wrong, unrealistic picture. But, as one who prays, one can still live for a long time in a really active sense, even if one cannot or not anymore change things humanly or politically or socially or if one becomes physically frail, old and increasingly understands oneself as in the waiting room to move to eternity. For whatever reason this waiting time is sometimes so long and arduous; seen in this way, it must at least not necessarily be experienced as meaningless. In any case, this is something that can be shared with anyone who wonders for whom and what his life still makes sense.

And finally: Who knows? Perhaps even being dependent on others can be accepted in some mysterious way as a service—in the sense that one becomes a challenge for others to mature and grow in the task. At the same moment as I put this into words, I feel the unwieldiness of this thought. It is a tricky tightrope walk between functionalizing suffering that way on the one hand and drawing blessings from it in the sense of Romans 8:28 on the other. ("And we know that in all things God works for the good of those who love him.")

Music!

February 22, 2015

V. Mangalwadi makes a very interesting remark in *The Book that Made Your World*: Among the indications of God's existence is music. Music is a matter of the mind; from the evolutionary point of view it is an enigma, ineffective, with no apparent purpose in terms of survival.[1] Music has also a lot to do with mathematics (with regard to J. S. Bach someone told me this before); harmony, tones are based on a "code."[2]

I continue to think; some associations:

One reason that praise of God is ordained (after all, God is definitely not dependent on it like a self-centered Emperor Nero) is probably that truth is expressed in this way; the eye is drawn to the greater truth or story, and in the heart such truth is best ingrained through music. Medicine against the unwarranted forgetting of beauty, harmony, joy.

Interesting for comparison: Islam has problems with music in many cases, out of general suspicion that music serves debauchery.

Buddhism aims at control over the breath to silence thinking and to enable the experience that there is no soul, only nothingness.

Heavenly nudge: Evening service later.

Prelude: Wonderful piano piece of Bach.

Postlude: Hymn: "Where else should I go …"

Topic of sermon: responsibility.

Take-away: mirror-foil with this sentence: "Here you see the person to whom God gave the responsibility for your life."

Joy Triggers
July 12, 2015

As I lay awake once again at night, the question crossed my mind where joy breaks through, quite directly— collecting joy-trigger situations, instead of counting sheep, so to speak. The terms stand only as summarizing placeholders for corresponding range of situations.

Examples:
- spontaneous unexpected gestures of help
- tenderness
- comedy
- understanding
- sharing
- creativity
- music
- beauty
- originality
- discoveries
- size (starry sky, etc.)
- children running through puddles
- cocky dolphins
- body awareness
- order (in nature, purposefulness)

- self-absorbed play
- "purposeless" activities, lying in the grass and smelling hay, etc.

(And don't forget: Joy is doubled in sharing and gifting!)

Playfully Creating
August 30, 2015

What I keep losing sight of, which is obviously somehow not really rooted deep enough yet:

There, where I
- feel joy
- and share joy
- and bring joy,

I participate in the original meaning and the final goal of creation.

The childlike self-forgetful joy of play and of playfully creating a world of our own, or our joy when we participate in the expanding journeys of discovery of little babies and children, reflects our Creator's joy in his creation, thus is a reference back to his essence and his deepest intentions. He created diversity—certainly not for us to disdain it and prefer hallelujah marathons.

Numinous Nearness
March 1, 2016

While reflecting on the greatness and incomprehensibility of God, the distance between him and us, it occurred to me that for many people this very feeling is the first and obvious one from which they move on —if things go well—to the experience of God's nearness. With me it tends to go the other way round. I have experienced God predominantly as near (looking back on life so far), but now there appears an even deeper feeling of his unfathomability and "strangeness"; the experience of the numinous, the at the same time fascinating and frightening, which people feel towards a divine being. I don't know whether that term (numinous) has ever crossed my mind before. Now it suddenly imposes itself. Strange.

I rummaged in earlier entries on the subject of joy. And got my reflection into view anew:

"Perhaps the challenge is simply to let joy and sadness stand side by side without measurements; perhaps it is diabolical seduction to think one should feel a permanent preponderance of joy, if faith is true" (November 14, 2014).

I think this makes sense. "Rejoice always" cannot be meant as a pious pressure to perform. Jesus sweated blood in Gethsemane, not belting out worship songs at the top of his lungs (Luke 22:44).

Contagious Joy of Life
May 7, 2016

Reflection while reading the book *Delighting in Trinity* (topic Trinity), especially regarding the—at first little concrete—statement, "God lives as overflowing love, and wants to let us participate in it."

What moved God to create the world? If we are his image, it makes sense to assume that there is some kind of echo of this in our world of experience. Scenarios like "Jungle Camp" (television show) or even "Tribute to Panem" (cinema) and the like, where everyone tries to come out on top at the expense of the other, are out of the question. But maybe something like this: Give a group of kids a bunch of Legos and let them design a world together. When we as parents see what comes out of it, how imaginative the kids are, how they help each other as a team, how they contribute their different gifts—that brings us joy. We get nothing out of it except simply joy. Or, to take an image from the last few days, when a professor like Mrs. S. experiences with her students how a conference is designed and carried out, how difficulties are mastered and afterwards everyone is amazed at what a good experience it was on all levels for the organizers as well as for the conference subjects: There is simply joy. Mrs. S. experiences the fruit of her efforts for each student, and I rejoice with all of them from the bottom of my heart, although I am only an observer from the outside.

These things happen every day all over the world, sometimes more, sometimes less (and they are as real as the evil that tries to destroy!).

This has to do with experiencing meaning, satisfaction, joy. It is an echo of the nature of God, who is also a playful God in the best sense. With immeasurable joy in creating, in creations, also to this a human echo is found in music (on the car ride today we listened to the musicals "The Fiddler on the Roof" and "Les Miserables," both so impressive in such different ways), architecture, writing, theater, technology, gardening, cooking.

Further thoughts were triggered by thinking about why one looks forward to a baby. Apart from the fact that it is a marvel in itself, it is exciting to witness how a new being discovers this world and what the child makes of it.

It continued to remind me of friends' dogs: With what exuberance they romped across the meadows on a walk—just like that, for the sheer joy of running. This can also be understood as an echo. "Because I live, you also will live." (John 14:19) God's motivation is contagious joy of life.

Joy, Relationship, and Hope
August 23, 2016

Even tidying up can be used by Jesus for timely communication. Unexpectedly I found an older birthday card.

"But this is my joy, that I cleave unto God, and put my trust in the Lord God, that I may declare all thy doings." (Psalm 73:28, according to LU84)

Joy is related to a relationship, *the* relationship, and it has to do with hope. As Kay Warren says in her book *Choose Joy: Because Happiness Isn't Enough*,[3] it is about something other than moments of happiness. It is about more. A deeper, quiet confidence in God.

Playful Echoes
August 29, 2016

In the afternoon we were a bit in the forest for geo-caching, a playful "treasure hunt" for adults. At one point there was a letterbox with very lovingly designed innards. The highlight was supposed to be the Pettling House, which housed a huge number of these little cans (pettlings). It went through my mind: As far as we know, only humans do such things, simply just for fun, for the joy of playing, more or less purposeless, at any rate not oriented to utility or purpose.

An echo of the creator, a kind of God's hint that nature is not sufficient to explain everything that is. For nature is purpose-oriented; it knows play, too, but almost only as a means to learn the skills that are necessary for survival.

What Really Is Gratitude?
May 4, 2019

Is gratitude (see the mood in the Psalms of Thanksgiving) the same as carefree rejoicing? Which rightly puts pressure on me if I don't feel that way? Probably not. First and foremost, gratitude is perception and recognition of reality, conscious appreciation of the good parts of life. Broadening of horizons.

Lord, What's Next?
June 22, 2019

When, on the one hand, I see the beauty and positive things of this world and how much more beautiful it could actually potentially be for so many more people, and on the other hand, how much negativity there is, then I cannot avoid the question of my contribution, my responsibility. I can withdraw in frustration or indifference, but then I have already allowed the poison of evil to access my roots; then I have cancelled the trust and the allegiance to Jesus, instead I have made my limited ability to assess sense and effectiveness and proportionality of the standard. Or I go up against that as well as possible within my living space, thus try to sustain and keep up faith, hope, love, to be salt and light. Because in the end, the destructive is not dependent on the few chaotic people in leadership positions, but on the many who allow themselves to be led without resistance (see also Scott Peck, *The People of the Lie*,[4] where he deals with the question of how the massacre of MyLai in the Vietnam War, among other things, could be possible). But salt must be added to the soup, light to the darkness. We are challenged to live communal life and to follow the example of Jesus's self-sacrificing devotion and love in all relationships possible to us. A self-chosen retreat into one's own small, lonely, "perfect" world is a denial of this calling—even if we ourselves could perhaps live well or better without others, the others should not live without us.

Everything has its time. What may be perfectly okay or even desirable in some circumstances—striving for and enjoying God's good gifts—may be subordinate or out of place in other circumstances. In war, many things must be put on hold for the sake of more important priorities. And war does not begin only when the weapons speak. Our contemporary efforts to achieve balance in life (work-life balance, among other things) must always be questioned by us as Christians; they are not an absolute value. Rather, the question that takes precedence is "Lord, what's next?" After all, we still have eternity ahead of us. Such a reference, however, easily has something objectionable, a note of spiritual escapism, so that nowadays Christians almost reflexively add that we should, of course, also gratefully experience the beautiful here and now. Which is undoubtedly true. But it can also be a good hiding place for the fact that in reality our faith in eternity is rather theoretical and we instinctively prefer the sparrow in the hand to the dove on the roof!

What Helps to Persevere?
July 15, 2019

Waiting time cannot be accelerated, and new perspectives cannot be forced.

I once looked up in a concordance the keyword *waiting*. Among other things: "My soul faints with longing for your salvation, but I have put my hope in your word." (Psalm 119:81) In other words, waiting is *not* joy.

"The prospect of the righteous is joy." (Proverbs 10:28) Waiting *leads to* joy—if you don't give up.

What helps to persevere?

Reassurance that it is worth it.

That waiting time is not wasted, empty time.

That promises are not empty.

That God is faithful.

To remind one another of that when we run out of breath.

How many people in the Bible have had to wait how long? And we may —unlike them, when they were still on the way—know the result, as encouragement already on our way.

I think that I must learn to internalize this change of view far more, away from the sheer duration and the unpleasant in-between time (which I don't have to gloss over) to God's character. This might be the best remedy against the weeds of resignation, fear and whatever else wants to grow like horsetail. Possibly the only one. And effective. Whereby in the case of horsetail one must consider the roots are long and deep. Stubbornly tearing off again and again is possibly the only realistic possibility against further multiplication.

In the evening I read again the day's watchword; I had forgotten it: "… we know that suffering produces perseverance; perseverance, character; and character, hope." (Romans 5:3–4) Appropriate.

Wonderfully, Mysteriously
October 7, 2019

Apart from creation, I can only discover God's traces in concrete human lives, and the closer they are to me and my own everyday life, the more credibly this has a reassuring effect on my faith. For this reason, too, people are gifts and tasks to one another.

Psalm 23: There are only two kinds of ways.

Either we are on our way *to* a pasture or we are on our way *on* a pasture. In both cases: We are not alone.

A quote I saw somewhere on Facebook comes to mind again:
"If you can't change things, why worry?
And if you can change them, why worry?"

The following outline can be helpful in making sure that giving thanks is appropriate and not synonymous with blue-eyed euphoria:

We are wonderfully mysteriously
- made   > past
- saved   > past
- accompanied   > present
- redeemed   > future

It is worthwhile to look for and list as many concrete details as possible on these points. The list could become amazingly long.

Brushing the Soul
June 13, 2020

Yesterday evening in bed I consciously tried to make myself aware once again:

We have eyes to see the never-boring breathtaking color play of sunrises and sunsets.

We have ears to hear tireless birdsong and moving compositions by brilliant musicians.

We have skin sensitive to soothing touches from people and animals (fur is such a great invention!).

We have olfactory nerves that trigger memories of happy moments (mountain air and beach) or make us breathe in with joy in the present (after a refreshing rain shower or in the autumn forest).

We have taste buds that give us pleasure from food (nerve food or soul food).

We have senses that allow us to experience the beauties and preciousnesses of this world in both large and small things.

Beauty is real. Not only the chaos.

The Creator behind it is real.

This is what I want to go to sleep with and wake up with.

That has to be firmly and big on the door of the snail's shell, as a friend would say.

Brushing teeth is important, brushing the soul even more.

One thing is certain: I take myself with me everywhere. If I don't manage the return to joy here, I will most probably not manage it elsewhere either. I need a certain independence from the external circumstances for my inner health. The heavenly reference point, the faith relationship must be the basic and decisive food source. There is no other way. This cannot lead to the underestimation or devaluation of the earthly, but to the appropriate, realistic evaluation and appreciation, and safety from external overestimation and overestimation.

5
DOUBTING AS TRAINING FOR REASSURANCE

Most Christians know doubts. Not all of them dare to face doubts. Still less to talk about them. Doubts can be very painful. But they can also be useful to learn about pathways out of the inner jungle, temptations to give up, and what helps us to go on.

~

On What Is Hope Based?
July 28, 2011

So much in this world is incomprehensible.

So much that God does and does not do is incomprehensible.

But in the end (Revelation 21:4), he himself will wipe the tears from our faces—that is, he lovingly keeps each individual in view.

On what is this hope based?

On the nature of Jesus, who saw the individual, who washed the feet, who took injustice, who gave a chance to the outsiders.

He healed, yes, in that he set signs of what his real will is and that he has begun his messianic ministry. But he did not—yet—fundamentally eliminate disease.

And he did not simply change the often at least equally agonizing social circumstances that afflicted people; that is, it was clear that life in this world would remain a life of struggle and hardship, but with him at their side.

Interesting: God basically legitimizes the question of *Why?*, namely asks it himself, the other way around, and what is decisive is what consequence we draw from what disturbs us.

"They have turned their backs to me and not their faces; yet when they are in trouble, they say, "Come and save us!" (Jeremiah 2:27)

"They did not ask, "Where is the Lord, who brought us up out of Egypt ..." (Jeremiah 2:6)

There are two opposite views.

Look at this terrible event—there you see, what God is really like! (devilish whispering).

Or:

Look at the whole history and nature and above all Jesus. There you see, how I really am.

Listen to my word, persevere; your personal Good Fridays are followed by Easter Sundays! (God's guidance).

Whether specific tasks or larger experiences, we tend to see the senseless and displace the senseful. But there is another picture where we find hope.

If I Were God ...
June 23, 2013

Sometimes, when I watch the news on TV, for example, the following flashes through my mind:

"If I were God, then wouldn't I ...?"

Not a very sensible thought.

Particularly since behind it an equally sense-poor short circuit lurks.

As God's behavior obviously is not what I would expect as natural from such a powerful and loving being, maybe he's not there at all?

Nevertheless, these doubtful thoughts unfortunately have something in common with horsetail—to simply eradicate it does not really work. The stuff has stubborn survival strategies.

So I'm getting into it more thoroughly. You can think it through to the end on a different level, "one size smaller."

"If I were president of ... then ...," yes, what exactly would I do then? Depending on the "I," the right, meaningful action would turn out very differently, depending on the country, culture, age, gender, knowledge, biography, place on the timeline of history, and so on. And what would be right and good for the one people, it would not necessarily be so for another one!

In other words, just because I, as a German, do not understand what an African president considers sensible, that does not necessarily mean that his decision is senseless and that he is a bad president. Things are much more complex.

Related to doubts of faith:

My ideal conceptions of God may be still so well-meant (and partly even quite shaped by God), but how absurd is it to take them and my limited horizon as a yardstick and try to justify doubts: If God is so other than I am, this can only speak against his existence.

What Do We Actually Know?
July 4, 2013

Our dog limps towards his last days. It is heartbreaking. Twelve years of amazing loyalty, trust, fun and so much more. "Only" an animal? Definitely not—not in the eyes of his Creator, not in our eyes. And a lot more is going on around us, as usual.

(… message we have heard from him) … "God is light; in him there is no darkness at all." (1 John 1:5)

How does this image of God fit with our experience of distress and disturbed or destroyed life?

The old theodicy question.

There is the God who actually does not want evil with all its concomitants. Who proves this "actually not wanting" in Jesus's healings. And who promises the coming of the day when he himself will wipe all tears from our eyes.

But who seems to have looked on or looked away for such a long time before and continues to do so outside of Israel during Jesus's lifetime and again afterwards—doesn't he? At least, that's how it often seems to us.

So how does this fit together?

"Simply believe"? But it is not that simple.

What do we actually know anyway?

Taking time to come up with a list of answers that are as specific as possible can be very helpful.

My bottom line: Not much.

And yet enough to be able to trust with good reason.

And yet again too little to ever be finally above all conceivable doubts on this earth.

And above all too little, in order to set up an absolutely conclusive system.

In other words, the only thing that works is to accept: We can only approach the whole truth, the contradiction-free understanding on the one hand, but on the other hand we can do at least this after all, and again we cannot reach it in this time. And therefore not to be frustrated, but to live with conviction step by step in this time present with Jesus, to enjoy joy *and* to accept difficult things as a challenge, not to let ourselves be pulled away from him ... in the best case thereby sensing or in the certainty that all alternatives are only worse than what doubts or unbelief whisper to us.

The "At Present Unsolvable" Pile
August 18, 2013

My head long knows that we will not find a satisfying explanation for many unfortunate experiences in this world. Nevertheless, it is so difficult to simply leave this question on the "at present unsolvable" pile, not to fight nevertheless again and again for a kind of mental system, in which I can accommodate somehow everything more or less plausibly. But God obviously resists that, even if it is about a well-meant biblical system. I therefore ask myself what I ultimately expect from it; what I am missing. Probably a greater sense of security, of control. Whether such a system would really achieve that is an open question. After all, there are situations where we have explanations, and yet they are difficult to bear—if someone has permanently damaged his lungs through chain smoking, the difficulty in breathing is not made easier to bear by the fact that he knows the cause.

Perhaps God refuses to give us some answers because we would not yet understand them; also perhaps because he knows that they would not help us as much as we expect them to. But he knows above all that we need him, the community of life, not a mental system; that the constant dependence on him ultimately opens the best possibilities of life and thereby also forms our personality especially in the difficult situations.

The Silence of God
August 20, 2013

Somebody called. Tears. Despair. Unfair attitude of others on top of the pain. Time was pressing for the other one, but at least I could offer my ears. Some of my ongoing reflections afterwards:

About the "silence of God" with regard to the insanity in our world: actually this is a misleading expression. He has not been silent, but has said everything in different ways and more than once, what has to be said—how life is meant, how it can work—and basically everyone who thinks knows that we would have paradise if we kept the commandments. But that's just what's lacking. The same goes for actively advocating the spread of the Christian faith. This contradicts the spirit of the age, which believes that all people should seek heaven in their own fashions (which, in the final analysis, means that Islamists should also be granted the right to forced Islamization).

A more correct expression would be:

By and large God seems not to enforce his expressed will, not to intervene or at least to limit the worst manifestations of evil, at least not in such a way that this would be somewhere clearly recognizable.

Decision Day
September 1, 2013

Doubts should be pursued as thoroughly as possible, thought through to the end, alternatives should be examined. In the interpretation of world and life experience, no one has 100 percent certainty; there is always a belief against another belief, not belief against knowledge. But if one wants to remain coherent in thinking and acting, and ultimately be viable, the day must come when a decision is made to which one adheres and to which one refers back again and again: Because everything has already been weighed to the best of one's knowledge and conscience.

Constant wandering between worlds is no solution. There is no "no man's land." That is a devilish illusion. I live in every moment, and the only question is on which side. To delay the decision only means to increase the practical schizophrenia in everyday life, namely to function on different levels sometimes as a Christian and sometimes to think as a doubter and thus to live inconsistently.

It can also be helpful to keep in mind that doubters, atheists, agnostics such as Camus, Nietzsche and others cannot unleash freedom, courage, hope, fighting spirit by their views as it has happened and happens again and again by Christians.

C. S. Lewis has described a very wise guideline in his Narnia stories. *The Silver Chair* is about a prince who has been kidnapped and enchanted into the underworld. Every night he experiences an hour of altered consciousness—an hour of truth, but which the witch sells to him as an hour of lies and has therefore ordered his shackling during this time "for his protection," which the prince accepts. Finally the children come to help free him after strong doubts on his part about what the correct view of the things is (can the *one* hour contain truth, if 23 speak against it?). The witch comes back, recognizes the situation, and tries again to subject all to her spell (and à la Feuerbach to make the upper world implausible as wishful thinking). What is really true—that is the struggle at stake. The witch says, "Your experiences are illusion." Finally, Mourning Puddler says:

> Suppose we really dreamed all these things or made them up—trees and grass and sun and moon and stars and Aslan himself. Suppose it were so. Then I can only say that the made-up things seem to me to be a good deal more important than the real ones. Suppose this black abyss of your kingdom is the only world. Well, it seems quite poor to me. And it's a funny thing when you think about it. If you are right, we are just children playing a game. But four children playing a game can create a fantasy world that dwarfs yours. And that is why I will stick to that fantasy world. I am on Aslan's side even if there is no Aslan. I will live as well as I can as a Narnian, even if there is no Narnia.[1]

Lewis is worthwhile. Again and again.

And People in the Universe
December 25, 2013

Crazy weeks and days. In the end, both of us were involved in three Holy Eve services, Andreas even with an infection. And now, only a few hours later, we are finally sitting in the plane on the way to the US for the wedding of our daughter. Surreal. And then:

This infinite vastness ...

God creates the biggest and smallest parts of the macro- and microcosm. And we: We despair at the impossibility of being able to classify the little piece of the puzzle that we survey—which is, after all, a somewhat megalomaniacal enterprise. Reasonable would be to let go of the small and big things of my life again and again trustingly into God's hands.

The following consideration can be helpful for this:

Ants understand their small world. And understand each other. Bees also. But ants and bees already don't understand each other. Even less do they comprehend the larger context in which they live and are arranged. The felt tininess in itself and the limited horizon does not speak against the existence of meaning, does not compel to think that there is also no higher context on the next higher levels. To believe that, to understand oneself as another "ant people" in the universe, is perhaps a perspective which helps to find realism, reasonable humility, better than to sink into unbelief and agnosticism.

"Why Did God Let This Happen?"
February 1, 2014

"Why did this happen to me? Why did my son, of all people, have to die in this accident?" "Why did I have to get such a mysterious disease?"

And the like.

A few thoughts on how to deal with such a question.

What can we assume?

1. God can "make good out of evil," he can even use evil to teach us good, no question.

2. But he does not do evil, otherwise he would be the devil or the Roman god Janus with the two heads, but not the God in whom is light and not darkness.
3. Again, but at the same time, he still has control over evil.
4. Thus we end up with a paradox—the age-old question of theodicy, which we cannot solve on this earth.

There are always people who—perhaps with good intentions—use the consolation contained in the first point to say to themselves or to others: "God is not afraid to send someone suffering because of their lack of faith or some offense." For example, I remember a Catholic woman telling me: in earlier times, women basically had to go through special penitential rituals after a miscarriage. Miscarriages were thus obviously understood as a consequence of personal sinful misconduct. That this had a very negative effect on their image of God should be understandable.

How I deal so far with the search for causes of experiences of suffering:

I am very cautious and reserved when people use phrases like "God did this or allowed this to happen so that ...." That sounds too much to me as if an individual failure could be the only reason for a situation, behind which, in reality, there might be a more or less complex network of causes and goals. The painful experience of the person in question is, after all, only one of the puzzle pieces in a much bigger picture; not everything in life is simply about me, and I usually cannot analyze Satan's role in it, nor have I insight what God's goals are. That's why, in counseling, I usually try to get away from the fairly automatic question of "Why did this happen to me?" Instead I ask, "What can I do and learn from this with God's help?" The question of who caused the problem is backward-looking, is an unpromising guessing game and costs unnecessary resources. It is usually more helpful to look forward, to face the existential challenge and not to burden oneself with diffuse feelings of guilt on top of everything that is already difficult, where no clear connection can be seen. (If a chain smoker gets lung cancer, that is a different situation; there are tangible approaches for connections.)

And even where I can say for myself in retrospect, "I learned this from the crisis," or "That has become surprisingly helpful to me in dealing with others in a similar situation sometime later," even there I am wary of saying, "That's why God let me go through this." To be able to judge whether that was the meaning, especially the only one— for that I would have to be able to see things from God's comprehensive perspective.

Appropriate: What is good luck–bad luck?

A parable from China tells of a poor farmer who cultivated a small field with a tired old horse and lived more poorly than well with his only son. One day his horse ran away. All the neighbors came and pitied him for his misfortune. The farmer remained calm and said, "How do you know it is bad luck?" The next week the horse came back and brought ten wild horses. The neighbors came and congratulated him on his great good fortune. The farmer replied thoughtfully, "How do you know it is good luck?" The son caught the horses, took the wildest one, and rode off on it. But the wild horse threw him off and the son broke his leg. All the neighbors came and wailed about the misfortune. The farmer again remained calm and said, "How do you know it is a misfortune?" Soon a war broke out and all the young men had to join the army. Only the son with his broken leg was allowed to stay at home.

We often see good luck and bad luck only superficially, inaccurately and wrongly. We think—like the neighbors—only of the visible and present. But things are often quite different and deeper and belong to larger contexts. God sees the events quite differently. He sees the background, the connections and the effects. More important than understanding is then trust![2]

So Many Why Questions
February 6, 2014

On YouTube, there is a video that tells of an African girl and her uncanny story of illness ("My face is eating me alive.")[3]

While watching, everything kept cramping up for me.

One side:

Why does God allow such a thing?

Why does God literally take so much time?

Why this roller coaster of hope and new tumor growth?

There is no answer for us in this life, even though everything in you is literally screaming for it.

The other side:

If they had not had faith (which is ultimately a consequence of mission over x stages!), they would have given up long ago. Then not so much love could have been given.

Then not so much love could have been experienced.

Then the hope would have died long ago and the girl too.

Literally incomprehensible in every respect.

Later I had the thought (abbreviated): The girl could have been operated on (both times) much sooner, if, for instance, the financial help had come faster (that it came at all, is already a miracle in itself, a sign that God pushed some people, made pressure, even if almost at the last moment).

This shows: To look only at the disease and then spontaneously regard God as the culprit who is ultimately responsible is not true to reality. Also human failure plays a role—the general inadequate willingness of mankind to share with each other in such a way that everyone can live as well as possible and get help. And how bad is it that even such an insane tumor does not get more people moving. How jaded we are already today.

And: If you look at what "less bad" terrible suffering relief organizations like Mercy Ships try to alleviate and how they are constantly confronted with the agony of choosing who to treat, I wonder how many of us Christians have probably overheard the call to "Go into all the world." Of course you can ask again why God doesn't just give his people an appropriate kick, I know, but somehow things are obviously much more complex after all.

An Intertwining Image
April 3, 2014

I came up with an image of the intertwining of divine, devilish, human will and action.

A polar bear in the polar sea: He finds worse and worse living conditions. If he were able to think about the observation of the change, he would not be able to analyze what are "normal" variations and what is due to human interventions. He may not even know of the existence of human beings, and even if he did, he would have no idea of their role in the whole, of their abilities, motivations, and so on.

Thus, also we can hardly—or not at all—get a grasp of what is happening in the dimensions above us, cannot analyze in a differentiated way which factors and actors have caused and made possible, for example, a bad event.

Exit from Doubt
April 15, 2014

The Christian fool is the person who considers every security to be extremely uncertain

... who relies on an invisible as if he saw him

... who hopes in death and dies in life

... and with all this makes himself ridiculous to the wise. (Tatyana Goricheva)[4]

Doubts can play a constructive role—if they lead to research and thereby to more clarity and better grounded views. But they can also play a very destructive role. Images from Tolkien's novel *The Lord of the Rings* come to my mind, when the ring owners have difficulties, even into the physical, to resist the attraction of the ring and let it go.

These scenes expose the potentially destructive and mendacious nature of doubt, which can develop a diabolical momentum of its own. It likes to try to present itself as a neutral, factually necessary or, in any case, to a certain extent harmless instrument for finding the truth, even when no more new information is to be expected, and the time finally had come for consideration, decision, and choice of standpoint.

Perhaps we hope to be protected from mistakes, from disappointments, by remaining in a state of limbo. Might we not have overlooked something after all and should therefore rather not commit ourselves? But this is a deceptive self-protection. Once again Tolkien: There are rings, chains of thoughts, which are themselves the worst.

They start at some point to give off a creeping poison that generally makes the ability to trust dwindle.

However, the problem arises: to notice when the friend becomes the enemy, to find the right time to separate. Thinking to the end can probably become an essential helper in this dichotomy.

In this case this means to ask: What is it in concrete terms that blocks my exit from phases of doubt? Why can't I make the decision: "So, that's enough now, actually everything that can be clarified about the sustainability of the Christian faith has been clarified, and therefore there must be an end to the musings"? Can I tell clear *reasons* for my hesitating? Or does it simply still *feel* somehow artificial, erratic, spasmodic to decide for exit?

And in the latter case I can ask one more question: Would waiting really change anything? Would I ask for more time to think? For what? I know in the end: none of this would make sense.

Why should I have a right to a thorn bush experience like Moses or similar spectacular things?

And even then, the next valley would come anyway; to build on mountaintop experiences makes little sense, I should know that by now.

And: Jesus just does not impose himself. In fact, he has already been embarrassingly patiently present in my life again and again. Actually, I have therefore got on much further compared to the situation in which people always are who are encouraged at ProChrist-evangelization and similar events to take the one step that is up, no matter what it looks like in you, and to leave the rest to Jesus.

To be an "arsonist" in a positive sense—yes, I wanted that from the beginning (a small booklet with this name, which was the program, was my companion after confirmation for a long time). It is strange that exactly this topic came up in the Passion devotion today.

In addition, this morning while reading the Bible, in John's Gospel, I stumbled over the verses where Jesus tells the disciples something three times expressly in advance, so that they will remember afterwards—an indication that rational guardrails are also important to him, that he wants to give us help on several levels.

And then there is the sermon that was sent to me "by chance" this evening. Increase your entrusted talents and use what God has entrusted to you." How many more broad hints do I actually want?

Avoiding Decision
April 16, 2014

Once again, avoiding a decision is unreasonable.

What would I do in the event of a serious illness? I cannot constantly ask whether I want to take medicine or rather give up. I must consistently pursue a strategy and subordinate everything else that wants to oppose it to the corresponding decision and stick to it in the long term regardless of short-term bouts of weakness.

Watchword today:

"By day the Lord went ahead of them in a pillar of cloud to guide them on their way and by night in a pillar of fire to give them light, so that they could travel by day or night." (Exodus 13:21)

"I am the light of the world. Whoever follows me will never walk in darkness, but will have the light of life." (John 8:12)

To turn away from you, O Lord, is to fall;

to turn toward you is to rise,

To live in you is to endure forever.

Give me your help in all tasks,

your guidance in all uncertainties,

in all suffering your peace. (Augustine)

How appropriate.

How Can We Make a Difference?
June 22, 2014

Psalm 34 was today's worship psalm. The pastor preached about Rich Man-Poor Lazarus (Luke 16:19ff). We are the rich; do we open our eyes, notice the needy at our door, who cannot help themselves ? A hundred Syrians have come to our little town of Minden as refugees on the weekend.

Yesterday, an American friend wrote (I think she is also dealing with the chaos around us right now): "The question is *why*? are we at the highest point globally since WWII in terms of migrants fleeing their homelands?"

I had just read a newspaper story about gross mistreatment of refugees when they arrived in Europe (early days of the refugee crisis).

My response: Europe. Formerly "Christian Occident."

Twenty-first century: *Really?*

Every time I think about these questions, I feel intense tension—and that is more than often. The photos and reports of what happens at the borders of Europe are and remain shocking. And the biographies and frustrating perspectives of those who manage to reach our cities here and eventually our neighborhoods are generally tragic as well. In most cases, dreams burst like soap bubbles. I know names, faces. Not many, but I know they are representative, and that's all I could carry right now. And I can't even help these as I would like to. This stirs guilt in me, even though I know it's an irrational feeling.

I can't see any answers or solutions to these problems—human-made, but transcending human ability to overcome them. As Goethe said in a famous poem ("The Sorcerer's Apprentice"): "Those I called, the spirits, I now cannot get rid of."[5]

We absolutely need a revival, yes, and it would also have to be a worldwide one of immense proportions. I don't see what else could help, and even that would only be a beginning.

But I also don't see how it should come about; rather the opposite is predicted for the end of days. And so many people suffer who—at least from a human perspective—never had a chance worthy of the name.

I also don't see any alternative to Christianity, neither on the theoretical level nor on the existential one. But I still don't see how we can make a difference either, except at best for a very few people around us. And even there, in my immediate context, I often feel an overwhelming, paralyzing helplessness. Fighting that takes most of my strength, and it doesn't get better with age. I still know we can be a blessing to some and that everyone counts. But facing the exponentially growing masses of people who can't be reached and healed and supported is just awful. And I can't even avoid contributing to some of the problems, even though I see them. I'd give a lot to be able to stop thinking, to get rid of the burden. But it looks like I'm not allowed to do that.

Perhaps in the future, for our children, this will become more and more a part of the Christian life—at least not to close our eyes (as so many already do) and to speak out for those who cannot do so themselves, even if the words are few and weak; at least to help one or the other and thereby give an indication that with God every individual counts; at least to pray for those helpless and oppressed masses whose names and faces God alone knows. And thus, to a limited extent, of course, to share the sufferings of Jesus. This certainly does not reflect the mood and attitude of the many who adhere to Positive Thinking and the Prosperity Gospel (I've had to deal with some of that recently), but biblical realism.

I suspect I'm not making your heart any lighter with these words. But still, maybe it's at least helpful to know that others are fighting similar battles.

Humble with the Truth
July 13, 2014

A student of theology from Asia is struggling with how his culture's mindset and way of thinking is so different from ours and the Jewish or biblical one. We have long discussions. The pain is real—how can at least information and basic communication be possible or successful under these circumstances? I can't get the discussion out of my head.

"Go and make disciples of all nations …"(Matthew 28:19)

If there is a truth that is valid for all, there must be a communicable elementary core. We cannot produce faith even with perfect communication (if it existed), but the information to whom and to what faith should refer would have to be communicable.

I think that with regard to some of the questions our life raises, it makes sense to think fundamentally about the nature, possibilities and limits of our ways of thinking. This can help us to remain humble and cautious on the one hand, and on the other hand, perhaps, to discover new aspects of our complex reality or to see familiar things in a new light.

But: In my opinion, the essential elements of the gospel would have to be quite independent of this. Otherwise it would not be a worldwide message of salvation for all peoples, all cultures, all languages, educated and uneducated, healthy and sick, young and old, rich and poor.

Opposing Spontaneous Distrust
November 19, 2014

In *The Hope of the Gospel*, George MacDonald writes: "Obedience is the soul of knowledge."[6]

Spontaneously, I react ambivalently, even rather negatively, although I somehow also find the expression "soul of knowledge" very good. Why ambivalent? The idea that obedience is the appropriate response to truth is found several times in the New Testament. In me, however, the primacy of obedience triggers the fear that with it my possibilities of finding truth might be restricted, filtered, as if I were put into a tunnel or into a one-way street.

But I must debunk this notion as false.

It is rather the other way around. Take via ferrata, for example: I can read endlessly about it. I only find out what it's like when I get involved with a rope team. The practice does not narrow my horizon, but expands it, involves further senses. I have to oppose this thought of spontaneous distrust.

Facts and Emotional Doubts
November 24, 2014

Struggling with doubts is exhausting. Being alone with it makes it even more difficult; it is all the more helpful when one meets experienced companions who are similarly wired and struggle with the same problems. This is what happened to me with Gary Habermas,[7] an American theologian. I came across him "by chance" (and at a very appropriate time), in the appendix of a book on a completely different topic. And it turned out that in years of struggle he developed practically identical thoughts and strategies as I did: Keep factual and emotional doubts apart (the existence of negative emotions says nothing about the truth of the facts, that is two different things).

Clarify factual questions and record the result; make memos and carry them with you; write down important thoughts and experiences every day and go through them again and again; counter the stubbornly recurring doubts just as stubbornly with the answers and mnemonics found up to then.

I often feel that being dependent on such aids is shameful, somehow childish. To see that someone like this professor knows nothing else and certainly nothing better, is therefore very relieving.

To the possible objection that this could all amount to a kind of self-organized brainwashing, in which I try to hammer into my head what I simply want to believe in spite of reality, I came up with the following comparison:

If you want to climb a high mountain, you not only have to prepare yourself thoroughly for the conditions of the mountain, but also familiarize yourself with possible reactions of the body in extreme situations. The fact is, at a certain altitude, oxygen becomes less available. This can lead to misjudgment and misbehavior in certain situations. I have to condition myself beforehand so that I can behave correctly in danger—based on facts and not on feelings. It is not about "The Emperor's New Clothes" (a German fairy tale in which noble clothes are pretended to be there and seen, which is all a lie), but about appropriate and necessary behavioral training.

Related to struggles with doubt: The greatest possible clarification of the factual issues is, after all, at the beginning with good reason and is consciously sought.

Enduring Powerlessness
December 28, 2014

The comforting and confidence-boosting thought that crossed my mind today in worship was that Jesus must have gone through this emotional distress of theodicy-issues himself. Before he began his public ministry, he certainly experienced much hardship around him without intervening. So he has consciously endured powerlessness—children with pain and illnesses that cannot be treated, poor people without perspective and social network, and many more. So at least he knows how we feel and what it means that sometimes your stomach just turns. At the same time, you get knots in your head trying to imagine what might have been going on inside him.

Perceiving
February 23, 2015

Very good impulse:

"According to a Buddhist parable, five blind men try to describe an elephant. One palpated its feet and proclaimed, 'The elephant is like a pillar.' The second leaned against the elephant's flank and scoffed, 'This is nonsense. The elephant is like a wall.' 'Not at all,' interjected the third. 'The elephant is like a rope', and held its tail. The fourth angrily declared, 'None of you have grasped the truth! The elephant is like a fan', and cooled with its ear. The fifth thought all four of them were out of their minds. 'The elephant is like a pointed, polished stone,' he said, stroking the elephant's tusk."[8]

The author Mangalwadi continues: five blind men and one elephant— what if there were a sixth man who could see and help the others perceive the other parts of the elephant (with senses other than the eye)? "That would be tantamount to a revelation."[9]

By the way:

People who see all religions as equally inadequate to grasp the whole truth often use this image in order to fight arrogance and call for tolerance. But whoever does this regards himself at that moment as the only one who sees correctly, who has a bird's-eye view of the religions. Why is this self-image not arrogant? One seems to call to modesty, but in truth one takes thereby just a point of view which one wanted to reject actually as super-human.

Life after Birth
May 12, 2015

Days of sorrow, grief in our family. Time for thankfulness, hope, but also for doubts once again trying to creep in here and there.

The old story comes back to me:

Is there life after birth?

A pair of unborn twins are talking in their mother's womb.

"Tell me, do you actually believe in life after birth?" asks one twin.

"Yes, definitely! In here we grow and become strong for what will come outside," answers the other twin.

"That's nonsense!" says the first. "There can be no life after birth. What would that look like?"

"I don't know that for sure either. But it will certainly be much brighter than here. And maybe we'll be walking around eating with our mouths."

"I've never heard such nonsense! Eating with your mouth? What a crazy idea. After all, there is the umbilical cord that feeds us. And how are you going to walk around? The umbilical cord is much too short for that."

"Yes, I'm sure it will work, it's just that everything will be a little different."

"You're crazy! No one has ever come back from after birth. Life ends with birth. Period."

"I admit that no one really knows what life will be like after birth. But I do know that we will see our mother then and that she will take care of us."

"Mother? You don't believe in a mother, do you? Where is she?"

"Well, here. All around us. We live in her and through her. Without her, we couldn't be at all!"

"Nonsense! I've never noticed anything about a mother, so she can't exist."

"Yes there is, sometimes when we're really quiet you can hear her singing. Or feel her caressing our world." (told by Henri Nouwen[10])

God Does Not Need Memory Chips
May 25, 2015

Today, we are an open book for surveillance services. There are computer brains that can store gigantic amounts of information and filter it in a short time. The movements of a "bugged" person can be recorded exactly. What a computer brain still lacks in comparison to a human being, is the consciousness of itself, the ability to face itself to a certain extent.

But if all the other things are already humanly possible, then modern humans should actually have much less difficulties with an omniscient God than our ancestors. That the Creator, to whom we owe our existence and abilities, is above our possibilities, is no longer just a logical, but still completely abstract thought; modern technology provides our imagination with mnemonic bridges. For example, the Creator could have built into all of us an as yet undiscovered "chip" through which he keeps us in view, but even more likely he does not even depend on it.

Feeling at Home
May 26, 2015

Maybe sometimes doubts can be overcome to a certain degree by "simply" living through them! Like living through a bad weather episode!

Anyway: Not only doubts tend to do their work partly under the surface of our consciousness; the Holy Spirit does so as well. It is difficult to describe, but after many rather unsettled weeks the guiding perspectives in my heart seem to consolidate again. It has to do with emotions, but it seems to be more, somehow. How dangerous it is to build on feelings I know only too well; but again, to live without them or with the wrong ones is not possible in the long run either. Something like a basic "feeling at home" ("Heimatgefühl"), related to Jesus and following him to the eternal goal, is fundamentally important.

A metaphor comes to my mind: It makes a big difference whether I can see myself as an exhausted child in the arms or on the back of the strong father or whether I see myself as a worn-out hobbit in front of the huge closed entry of the mountain without any idea how to open the door.

For further reassurance on the rational level, I find it helpful to remind myself few questions agnostics have to face:

Why is something—and not nothing?

How can life arise from lifelessness?

How can ethics arise from nature?

I can't see a convincing alternative to the Christian answers.

Cautious Conclusions
July 1, 2015

Yesterday was bad. Not outwardly, but inwardly. The vehemence of the negative thoughts and feelings was immense; deep passionate aversion against life ("things simply shouldn't be as they are"). The triggers for this phenomenon are exchangeable, of secondary importance, can be news, problems in family or church. The decision to prefer a peak tour in the mountains over against a more harmless hike was helpful; the physical challenge at least reduced the inner tension a bit. I do not understand why I still face such attacks.

So I try anew to remind myself of these truisms:

I cannot understand the problems of the world, still less solve them.

I cannot solve the problems of those whom I love.

I cannot even solve my own problems.

And Jesus could, but obviously he has very different ideas regarding that. There seems to be only the choice between two sorts of "surrender"—confidently or with gnashing teeth.

Problem: If obviously I cannot make peace with this permanently—how can I dare to tell others? But then the next question arises: What is the meaning of my life? So far I have seen that in being a land-post, a witness to Jesus.

So this kind of crisis attacks my basis.

Dangerous trap: to conclude from the obvious or supposed deficiencies of Christians the unreality, untruthfulness of faith. In such a moment I see through a filter, see only the deficiency, not what would be if the person in question was not a Christian! Consider the Epistle to Thyatira in Revelation 2:18: So much life, and yet also great danger. Jesus does not conclude from the existence of the false and sinful the inauthenticity and hypocrisy of the right—both are really there! That is true for myself as well.

Truth Proves Useful
July 30, 2015

The truth does not become untrue because people do not live up to it. This also applies to Christians who fall short of what they should and could live. On the other hand, the truth proves to be useful for life where it is followed. Actually, this should be self-evident. But I sometimes tend to forgetfulness or to wrong conclusions from everyday experience and thereby open myself to the doubt an unnecessary gateway. "If not even the Christians …" is a fatal trap.

Bridge to Invisible
August 28, 2015

Is there really more between heaven and earth than we can comprehend? Often our feeling or perception of life deviates from this view and triggers corresponding doubts. When thinking about this, the image of the embryo in the womb came to my mind again as a mnemonic (habitat womb thought of as a comparison to earthly existence, habitat earth as a comparison to eternal existence). This is helpful under the point of view that in the womb some things are prepared which are not used there yet (lungs for breathing, for instance), but the "size" relations, the enormous measure of the differences hits the comparison nevertheless only inadequately. I notice, however, that on the emotional level the knowledge, or better the idea of the size, of the universe works again and again unsettling, why this mnemonic need announces itself again and again.

Then it came to my mind: What would be, if a deep sea fish had consciousness, and heard of stars? Life on solid land alone would be beyond its imagination, not to mention outer space. Life outside water means life in other elements; land and air as habitats are unimaginable, not to mention space travel. Nevertheless, the fish is surrounded by it and influenced by it without being able to perceive it in detail. Not even a completely developed creature is able to live everywhere within the different habitats of our space-time dimension or even has an idea of them.

Similarly, we cannot perceive the invisible dimension surrounding us. But to conclude from this that it does not exist would definitely be a short-circuit!

Such pictorial mnemonic bridges help me to oppose the emotional aspects of doubt thoughts (which are also triggered and shaped by impressions, snippets of our reality) with something more impressive than the simple abstract statement that we cannot grasp God with the mind. Mnemonic bridges provide meaningful substantiation, vivid reasons for the abstract statement.

Ants, Bees, Bats—and Us
September 25, 2015

At some point, probably triggered by the topic of eternity and in view of problems understanding each other, the thought of ants popped into my mind again, but in a modified form: Ants, bees, bats all have functioning means of communication. If each species would set its way absolute in the sense that it considers other ways unreal, then we as "above" them would know that this is nonsense. But this logically means that it is a perfectly reasonable assumption that there can be means of communication above *us*. We do not understand in detail how prayer works. But that it is another such means within creation, we can even experience that, and thus we know more than, for example, ants can know about bats.

What is important for me with this thought is to perceive how complex already our visible or better humanly (increasingly) accessible reality is—and how well the spiritual dimension fits into it as another level and is not simply something completely abstruse, completely different. This builds up a quite reasonable counterweight to the otherwise easily overwhelming impression of the unreality of the dimension of God.

The Certainty of Story
January 9, 2016

Looking back to a discussion in a Bible study group.

In the Bible, it is quite naturally assumed and reported that God occasionally intervenes in this world in a way that contradicts the laws of nature known to us. The Creator, who has given structure and rules to his creation, keeps open exceptions to the rule behavior. Those who cannot assume on scientific grounds that such a thing is possible must interpret the corresponding stories differently. The common method in modern theology is to understand the miracle stories as pictures and to imply that the biblical authors tell us that Jesus, for instance, had stilled a dangerous fall wind on the Sea of Galilee, but that they actually did not mean it that way, but wanted to say that Jesus has control over our problems at any time—over the storms of our life in the figurative sense, that is. Or: Jesus did not actually raise Lazarus from death, but the disciples wanted to say that Jesus had power over the death, and we can and should also believe this as modern people. What factual basis remains there for this, is a question that is not asked. Whoever understands the stories in such a way finds a certain peace in the fact that for faith, some things can be true which are not real or possible on the normal natural level, and seems to have solved thus the conflict between Bible and natural science, without having to decide for a side.

I certainly understand the initial problem. But I always get knots in my head with this "solution." That it is not provable what is thought to be possible out of faith is undoubtedly correct; but instead to prefer to think that something is impossible in this world, but is to be believed on another level, leads for me to a curious split understanding of reality. If the visible reality is part of a bigger reality—though at the moment still hidden to us—then the judgment "impossible" can be only a too short-sighted misjudgment. Since our knowledge about the relationship between the invisible and the visible, between whole and subset, is still insufficient, it is reasonable to assume that they do *not* stand in *truly* irreconcilable opposition. It can *appear* to us that way, so we must be careful not to jump to premature conclusions.

The old question to liberals: What reason should have led the evangelists to invent the infancy stories or other miracle stories if what they are trying to say about Jesus is not triggered by and rooted in real events in space and time? What would then still distinguish their faith from pure wishful thinking?

Continuation from an older note:

God is the creator and sustainer of nature was familiar to the people for a long time, so this was not the unexpected, special thing that they now had to pass on as news. What was new was that Jesus obviously shared in the creative power of God. Judging by the story, this was unexpected and at least at first caused horror and the feeling of the uncanny.

If this story had not happened at all—what new news remains? And how did people come up with it? Did they sit down and philosophize? And then developed this story from that? A story that feels to any unbiased reader like an account and not like a parable? Why then did Jesus's enemies not later use the opportunity to prove him a liar, when they were desperately looking for incriminating material? At the wine transformation or at the bread multiplication, there were a lot of witnesses!

Is Faith Rational?
March 12, 2016

Mathematics professor, philosopher of science, and Christian apologist John Lennox (Oxford) gave a lecture[11] on the new atheism in 2015. A few thoughts from it.

He had been to Delft, in Holland, not long before and in a related discussion it was implied that belief in God was the same thing and as unfounded as belief in Santa Claus. Lennox then asked the students who had come to believe in Santa Claus as an adult. Not a single hand went up. "And who has come to believe in God as an adult?" Hundreds of hands went up.

Furthermore:

Psychological theories (e.g., Freud) which interpret faith as projection of wishful thoughts are not useful for finding the truth. Other reasons must be given, because the projection argument can be used just as well against atheism. Then atheism would be a projection of the wish not to have to face God one day and to give account for one's own life. Milosz, the Polish Nobel Prize winner for literature, puts it this way: "The true opium for the people is the belief that nothing comes after death; the great comfort of thinking that we will not be condemned for our deceit, greed, cowardice, murders." One avoids having to take one's own responsibility.

Stephen Hawking was asked by a British newspaper what he thought of religion. He said, "Religion is a fairy tale for people who are afraid of the dark."

Lennox was also asked. He said, "Atheism is a fantasy for those who are afraid of the light."

It is problematic to equate rationality with natural science. Then all faculties of the humanities would have to close immediately because they cannot produce any knowledge.

Albert Einstein had pointed out that one can talk about the ethical foundation of natural science, but not about the scientific foundation of ethics.

If someone says that only natural science can grasp truth, then he utters a non-scientific sentence, and thus scores an own goal.

More Pieces of the Whole
March 25, 2016

It was a crazy week due to problems of people around us. I realize: My strong sensitivity of finality and mortality often resembles more a steady river in the underground than a thunderstorm, which as an exception to normal weather disappears relatively quickly again. I ask myself: Am I morbid? Or does that prove a realism which I only have avoided facing for too long? But if that were the case, how can I then avoid that my knowing of eternity is not drawn into something surreal? Why do all my strategies not work at least predominantly? Actually, shouldn't the familiarity with the biblical perspective and the acceptance of life as it is, not grow with age, and grow deeper roots? Instead impressions of the mysteriousness of life even unto its absurdity push themselves into the foreground. What leads to question the authenticity and reliability of my faith? That I do not know anyone who is struggling with similar problems, doesn't make it easier to accept my "skin."

Attempt at a mnemonic:

When a dad tries to answer difficult questions for his little child, he will have to simplify greatly. He won't want to lie, but he knows that in the little head, distorted images of reality naturally arise from the simplifications, and he has to put up with that. When the child grows up, the woodcut-like, schematic increasingly dawns on the child, the horizon becomes larger, the previous knowledge becomes more differentiated, more complex.

However, the knowledge about the fundamentally fragmentary nature of our cognition will also remain with the adult. A seemingly smooth complete system would rather indicate that something is faulty, because reality will always remain ahead of us.

In other words: If the basic lines of the biblical worldview seem to us too simple a schematic, this does not speak against their truth, but only that they are adapted to our limited horizon and point beyond themselves in what we *feel* to be inadequate rather than being able to formulate adequately. (Another important consequence of this: If I draw from my respective woodcut version the justification or necessity to throw everything overboard, I take it, as it were, too seriously in a wrong sense, as if it were identical with reality; I forget the provisionality.)

Example: Atonement, a biblical and worldwide concept, but one whose necessity I ultimately do not understand (unlike punishment, whose functions as deterrence, as protection for society, as education and reparation appear reasonable). Why "must" atonement be? Why are confession of guilt, request for forgiveness and granting of forgiveness not sufficient in principle to eliminate guilt? Why "had" there to be blood for reconciliation between God and humans? I do not know. Now, if I were to assume that because *I* see no point, there *is* no rational reason for it, then this concept, and thus ultimately God himself, must seem irrational and somehow arbitrary to me (though it should be a warning to me that most people and cultures intuitively agree with the idea of atonement). But I then forget that the fault lies with me because of the insufficient basic assumption, since I take my limited insight, i.e., a partial piece, for the whole. There is just more between heaven and earth than we know. The other mistake would be to reject the part because I do not know the whole; also this would be out of touch with reality.

The whole thing boils down to the fact that on the one hand we need dogmatics with a claim to truth, summarizing representations of biblical statements, and at the same time we have to keep in mind their provisionality. It is also indispensable for the existential faith implementation, because there are interactions; on the other hand, living the life always remains ahead of reflecting on it.

Another topic that concerns me more often: How can people who find more intense reflection difficult consciously live discipleship?

Once again Tolkien's *Lord of the Rings* helps me. Very few hobbits are suitable as politicians. But they know what counts in life, in contrast to the evil creatures created by Sauron. There, too, are parallels to being a Christian. Many people think in simple terms. But this does not speak against the possibility to have a sense for the true and essential.

Another thought in the aftermath of the attacks in Brussels:

Once again the power of evil is shown, but also that nothing would be better than to follow Jesus. No other religion or philosophy has as much theoretical and practical potential for good as the Christian faith.

God Is Not Made of Wood
April 19, 2016

Lost and Found:
> God is not made of wood
> If the thought comes to you that everything you have thought about God is wrong,
> and that there is no God,
> do not be dismayed by it.
> Many people are like that.
> But do not think that your unbelief is because there is no God.
> If you can no longer believe in the God you used to believe in,
> it is because
> that there was something wrong in your faith,
> and you must make a better effort to understand what you call God.
> When a man
> stops believing in his wooden God,
> it does not mean that there is no God,
> but only that the true God is not made of wood. (Leo Tolstoy)[12]

Eternity in the Heart
April 23, 2016

The dress rehearsal of the children's musical Bartimaeus (Mark 10:46ff) got under my skin. What a life of longing that must have been for blind Bartimaeus. This then triggered further thoughts. The basic longings of all people are the same, and how many have to endure that even basic ones are not fulfilled. The intense capacity of human consciousness for self-reflection also has its dark side—knowing what could be; and also knowing one's own finitude. Animals also certainly know sensations far more than we often realize; love, sadness, loneliness, joy: Clear examples of these can be found in at least some species. But I am not aware of any animal species that is capable of suicide (at least not in the sense of individual suicide). I conclude from this that the consciousness for finiteness, time, meaning and thus also meaninglessness is not as present as in humans. This again can mean that a hint to God is hidden here; why should nature develop such a consciousness, which implies self-destructive possibilities, in humans, which more or less burdens the life of countless individuals of this species? But if the spiritual hunger were made analogous to the physical one to be satisfied in the end, at last in a life after death, then it would make a certain sense to keep awake the probing question whether this life is really everything, and to look for answer. "He has also set eternity in the human heart." (Ecclesiastes 3:11) And obviously already the early primitive humans assumed that life goes on. They buried. And in the middle of time one came who said it quite clearly that he can and wants to fulfill the longings, sooner or later. Jesus.

The Anchor Holds
May 3, 2016

Attempt to find a reliable starting point.

Jesus lived.

People heard him and had experiences with him. Extraordinary experiences. Undeniable experiences.

He was executed.

The disciples were in despair.

They experienced him as risen.

They were changed.

Were so certain that they could die as martyrs.

Paul went from being a persecutor of Christians to being a herald.

From this follows the reliability of what Jesus proclaimed.

Yes, it may seem fabulous.

But scattered throughout history are clues that make a thread. Facts. And interpretations of those facts. The Old Testament.

And since Jesus, history contains other clues—the New Testament, church history.

All this (plus existence of ethics, of music etc.) an agnostic would have to be able to explain differently and more plausibly, without the existence of this God.

Possible trap: When thinking about reasons for or against faith, to treat them too flat or equally, so to say, to compare mainly the respective quantity. But there are arguments more weighty and less weighty. And if the main pillars of faith are reliably strong, then other as yet unanswered problems can and must be subordinated without posing a threat to the whole.

Today I pulled out again the essays of G. Habermas on the subject of doubt.

Interesting experience of C. S. Lewis: "Now that I am a Christian, I have moods in which the whole thing looks very improbable; but when I was an atheist, I had moods in which Christianity looked terribly problematic."[13]

Believers as well as non-believers have the same dilemma that their conviction can become doubtful to them.

Habermas goes on to describe a striking image[14] of what the witness of the Holy Spirit can be compared to in the believer. Let us imagine an anchor that is firmly embedded in the rock. When the boat starts to drift away, first the loose part of the anchor chain starts to move; but this only works until the chain is taut. Within the range given by the length of the chain, the boat can drift around, but it cannot break loose. Habermas experienced again and again that his chain of faith drifted off in different directions, but realized by this that he nevertheless could not deny Jesus or exchange him for someone else.

This helps not to look for the traces of the Holy Spirit in the wrong direction, as in fundamental steadfastness; it takes seriously that not only the doubting questions are to be considered as a fact, but also the reluctance (no matter how great or small) of the heart to give up faith in meaning, love, and hope, grounded in experiences such as the spontaneous "warm heart," the assent when reading the Gospels and contemplating what Jesus says and does.

Where God Is Not Worshipped
May 10, 2016

Where God is not worshipped, other gods or people or ideas are idolized.

Without "heroes" and subordination (voluntary or forced), life obviously does not work; neutrality practically does not exist.

Not even a rule of science would be able to provide that. It does not even potentially mean objectivity for all. Because: Values are not their field of expertise, and without them it does not work. Today we already see the problems of bio-ethics clearly enough in the eugenic discussions about life worth living, and also that in the context of artificial intelligence morality proves to be actually necessary (for instance, with autonomous driving: Which life should be given the highest priority if there is a risk of an accident?).

And secular politics cannot do it either. Without absolute values, only rule by some elite remains. The "little" people will always be victims, patients, bargaining chips—certainly not "king's children."

Have I overlooked an alternative to Jesus worth living for, which would theoretically be good for all people?

For what or for whom else would life in all circumstances (sick, disabled, unborn, old) be an inviolable good worth protecting? Far and wide nothing tenable to see. Except Jesus.

A book about the Trinity also still goes with me.

Where are traces of God's love visible in this world? Of his overflowing nature and will? Everywhere where good happens, consciously or unconsciously, it is an echo of him. Why would it be there if he were not?

All-or-nothing thinking is unrealistic, literally. The world is complex, differentiated, for all people; even for those on the dark side of life, not everything is just permanently pitch black. Yes, "overflowing love" as the essence of God is certainly not so easy to read out of the world; but neither is the opposite.

Thinking game: Even if I should have given false hopes to people by my faith (in case this faith would be error), all alternatives would have been worse all the time, would have hardly made them more viable, happier people.

I realize that I would like to read more intensively in the Bible again (instead of mainly about it), in order to get a more comprehensive picture again. But immediately parallel to this the concern arises that intensified reading especially in the Old Testament could immediately unleash avalanches of new questions. Therefore, I have to keep in mind that Jesus testified to the authority of the Old Testament as God's reliable self-revelation, and that the truth of this testimony does not stand or fall with my (in)ability of interpretation. There will always be discussion about details; but the broad lines must not automatically become questionable because of that. That would be short-circuiting. To keep the core statements is a priority, even if the details may be disputed: God has created everything, the world is no longer as it was and should be, but a new world is on the move, etc.

"Self-therapeutic" consequence: I try to imagine very consciously what I would do if I traveled back in time and met Jesus and were faced with the decision to follow him or not yet for the time being, as long as not everything has been clarified enough. And I have to realize: The subjunctive in the last sentence betrays an illusion. For I stand before him in every moment, whether I want to admit it or not. I remember my spiritual vows that I renewed to Jesus some time ago. A shameful idea, a hint the size of a fence post—gracious and challenging at the same time.

Clarify Who Jesus Is
May 15, 2016

Why should I believe God's overflowing love and longing for relationship in the face of billions of creatures from whom he seems to have successfully hidden?

The fact is: If Jesus is God in human form, he is at least a very empathetic and self-sacrificing God with an eye for the individual and especially for those who are on the dark side of life. This means I have to clarify who Jesus is. Either Jesus is *not* God (and I then have a lot of other unanswered questions to deal with) or he *is* and I must then trust him that we still understand too little of the big story.

I have to believe him that he is not indifferent to all these people—against appearances—but that he will still realize other plans with them; that with their death not everything is lost, even if we rather get knots in our head than a clear idea when trying to imagine something; that also for them eternity will outweigh the sufferings of this time. (As a side note, life expectancy has only increased so much in the last few decades).

Trust in a loving God can only come from one person in history: Jesus.

Why Is He Hiding?
May 18, 2016

Homeless.
So helpless.
God loves them more than any human could!?
Why is he hiding?
Well, he is only partially hiding.
He says what he thinks.
And what he wants.
And that humans are responsible to help each other.
But his love for the poor still seems ineffective …
Or maybe, even more precisely, exactly because of that …

Until Eternity
May 30, 2016

In dark hours of questioning, the same rotten game plays itself out emotionally again and again: If God does not behave as I think he should, this immediately speaks against him in my feelings, either in the sense of emerging doubts about his existence or of such great perceived distance that familiarity seems impossible.

But: If I despair of the mass of those suffering from poverty, war, expulsion, discrimination, and so on, should my compassion, my sense of justice, my love be greater than that of God, who has given me these abilities? Who created eyes and ears and compassion—should he not perceive accordingly?

Senseless insinuation …

The "solution" must therefore lie somewhere else. Probably until eternity.

Jesus Tells the Truth
July 16, 2016

God, the creator of a gigantic universe, has every single person in mind, his heart beats for every single person, he hears every word, feels every sensation. Isn't that a completely fairy-tale, childish, self-centered and unrealistic idea?

Counter-argument: The impression of the devious has much to do with the fact that we lack suitable comparisons from our world of experience and that things are different in our world:

- The rulers of this world pay attention to distance from the people. They live in their own world.
- And as far as the proportions are concerned: We can perhaps imagine to still know the individual animals in a larger flock of sheep, but "already" an anthill shows us our limitations.
  Certainly, logically seen nothing is impossible with God. But one gets such knots in the head with the attempt to imagine this even approximately.

So you have to consciously give up these attempts to get an idea and "simply" practically get involved with the fact that Jesus is telling the truth: Our hairs are numbered. Our Father in heaven knows what we need and what is going on in our hearts. The whole universe is so finely tuned to each other that alone the still completely inadequate idea of the extent of this fine-tuning should be indication enough for us that this trust can refer back to and be based on meaningful rationally tangible facts with good reason.

Truth in Eternity
August 6, 2016

Suicide. The topic was triggered by an email prayer request for a family left behind.

In his diary, the writer and songwriter Jochen Klepper (who eventually prevented his family's deportation by the Nazis by committing suicide together) writes: "Sometimes one thinks that God should give one a visible sign to help one in all the opposition of one's work. But this is precisely his sign: That he lets one persevere and dare and endure."[15]

Later I asked myself: If this is true—which I believe—how could suicide have happened? Did God stop carrying the family through this method? Not imaginable. My thought: Maybe in a certain sense God allowed Klepper's terrible decision as an act of mercy from God's side—as an individual escape route from insurmountable despair! A very daring and speculative thought, I know. We will know the truth only in eternity. The relationship between God's will, our will, Satan's will is too complex for us to grasp with the simple concepts of "free will" or "unfree will." Anyway: God is a gracious and compassionate God. We don't have to worry that he will turn his back on us or leave us in the lurch because we can't handle the challenges we face in a perfect way. He knew beforehand that we would not be able to do so. We can rely on the rainbow even on a personal level.

"Tell No One." Why Not?
September 8, 2016

"Jesus commanded them not to tell anyone." (Mark 7:36)

Why would Jesus do this?

First, Jesus fulfills promise of salvation: "Then will the eyes of the blind be opened and the ears of the deaf unstopped." (Isaiah 35:5)

Second, Jesus forbids the person who was healed to tell—the famous "Messiah's secret" in Mark. Doesn't Jesus know that by doing this he achieves exactly the opposite and that it doesn't work anyway, because word naturally gets around about such serious changes? Whoever accuses Mark of a stylistic device here keeps the naivety away from Jesus, but ultimately shifts it to Mark. Perhaps the solution is so simple that it is therefore overlooked: Maybe Jesus simply wants to make it persistently clear through these repeated statements that he is not out for propaganda and publicity; perhaps he wants to set a clear sign against the usual human behavior of basking in the center! He does not call loudly in the streets (Isaiah 42:2), of course not in the absolute sense; otherwise he would not be allowed to preach, but in the relative sense.

Third, moreover, Jesus behaves differently—just as people and families and village situations are different.

What Does the Lord Require of You?
November 8, 2016

When I look at the diversity of inner-Christian beliefs and faith practices worldwide, I ask myself how the same God and his concern that all people find the one truth can stand behind all this diversity, the manifold inconsistencies and opposites. This obviously appears as a historically and globally failing endeavor. And it can therefore so easily trigger or strengthen the impression of the unreality of God; the impression that these are probably rather religious (empty) formulas, but behind them there can be no serious revelation of a living God. This consideration challenges to examine whether this is not hasty judgment.

Isn't there perhaps something that the various Christian faith practices of all times and cultures have in common that distinguishes them from other religions and ideologies?

It cannot be a dogmatic concept as a whole; neither a lifestyle that would be as easily recognizable as a school uniform.

And yet: Perhaps we can learn from our Jewish relatives and faith ancestors.

The Jewish faith has always been very much related to the practice of life. In the Old Testament, there is nothing like dogmatics in our sense, which people are supposed to adopt in order to be God's covenant partners; no comprehensively formulated body of doctrine that deals with all areas of life. Rather, at its core, it is always about narratives of relationships, about love, trust, doing justice to God and one's fellow humans, and what guidelines serve to do so.

A helpful core word is "He has shown you, O mortal, what is good. And what does the Lord require of you? To act justly and to love mercy and to walk humbly with your God." (Micah 6:8) Also: "The goal of this command is love, which comes from a pure heart and a good conscience and a sincere faith." (1 Timothy 1:5)

Of course, this life-practice does not work completely without theological theory. But "having the (follower's) heart in the right place" (wanting to be aligned with God) is something very elementary in terms of emphasis, and this becomes outwardly visible, as a basic orientation in life, to some extent independently of "correct" theological terminology. A kind of basic attitude, then, which can presumably be found throughout the diversity mentioned at the beginning? And which ultimately only God, who sees into the hearts, can judge.

The question of who is a "real" Christian thus remains a question that is always relevant and at the same time can never be answered conclusively. For example, to apply to Coptic Christians the standard of the "four spiritual laws," as they were formulated in an American student movement of the 20th century as an aid for missionary conversations, would be mistaken.

The question about the meaning and weight of theological thinking is about a tightrope walk between too much and too little systematization; but a "tightrope walk," where there is only complete crash as an alternative, is probably not an adequate image; perhaps better is the image of a hike through a bog, where one can drift further into increasing mud, sometimes to the right, sometimes to the left.

But what then is unity, being one—a goal that Jesus himself set before his church? If you look at the multifaceted crew of disciples, then it is not about eliminating individuality and originality, i.e., not about conflict-free equality; and even at the church leadership level it may not have the priority with God that we usually assume and desire ("at least there it should work out …"). Influenced by the effectiveness thinking of modern management, we feel that this is rather ineffective. But maybe it is more about character training, learning to love and conflict management—to learn these things "ahead" for the community and then to pass them on authentically (including enduring when problems cannot be solved).

Love Rekindled
November 16, 2016

Back home after a vacation. Only few hours later Andreas was on his way to his visit to a grieving family, and another funeral is already set. Back to daily life. And this morning we heard of someone nearby who had lost a daughter-in-law by sudden death, leaving two little kids and her husband. Shock. How can one cope with such a situation—if one has no faith? Even with faith, it is terribly hard.

What open questions do agnostics and atheists have to live with? Attempt of a listing:

- Where does religion come from as a universal phenomenon?
- Where does belief in eternal life come from? (Humans bury since primeval times!)
- What is morality based on? Where does goodness, selflessness, care for the sick and elderly, love come from?
- Where does music come from?
- How are complexity and "fine-tuning" from macrocosm to microcosm to be explained?
- Where does humor come from?
- Where does the unintentional, oblivious joy of beauty and play come from?
- Problem of suicide, which is not known in animal world in comparable way; why should nature produce such a thing?
- Animals don't need meaning, as far as we know. Why human? A human being needs: Food, home, friends, love, livelihood or work, a higher goal or meaning.

It may perhaps *feel* more realistic to fade out God and his incarnation and the fairy-tale appearing aspects of the invisible dimension; this rather fits the common scientific-technocratically influenced and objectivity-suggesting mainstream. But in view of the faded out problems or questions, purely rationally seen, this is definitely not simply the "rational" solution against the "irrational" one of the faith.

I have to keep that in mind that just as truth is bigger than what a dad can explain to his child, not smaller, so it would be foolish to shun prayer as too naive or meaning-poor, "ineffective," and thus give in to the impression of distance. However and whenever the first love (Revelation 2:4) will return where it has been lost, to keep distance, not to seek the personal encounter with Jesus at all is certainly the most senseless behavior; it makes sense, on the contrary, to persistently seek his nearness.

I am looking for an image for God's restraint towards his creation. His love, which is actually overflowing by nature, limits itself so much that it sometimes seems almost unrecognizable to us. He intervenes, but possibly (and often contrary to our desires) rather as little as necessary, whereby his and our definition of *necessary* on top of that diverge unmistakably. What pledge do we have that his love is real, tangible? He lived a life for us and gave it away. Only in contemplation of his life and death can our love in return be kindled; where else?

Open to Question?
November 29, 2016

To contrast which questions remain open depending on one's religious conviction is only one of the points that are important if one wants to clarify one's doubts.

What also belongs on the scale: how does an agnostic explain the experiences of me and countless others across space and time, which were interpreted as an encounter with Jesus, as hearing God's voice in everyday life? All just imagination and coincidence? Tonight this thought came to my mind again: "Just think back, only all what you recorded in the diary, what then condensed in the lecture about ways of heavenly communication. That would certainly give atheists some headaches."

Redemption through Beauty
December 11, 2016

Advent concert.

The music somehow felt good, was simple and beautiful. Typically, a critical question quickly came to the fore again: Aren't such concerts an escape into an ideal world, an escape from the difficult reality—and therefore actually only acceptable when there is no longer a reason to escape? But then I remembered that even in concentration camps or on the sinking Titanic music was played.

Next thought: can one or should one, at least as a Christian, not also see music as an active demonstration of the beautiful, protest against disharmony? Recently I came across two good quotes in M. Lütz, "God": "Beauty will save the world" (Dostoevsky) and the physicist Albert Einstein, "The most beautiful thing we can experience is the mysterious. It is the basic feeling that stands at the cradle of true science and art."[16] Redemption through beauty. Countering the pull of the evil, the oppressive, the sad. Beauty is ultimately a way of speaking of God, what his will for his creation actually is—joy, harmony, play, creativity, diversity.

Longing for the Invisible
December 16, 2016

The book by Philip Yancey, *Sehnsucht nach dem Unsichtbaren* (*Reaching for the Invisible God*) arrived yesterday. Liberating—how much I have thought the same way, asked and felt, up to similar formulations, up to "To my shame, I admit that one of the strongest reasons for continuing to believe in God is the lack of good alternatives."[17] This is a reassuring counter-attack against my often frustrating basic feeling: I see so much that others don't seem to see, and often fail to see much that others seem to see.

"Personal relationship" with God is definitely a term in need of interpretation, otherwise it easily leads to misleading expectations. Even all the "great ones" of church history have probably known their dark valleys. Other key points from Yancey:

- Consciously keep in mind: Faith is about *unequal* partnership. This can guard against false expectations.
- Form the relationship on God's terms, not ours. Yancey quotes the passage in Micah 6:8 ("He has shown you, O mortal, what is good. And what does the Lord require of you? To act justly and

to love mercy and to walk humbly with your God."), which has also become very familiar to me, and he states, "I do not first come to know God and then do his will; I come to know him by doing his will. I enter into an active relationship. That is, I give God my time, care for the people he cares about, and keep his commandments—whether I feel that way or not."[18]
- There is no path to immunity from doubt.
- His strategies against doubts sound completely familiar to me—a clear encouragement not to have overlooked something essential, but to be on meaningful paths.
- Yancey's experience: Life becomes more complicated with age, growth obviously does not "automatically" mean more steadiness, according to the experiences of spiritual ancestors or role models.
- "The soul must long for God in order to be inflamed by the love of God; but if the soul does not feel this longing, then it must long for the longing. Longing for longing also comes from God." (Meister Eckhart[19])
- "'It does not depend on you whether the work will be completed, but neither do you have the freedom not to begin it,' says an old saying from the Talmud. The work is God's work, working on a world that has been greatly damaged, with the aim of restoring and redeeming it. For both Jews and Christians, said work means bringing about a little more peace, justice, hope, and healing in everything our hands touch."[20]
- "Chesterton: 'Christianity has overcome the problem of fierce antagonisms by retaining them, and with equal fierceness.' Most heresies arise in the attempt ever to adopt a proposition at the expense of its opposite."[21]

The Cross Is a Pledge
January 1, 2017

What is the core question regarding the truth of faith? Whether Jesus has risen from the dead. The cross can become a pledge of his love for me only afterwards, because the corresponding interpretation of the cross already presupposes the Christian interpretation and the faith in it (from the outside one sees only a Roman execution).

From what can love, joy, wonder be nourished, in the midst of dark circumstances of life? From the hope of the future glory and the knowledge of his compassion and his protecting hand in the present—for which the cross is a pledge.

How ... Who ... Why
January 12, 2017

One can doubt whether God is as Christians believe him to be, and I have had to struggle with such doubts more than I would like. But atheism—the assumption that there is no higher being of any kind—has never seemed to me to be a serious alternative; it seems to me to be downright unreasonable. V. Vitale has brought this to the point very well:

"The how question (a question about mechanism) does not answer the who question (a question about actor), nor does it answer the why question (a question about intent). Why was Microsoft Office created? We will get an answer to this question only if Bill Gates is willing to share it with us, if the creator of the system is willing to reveal that. ...

The universe has a beginning.

The universe is recognizable.

The universe follows rules.

The universe is finely tuned for life.

I believe that these four facts about the universe are all best explained by the existence of God."[22]

Experiences of God's Truth
January 18, 2017

Thought splinter:

In what sense can I have experiences of God's truth?
- through unusual, "para-normal" experiences, which seem most coherently explainable by Christian interpretation
- by "functioning," by experiencing changes in the sense of the announced.

Stubborn Doubts
February 6, 2017

What to do when doubts stubbornly return? A time travel through my diary was very revealing for me, in several respects.

For one thing, it was frustrating to realize how many insights I simply forgot again in the hustle and bustle of everyday life. Over and over again. But: Even from different situations and with different emphases, I have ultimately always come back to the same elementary thought processes and insights, which speaks for the fact that the considerations hold water.

For instance, an astonishing quantity of "coincidences" occurred, unusual in different measure certainly, but among them more than a handful literally were really noteworthy remarkable ones. All kinds of the "heavenly ways of speaking" (in the sense of ways of communication) are represented, from quiet to actually unmistakable. Question: Coincidence or providence? Answer: Decision is asked. No other way. Actually, more precisely: Surrender, letting go of mistrust. Repentance. Turning.

At the same time, a new seductive escape thought now arises: "That's as meaningless as New Year's resolutions. The review proves: it will start over again and again." Yes. True. Unfortunately. But is that really a valid reason to run away from consciously reaffirming the basic decision again and again and again and just again? Would I also say to someone with marital or addiction problems, "Well, at least once or twice, yes, you can and should renew your promises, even if you messed up, but then if it happens again, it's no use!"? Hardly. The healing can only come from intensification, and if it were hourly or daily. Hopelessness springs from dark powers.

To ward doubts off by referring back to the promise of faithfulness and its renewal has a rational basis; I remind myself of that in the hope that this will have a reassuring effect on writing down such trains of thought step-by-step.

It is understandable to doubt and therefore a legitimate concern to examine whether Jesus told the truth, whether he is the truth of God in person. I can discuss this, I can and must weigh arguments. The decisive factor will be my result with regard to the resurrection.

If I realize the resurrection as the most plausible interpretation of the facts and so as truth, this means: The resurrected is indeed part and revealer of a greater reality. To learn to submit to him and his information is the only reasonable consequence. Any fundamental rebellion against the new framework of interpretation or essential parts of it is from now on irrational (so I should also immediately recognize and name it) and futile. Realities are as they are, and I should always remain aware of my limitations in the process of getting to know them. Humility is appropriate and wise.

From now I can counter the repetition of the doubts only by the repetition of the truth.

Important to keep in mind: the basic truths are not at stake with the correctness of any particular theory (e.g., how the Bible came to be, how the creation accounts are to be understood). The criminal on the cross next to Jesus did not yet know Paul's gospel explanations, nor Luther's Protestant rule of thumb "by faith (or grace or Word) alone," and certainly not the Chicago Declaration on Bible inspiration. He looked to Jesus with ultimate hope. That was decisive.

And all of this is not creating my own matrix. This fear is based on a false assumption that adopting the Christian worldview is like putting on a pair of glasses that can effectively block out, "make disappear" weighty parts of reality, whereas without these glasses I would see all of reality. Firstly, we only have the choice between glasses and not between seeing with or without glasses, and secondly, it will become apparent which glasses prove themselves better in everyday life. Admittedly, "prove" also includes subjective elements again. But not even the natural sciences can do without practical testing and are sometimes already happy when something works, even if one does not—yet—understand in all details why (e.g., with drugs). Good experience supports the probability that one is on the right track, which helps to move forward.

The Christian perspective includes the challenge to look closely. The "father of lies" (John 8:44) wants to blind, wants to brainwash, to forbid thinking; the God of truth wants to set our feet on wide open space, does not force, challenges us to examine whether he keeps his word and whether it is consistent with our lives. Jesus and, for instance, Mohammed are not on the same level just because they are both leaders; there are huge qualitative differences. Jesus corresponds to the paradigm of the experienced and reliable mountain rescuer who stakes his own life and who wants to make me his co-worker by challenging and training my thinking; Jesus expects obedience to (co-)thinking, Mohammed obedience against (co-)thinking. Jesus loved to the end. This makes him trustworthy.

In the New Testament it is often said that we should obey the truth —an unusual formulation, because an ethical element comes into it, a relational level. Truth as a philosophical concept, for example, requires only a rational recognition; truth as a person, however, requires loyalty, submission beyond that. And what I easily overlook or forget in the whirl of doubts: From such loyalty results a (rationally justifiable!) support against mental and emotional aberrations. Rebellion, self-pity, hopelessness, despair—everything arises from a wrong assessment of my situation and a wrong view of God, which I refuse to correct; is ultimately basically self-overestimation. In short, it's sin; is mistrust, which does not believe God, his love, and his word, and therefore hurts him. And it is helpful if I also expose this as such and can thus become realistic again. Otherwise, I let myself be ensnared and drawn into the maelstrom of evil. My feeling may be honest, but that does not make it right. The truth has been and is Jesus. He is the only reasonable point of reference.

The circle closes: When doubts gain the upper hand and want to paralyze, it makes sense to refer back to the starting point, the resurrection—better, the Risen One, and from there to ward off the destructive whispers of evil out of loyalty in conscious obedience with a clear conscience, without worrying to lose reality with it. The opposite is the case. To doubt a person (whose love and devotion demands respect even from many opponents!) is once again a completely different issue than to doubt a worldview; this holistic approach can protect from and lead out of narrow views, can broaden the horizon for a reality that is more complex than I can grasp conceptually. If he says that every creature is dear to him, then this must be true, even if I cannot perceive this empirically or only insufficiently. Not my perception is the criterion of truth, but the statement of the Risen One.

From all this, there is also another practical consequence for dealing with doubts. It makes sense to clarify right at the first appearance whether the burdening questions are of a kind that entitles to subject the original assumption once again to a critical examination. If this is not the case, I should make myself very aware that I am probably just once again succumbing to errors in thinking. And I can get away from an inadequate point of view only by repentance and return to reasoned, not simply blind, trust (as towards an experienced mountain guide).

How Can We See the Greatness of God?
September 19, 2017

From the universe we can see: God's power and genius is infinitely greater than ours.

We cannot see his love as we can see the universe. But the same is true for it—it must be infinitely greater than ours. Thinking bigger, not smaller—that's what we need to counter doubts with. The best which is possible to human character is tiny compared to God's version of it, even if it is just not as vivid as nature. But all goodness, all love among people is, after all, also a visible reflection of his goodness and love. Among people you just have to look a little more closely (than simply looking up at the starry sky) and consciously make the connection to the heavenly source. The open wound of the theodicy question ("How can God be love and just in the face of the existence of evil?") remains, of course. It exists in the first place only because of the statement that God is love. But a more adequate conception of the unimaginable greatness of God can perhaps help to better endure the theodicy question!

Truth or Power?
October 10, 2017

An aside in a lecture on the Reformation has a lasting effect. The speaker made it clear: Not content, but rather power interests were what counted with regard to whether and under what circumstances sovereigns joined the Reformation, and also for the population the question of truth or content was not so much in the foreground, but rather changes in dependency relationships.

We can ask for the truth. But to do so seems to be more or less subordinate to something else; power is more important. Why? A guess: Having power suggests one's own ability to control and know greatness. To be one's own master. To subordinate oneself to a God who reverses this order of values, fundamentally, and who does not only want to serve and show solidarity from case to case, as in the case of one's own discretion, seems to be a risk and is therefore difficult.

Speaking Hope into Life
October 14, 2017

Due to corresponding encounters, I remembered what I had read again in the book about a chronically ill woman the day before: It is about believing God's love despite life circumstances that are difficult.

And then it went through my mind: That God became man must also have burned into Jesus's soul, his memory, enough to be able to sympathize with us. When he calls us to share his way of suffering, it is often difficult; but the burden also means dignity: To participate at his side and in his way in the resistance of good against evil, of hope against resignation, of trust against bitterness.

The paraplegic Joni Eareckson (and other Christians who were not healed): What a difference she made! Of course, the question arises: Couldn't it have been easier? By our standards, sure. But from God's worldwide perspective obviously not.

A missionary told of her work during the terrible earthquake in a South American country in 2016, of practical help and pastoral care; she called the latter "speaking hope into life"—a phrase that came up several times and has stuck with me.

In emergency situations, the question always arises: Is it better to bear witness or to share the suffering of others silently, because the words want to stick in your throat anyway?

But when I think about it, actually this should not be a question.

In the minimal case: People experience human attention and closeness. At the next conceivable level in the perception of the sufferer, God's "shoulder" becomes tangible, concrete through the human shoulder of the messenger. At the highest level, the encounter leads to the start of one's own relationship, independent of the witness.

Another train of thought: If nature is goal-oriented and tries to adapt living beings optimally, it makes little sense to endow them with unfulfillable longings. Humans, however, have this deep longing for meaning and for the imperishable.

So: If otherwise everything that exists is somehow characterized by order, is laid out for aim and effectiveness, shows a certain rationality, (on this assumption and experience science and technology are based and function!), then it is not particularly reasonable to assume, despite the partial areas being recognizably and meaningfully arranged, that the whole is meaningless.

Dedicated to God's Reign
January 3, 2018

Sad, frustrating, but true—even what has already been understood can still become blurred in day-to-day business; "red threads" can slip away. It helps me to write down what I pray for, to pray in writing so to speak. And to pull my mini-card box with prayer and thought notes out of my pocket every now and then during the day, in order to consciously align myself with it.

Repetition to remember:

The first is the question of truth, the most plausible perspective. The second is the corresponding behavior as a logical consequence. Whether I would actually like things to be different is completely irrelevant.

If God came into his creation to set things right and have us participate in it, then dedicating ourselves to the spread of God's reign is the best thing we can do.

Why?

We behave "according to the plan," coherently.

We behave in a future-oriented way.

One Person in History
January 16, 2018

The size problem is a recurrent problem for me. And I repeatedly fall into the trap of not being able to distinguish between categories clearly enough; the levels of quality and quantity often become blurred. (The words don't really hit the impression yet, but I can't formulate it better yet).

Everything is supposed to revolve around *one* person in history. Unimaginable. But above all: How small he is in view of the greatness of God, even if God is within reach in him for a few years, what a small "section" of God is that! Doesn't the great awakening in eternity therefore *have* to come—disillusionment, the end of self-deception, how completely different God really is and how naive we were in our human imagination?

But: If the gospel is true, if God revealed himself and made his way to us, then I have to counter this impression: Size and expansion in time and space etc. do not allow any conclusion about his essence, his heart, that this is an inappropriate mixing of categories, no matter how obvious or inevitable it seems to be to us.

If the incarnation has taken place, the following applies: The part of God that meets me in Jesus, the "revealed" God, is the reliable core, reflects his nature so much that I do not have to fear that all that is still hidden and strange would completely question my present image of God once on the day of the encounter or change it in such a way that it will then seem to me that I had a completely wrong image. Rather, it will be like an expansion of the center, a confirmation. The Cross and the Resurrection will then not be put in the shade, but will come to the fore in all the more radiant light. The meaning of the Incarnation, no matter how it had "functioned" in detail, is not pretending, deception, but revelation, truth—God cannot lie. That would be a senseless assumption. That's why it makes sense, that's why it's not childish or naive to relate to Jesus as if he were facing me as in his earthly lifetime (that includes enough bulky stuff anyway to keep me from a handy, harmless image of God, provided I keep exposing myself to the Bible). This is not an arbitrary humanizing of God in an inappropriate sense. Jesus reflects God's identity. It is not our image of him that will change drastically when we are in eternity, but our image of this world and creation.

Ready with Oxygen
February 25, 2018

On the importance of feelings in faith crises:

There is no question that faith cannot be based on feelings, for various good reasons. But this does not mean that faith can do without feelings in the long run. If faith is in essence a relationship, it must be holistic. This is not only an at least intuitive spontaneous expectation of every human being to whom faith is proclaimed as a personal relationship with his Creator and the promise of his closeness, but it is also willed by the Creator, who has "knitted" us in this way, and in the first commandment, feeling is a component of holistic devotion. That is, the need for at least a predominant coherence between conviction in the head and basic trust in the heart is basically justified. Love can endure crises of feeling as episodes, but not as a permanent state.

To put it in another way: A mountaineer without a breathing apparatus must be prepared at an altitude of 7,000–8,000 meters for his perception to be clouded by the lack of oxygen. He can prepare himself for this because he has the comparison, because he knows what he should actually perceive, because he has the "real reality" as a yardstick and what can and must therefore be unmasked as an illusion if necessary. Head has priority over feeling.

In both cases one has to be prepared: The longer such states last, the more destructive power the missing feelings develop or turn into negative ones.

Limited Insight Is Not Infallible
March 28, 2018

Once again the thought of a polar bear helped me. This time on the subject of how we can imagine God's activity:

Let us imagine that one would say to a polar bear: There are supposed to be beings (people) who can talk to each other over distances of many days' travel without having a loud voice. How should he be able to imagine what telephone or radio is? He can't. He will think it is nonsense.

By the way, not even a Martin Luther could have imagined that—even the same kind of creature as us, but separated by a few centuries.

Our limited insight is not an infallible standard for what can be and what cannot be.

"Here I Am Right."
May 20, 2018

Once again looking for reassurance of the elementary. What can have a certain spontaneously convincing plausibility for people not trained in theology and philosophy? What can convey an idea of what Christians think and why they find faith more convincing than non-belief despite the problems they themselves know? Seeking for "bridges," apologetic approach.

Fact: We live. Without our contribution, our decision.

We are faced with the question: What do we do with it? What do we need?

Love. Hope. Meaning.

What difference does faith make? What distinguishes every simple Christian from a simple non-Christian who lives on his own?

Helping one another to find it all, in the right places, that don't turn out to be illusions sooner or later.

Encouraging one another to hold on to it, not to be misled. To be God's co-workers, "co-authors," "gritting and salting service in icy Narnia." Discovering, interpreting, pointing out God's traces.

I love because I am loved and know that love will have the last word. I hope because I know that the visible is not the ultimate reality. I believe that this world is unthinkable without a Creator and Sustainer, and that He has a human 'face' turned toward us—Jesus.

Bringing the bigger picture into view: This world is provisional, literally a pre-runner. Speaking hope into life: One is there who hears, who sees, who ultimately leads to the goal. These things —if possible, expressed even more simply—can also be grasped by an ordinary person; perhaps more intuitively than intellectually penetrated but therefore not less deeply.

And he can also share them in a simple way, e.g., by inviting. I often ask myself: What makes a house group, a church service, a beneficial experience for oneself and others, even if most of the details of the sermon usually rush by and can hardly be reproduced? Spontaneous agreement of the heart; to feel "Here I am right. In a healing environment. Here I experience truth, even if I do not understand everything by far and certainly cannot retain it. Here I am in good hands. Everything else will sort itself out."

The Gospel in Emergencies
January 28, 2019

Prompted by the death of little two-year-old year old Julen (Spain, fell into illegal well, parents have already lost a child):

What difference does the gospel make in concrete emergencies?

It would be best to compare concrete life stories.

But one can also make some general statements:

As non-Christians, we can only hammer against the wall in front of us with the fury of despair or remain sitting in front of it in resignation.

As Christians, we know about the existence of a hidden door and wait for it to show itself and open.

For non-Christians: the hunger for meaning is either satisfied with substitutes or remains a debilitating mystery of nature.

As a Christian, I know: I am part of a larger plan; I may not like it, but at least it exists, and one day I will understand it.

I may still be able to evade the question of meaning; but I cannot evade the question of good and evil. I have to take a stand every day, make decisions. Either I decide for the evil, possibly also at the expense of the others, or the good (risk: possibly also at my expense). Do I resist the pull of evil or do I let myself be drawn into it?

Bread for When God Seems Silent
April 13, 2019

Regarding the inner outcry in many situations, "Why is God silent?" Is he?

1. He says what he wants and what he does not want.

2. He has taken up the fight himself.
3. He calls people into his peacemaker army.
4. Our anger, our compassion are expressions of his anger, his compassion, in us, with the purpose of becoming helpers to others through us.

While reading, I came across a note from January 25, 2015, Bible Week: "I am the bread."

The exposition probably had been too unspecific for me. But how could concretion look like?

Bread is a source of energy that keeps us alive. The body needs physical food. What does soul or heart need?

Hope. Sense. Love. Peace. Security.

Three Pillars
November 11, 2019

Last night I was still browsing through C. S. Lewis, Christian Reflections, Religion: Reality or Substitute?

Lewis seems to know this sense of the unreality of faith, which is very comforting, and deals with it critically. What is the basis of what we really know? Three pillars: Authority, reason, experience. People who have lost their faith have rarely gotten to this point through rational thought. It is more likely our senses that play tricks on us. (Examples: swimming and mountaineering).

> It is your senses and your imagination that try to attack the faith. Here, as in the New Testament, the conflict is not between faith and reason, but between faith and sight. We can face things we know are dangerous, as long as they don't look or sound too dangerous; our real problem is often with things we know are safe, but which look scary. Our trust in Jesus does not waver so much when real arguments are made against it as when it looks unlikely - when the whole world takes on that bleak appearance that really tells us more about our passions and even our digestion than about reality.[23]

No Simple Answers. And Yet ...
December 4, 2019

A telephone conversation lingered longer, in which many heavy burdens were shared. We agreed, "There are no easy answers."

But then I did begin to question that phrase a bit.

Yes, in terms of the details of how we live our lives and the why of that very pain and suffering, the phrase is true.

No, in terms of what we need to cope with life, it is not true.

And it is important to distinguish between the two; otherwise, we may be depriving ourselves of important "means for survival."

At least some among those whose words we spontaneously perceive as cold, cynical, or thoughtless when we feel distaste for the adversities of our lives have grasped just that rightly, though perhaps more intuitively. They simply live in the childlike attitude of trust to which Jesus challenges us again and again and which we are currently lacking. The line between childish and childlike is certainly narrow, but it is not my task to find out and judge that. Perhaps they really lack the tactfulness in communicating the truth or the sense for the right time (which is really hard to find out, to be fair); but that does not change anything about the simple truth itself: God is.

And if God is, then God cannot be other than good.

And that is why faith, hope, love, no matter what gets in the way, are worthwhile.

In the short or long or longer run, for sure, this good God will reach the goal with us, if we don't give up on him.

And when we are in danger of sinking in the vortex of our feelings and thoughts, it is good when others, like a lighthouse, still have solid ground under their feet and can point the way to where the land is to be sought.

Another picture: Once we have really thought through the reasons for trust to the end and also have our own experiences in mind (for which an atheist would first have to find explanations other than God), then "simply trust" simply makes sense—just as our dog trusted us, even when we took him to the vet, or when we did such devious things with him as riding a chair lift, or when Andreas carried him up an unexpected and steep iron ladder in the forest in deep snow in the

Elbe Sandstone Mountains—all challenges that were completely abnormal for the dog, but for the dog the only thing that mattered was that we were together—that counts. That's enough.

Actually, that is the most beautiful thing that can happen to us, when we can maintain such trust even in the face of real difficulties and when fears don't get the upper hand.

I have asked myself why I often react so allergically, at least inwardly, to statements that seem too simple to me.

In the end, don't I long for exactly such a "simple" trust that cannot be shaken by anything? Wouldn't it actually be nice if I could save myself all the tedious detours and wrong tracks in the attempt to stabilize the roots of my trust?

Moreover, it may indeed be that the people with the simple answers have simple answers because they have a very naive image of God and do not really face the difficulties and the also experienceable strangeness and hiddenness of God. But again, even if so, this would still be a matter between God and them and perhaps not yet the right time for them just now; it would only be an indication that they have not faced certain things. In any case it makes no sense if I react aggressively to this. Perhaps I can give them a hint if I suspect that something like this could be the true reason underlying their words, and that it would lead to a more mature image of God to see how difficult it sometimes is to hold onto faith and that God does not always show us his closeness in the way we would like (because then they cannot be suddenly attacked defenselessly by such an experience one day).

Once again, why my excitement? The fact that we tend to accept simple-sounding answers from people when we know that they have been through a lot shows that it is not necessarily the answers themselves that annoy us, that seem unbelievable to us, but that our doubts are directed at the fact that the people have not yet tried it out in their own lives and that the answers could therefore be wrong. So it's always easy to mix up different layers which happens in seconds and makes us extend our inner spines. And whether we become fairer to the reality by that than the "life strangers" who live in their bubbles and annoy us is possibly very much worth to question.

What are the layers that can play a role there?

There is still a fear lurking in some corner of my heart that I might have overlooked something after all. It is also the longing to be understood, not to be alone in this pain. It is frightening to see that my ability to trust, which is actually so important, is so limited; and then it helps when I know from others that they have to struggle similarly (and those who don't have to struggle reinforce my frustration). Maybe shame comes into it too; or guilty conscience sometimes. Or just the will: I just want to be able to let my anger out. I simply still don't want to admit and accept that my unwillingness is ultimately insufficiently justified because of the resulting consequence. Holding onto doubt and indecision sometimes suggests to me, I think, such a last vestige of "I still have options in front of me" and therefore some control over what happens next. I hold on to the illusion in order not to have to take this step yet, which would actually be the logical next step—to "just" let myself fall.

Thinking Is a Gift of God
January 30, 2020

"Now faith is confidence in what we hope for and assurance about what we do not see." (Hebrews 11:1)

"(Moses) saw him who is invisible." (Hebrews 11:27)

Jesus says, "Blessed are those who have not seen and yet have believed." (John 20:29)

Does all this amount to saying that faith is irrational?

And that (according to an old prejudice) therefore the one who can leave his mind at the church door is especially well off? (That would include: Jesus is at war with reason).

No; on the contrary: because *he* is well off who manages to be rational: to trust his mind more than his senses. Faith is in conflict with seeing, not with reason.

Thinking is important, a gift of God (if used appropriately). C. S. Lewis writes about Jesus's sentence to Thomas:

> It is addressed to a person who (…) already believed,
> who had already been acquainted for a long time
> with a very special person and had proofs that this

person could do very strange things, and who then refused to believe another strangeness, which was often predicted by this person and vouched for by his closest friends in agreement. It does not contain a rebuke to skepticism in the philosophical sense, but to the psychological quality of 'distrust'. It actually says: 'You know me too well for that!'[24]

Furthermore, when we have doubts, we must not forget: God's presence and manifestation of that presence are two different things—His presence is constant, but he does not always show himself clearly to us.

"Faith is reason taken courage." (Thomas Graham)[25]

Where Jesus Is Found
April 22, 2020

Sunday: the sermon of Daniel (Hamburg Project Church) was again very good, about Thomas, John 20:24 and following. Good hint at the end, the point I have not perceived so far: How did Jesus know about Thomas' objection to the disciples, that he would believe them and Jesus only when he could put his fingers into the wounds? Jesus was just *there* all the time—invisibly. Later I heard a short impulse to the above story on Facebook; it put the emphasis on the fact that Jesus does not want to be found in the spectacular, special feelings, etc., but in the everyday. But there again in a certain way quite noticeably, e.g., in the Lord's Supper, but also where we care for his least brothers, the sick, the weak, etc. just where we follow his mission.

What Did Paul Gain?
September 30, 2020

Today's reading is 2 Corinthians 11:16–33. Paul, through his work, has repeatedly suffered many hardships, struggles, enormous physical and psychological injuries, with no prospect that this would one day change in this life. He has lost everything that gave his life meaning, prestige, and influence before his conversion. He has got no respectable position, no power, no financial or other benefits from his ministry, unlike many a prosperity preacher today, or cult leaders or Islamists. Not only his conversion, but also his continued life is a testimony to the truthfulness of his faith and to the reality of Jesus behind everything. If someone doubts the reliability of the first Christians, accuses them of wishful thinking or whatever, one must hold these things before his eyes and demand a plausible explanation.

Where Were You?
November 28, 2020

The problem of theodicy is addressed to the wrong address; God turns it around, so to speak:

"The righteous perish, and no-one takes it to heart; the devout are taken away, and no-one understands that the righteous are taken away to be spared from evil." (Isaiah 57:1)

People don't care, but God—he sees the righteous and cares, giving the peace that was denied him on earth. *When* God "looks away, listens, is silent," then, towards those who do not want to let go of their wrong ways (vvs.11 and 13). Actually God expects that people would notice it, would start paying attention, that there is something topsy-turvy, when the faithful men are snatched away (vs. 2), but they do not react. So basically God asks his people, "Why do you allow this to happen?"

To the unrighteous, God is indeed silent (vs.11), hoping that would lead to reflection; but it does not.

I am reminded of the reference in the book *Freiheit für Linh* (American edition *Terrify No More* on human trafficking), that the question of victims is not even necessarily addressed to God (Where were you?), but to Christians (Where were you?).[26]

God Saw
December 3, 2020

Is God blind to the injustice on earth? No:
Genesis 6:12 ... and God saw.
Genesis 11:5 ... came down to see

Isaiah 59:15–16... and the Lord saw it (contrast to before, there the blindness of men is complained about)

What is the "proof" that he saw?

His statement. And his reaction—even if his patience is often incomprehensibly long.

Jesus Did Not See Decay
July 17, 2021

Both Peter in his Pentecost sermon and Paul on his first missionary journey cite Psalm 16:10 as scriptural evidence that it was foretold that the Messiah would "not see decay." The first Christians did not only care about the resurrection, but also about the empty tomb.

That both cite the same scriptural evidence also indicates that there was probably a pool of scriptural evidence (perhaps as early as when Jesus was traveling with the Emmaus disciples?) that was used like a catechism for preaching and instruction. This is only a theory, but a very obvious and reasonable and quite possible one.

When I told Andreas about this, we got onto the subject of resurrection hope in the Old Testament and he referred to rapture of Enoch and Elijah. This triggered in me the next thought that it would also have been really strange if the Messiah, who after all is still far above these two, would have gone into eternity quite "normally." Actually, the Messiah would have to surpass all his forerunners in some way—and Jesus did it.

A Realistic Heading
July 19, 2021

Luke 5:33 and following: In the explanation in my study Bible under the passage it says that the figurative words indicate that Jesus is bringing something "completely new, which does not fit in with the old and the traditional and must not be mixed up." That sounds too crass to me, too one-sided, and raises the question of how we can describe Jesus's relationship to the revelation of the Old Testament more accurately.

A realistic heading could be: there is a tension between "not the smallest letter ... will by any means disappear from the Law until everything is accomplished." (Matthew 5:18) and "no-one pours new wine into old wineskins."(Luke 5:37)
- There are lasting things (God's character; God's directives; acts of God, experiences of Israel anyway).
- There are things that Israel misunderstood, that already the prophets tried to correct, unfortunately in vain (it is about heart and faith, not about rules and facade).
- There are things which were hinted at already but in a rather hidden way, which Jesus now says more clearly (Messiah; two phases of his coming and the nature of his reign).
- There are things that are changing (ritual law; extension to Gentiles; but that becomes still more clear *after* resurrection).

A Place to Stand Together
January 31, 2021

I started again with Metaxas's biography on Bonhoeffer, which I had read with enthusiasm some years ago. Striking:

> The church must confess Christ not only to the Gentiles, but also to the Jews, Bonhoeffer continues. It has the task of bringing the Messiah of the Jews to the Jews who do not yet know him. If it adopted Hitler's Aryan paragraph, it would deny itself this opportunity. Bonhoeffer's dramatic, almost shocking conclusion was: the church must not only make it possible for Jews to belong to it, but that is precisely its essence: to be the place where Jews and Germans stand together. Nor is it at all a question of whether our German-born parishioners today can still bear church fellowship with the Jews. Rather, it is the task of Christian proclamation to say: here, where Jew and German stand together under the Word of God, is church, here it proves itself whether church is still church or not.[27]

Bonhoeffer, the fighter *for* the Jews, is also *for* the mission to the Jews. This is certainly not heard gladly by everyone today. In 2016, for example, the then EKD chairwoman Schwaetzer said: "As Christians it is not our task to lead Jews to salvation, God does that himself."[28]

6
TEAMING UP TO BELIEVE, HOPE AND LOVE TOGETHER

The Christian life is designed as and for teamwork. It's a counter-culture that can be a foretaste of heaven. Incomparably precious. But still it remains a teamwork of sinners. This is why it also is a permanent challenge—and often very painful. It's about a unique kind of fellowship.

~

Little Candles in Life Houses
October 31, 2013

Visit in the Christmas museum in Rothenburg ob der Tauber—a fascinating place with tons of little lights everywhere, very special atmosphere. I think:

We would like to install a new lighting system in people's "life houses." But we usually only get around to it at best, to light a few candles of different sizes somewhere.

Measured against the great desire: frustrating.

Devilish tactics: Through the frustration of the impossible to paralyze the motivation for the possible.

Because also each candle brings brightness and warmth. For example:
- listen patiently
- just be there
- encourage
- take seriously

- strengthen
- comfort
- make you smile
- give a breathing space
- just give a helping hand
- give a loving nudge
- somewhere make a few minutes of everyday life easier for the other person
- be generous
- give hope
- trust
- confide

And these are candles too:
- *not* turn a deaf ear like many others
- *not* to intrigue like many others
- *not* to be disrespectful like many others
- *not* to make one's own advantage the standard
- *not* to insist on one's own right

And much more. At the end of a day, a whole lot can have come together!

All these small candles are living indications of the great light—for everyone who wants to see further.

Whether he does, is not in our hands. But without the small candles he does not have this chance at all.

What remains is love.

Strength in the Snowstorms
November 4, 2013

Is weakness a value in itself (because God has the weak especially in mind)?

No, certainly not. But it is an underestimated tool to recognize the truth, to become realistic.

Self-sufficiency, independence may seem like the thing that gives the greatest possible freedom. But I believe this is an illusion. The greatest freedom is where love is lived—and love is based on reciprocity.

Facing and admitting weakness is a very special kind of strength. The courage to reveal ourselves as vulnerable (which we *all* are but usually try to hide as much as possible from ourselves, or at least from others). For Christians, this strength is grounded in God's all-encompassing care in the process. And it gives others the opportunity to use their gifts and strengths for our good.

Theoretically, then, we might be the ones in this world who should have the least trouble facing the truth about our situation. But the fact is, nevertheless, it is much easier to think about it when we are sitting in a rocking chair than when we are trying to find our way through a snowstorm. But probably we can really only, or at least best, exercise our spiritual muscles when we are in such situations that seriously challenge us, and that means pain, sweat, and so on.

Life is not easy. And Jesus never promised that it would be, but that he would be with us. Again, we know this and yet deep in our hearts we long for paradise on earth. Good that his patience is so great and that we can never disappoint him, because he already knows beforehand what kind of people he has to deal with!

To me, the mystery of Christian community often seems like a kind of mobile hospital on the road to eternity; there is a reciprocal give and take at different stages of the journey. In the end, a deeply enriching experience if we manage to overcome the natural feelings of shame, pride and fear. God's way of making us feel his love through others. By the way, we have a good example: the Lord of the Universe was not afraid to ask his friends for prayer when he experienced his hour of crisis as a man, in Gethsemane.

God's Hidden Network
November 14, 2013

Not often, but several times in the past few months I have been surprised by inklings of God's normally hidden network of his praying people. To be able to see and share where God is working ...
- in different people
- in different places
- at the same time

- with the same goal (without them knowing about each other at first!)

... is a powerful weapon against temptations to let our trust in his open ears and eyes be shaken when God seems to be silent. For me, the encouraging effect of these insights has much to do with the experience of a certain "objectivity" of God's action. In times of uncertainty (thoughts like: "Am I possibly only seeing, what I want to see?"), such experiences are an additional help to realize that answer to prayer is rooted in reality.

It is the exception that God gives us such glimpses (I admit I would like a lot more of them), but they are a tremendous support to trust even in those situations where we cannot see—where we cannot *yet* see.

However, the experience requires the willingness to openly share with others what moves me. And to do so without being certain what will come of it.

A Balancing Act
November 20, 2013

Somebody shared on Facebook:

> Imagine being in a room together with people of all sorts of different ethnic backgrounds, with Protestants, Catholics, Amish, Conservatives, Charismatics, people with various disabilities, some singing in the same key, some not singing at all (according to their culture, not because of God), all ages, etc., praying, praising, listening to the Gospel message, and they are one church. Seems impossible, doesn't it? NO! This is exactly what our family experienced at the "Joni and Friends" family retreat. It gives a sense of heaven. True community. This is where you realize that we are truly one body in Jesus. Great thing.

My thoughts on that:

The first "church," first Christian community was the group of the Twelve, followed by the Christians in Jerusalem. Both were not governed from the beginning by a common overall sound and well thought-out doctrine and corresponding organizational structure. Not that such a structure or clear doctrine is in itself negative (some people today seem to think so); no community can live in the long run without such a thing, and Christ himself aimed at our growth in the truth. But precisely this is an important point: those who still have to grow still have to learn and should therefore realize and accept that others have been given a different timetable by the Lord himself, that they may have different priorities because of their culture or situation, make different mistakes, realize their mistakes at different times, or perhaps not at all until the end, etc.

So Christians face a rather difficult challenge, a balancing act: to strive for growing knowledge of Christ on all possible levels and to try to practice in daily life what they have learned (including congregational structures) on the one hand, and on the other hand to hold together as much as possible with other Christians who share only a part of one's conviction; and always to have an open eye, ear and heart to see if one can learn something from them.

This does not mean playing truth and love off against each other. We need both.

Zufall

December 6, 2013

It was a really bad morning. There was some stuff I just couldn't get along with, which literally made my knees weak and shaky in an unusual and scary way. I tried to force myself to do activities by cleaning. By lunchtime, the internal storm finally dissipated. I became calmer and firmer and able to work again, thanks to the Lord. It had been a very disturbing experience. At some point in between, a friend had sent me Paul's words: "To those who love God, all things must (!) work together for good" (according to Romans 8:28). Later, I wanted to briefly check something on Facebook, when I came across a picture on the home page that an acquaintance had posted a few minutes earlier: Isaiah 35:3–4: "Strengthen the feeble hands, steady the knees that give way; say to those with fearful hearts, 'Be strong, do not fear; your God will come.'"

Coincidence? Hardly.

Apt comment of the friend to whom I told about it: "Wow! We get what we need when we need it. No, 'coincidence' does not exist, but it 'falls to us' what we need; someone takes care of it." (There is a wordplay involved: The German word for *coincidence* is "Zufall.")

In His Hands
December 15, 2013

A strange experience in the church service. A deep conflict in the staff made me very uneasy. The awareness of disunity was like a tormenting shadow over everything. But I tried to fight it and still take in everything with as much concentration as possible. I knew that at about the same time a couple of friends in the USA were on a plane to another state. The sermon was about Revelation 3:7–10. In between I had several impulses to pray for the friends and to email the Revelation passage. Because I saw no connection or concrete occasion at all, I prayed, but otherwise tried to push away the thought of a message. However, it stubbornly returned. To finally get rid of it, I wrote a short message shortly after the end of the service: "Just sat in the service, Rev 3:7–10. Had several impulses to pray for you and to send this text. For whatever reason. Maybe you have some idea!"

A few hours later came the reply, "Can't write details right now, but that totally fit!" (The explanation came the other day.) God's ways and networks are mysterious …

Later, I came across an apt quote from Oswald Chambers:

"If you are to be used by God, he will take you through a series of experiences that are not meant for yourself at all. They are meant to make you useful in His hands and to help you understand what is happening in the lives of others. Because of this process, you need never be surprised at what comes your way."[1]

Faith Founded in Simple Obedience
April 18, 2014

Corrie ten Boom once said, "When I read the Bible in a scientific, theological or scholarly way, it does not make me happy. But when I read that God so loved the world that He gave His only Son that whoever believes in Him should not perish but have eternal life, then I am truly happy."[2]

Spontaneously I ask myself: isn't that a bit simplified? It can be that simple—should be that simple? But then I realize: all the great fathers and mothers in the faith that we have experienced in the course of church history and who have changed the world for the better have done so out of a faith that was founded in simple obedience to the biblical word. The Salvation Army could not have been founded by a liberal professor. Neither could the Wycliff Bible translators. Neither could George Müller's orphanage. Not to mention the many individuals respected for their spirit of love, extraordinary reconciliation, self-denial, strength in extreme situations such as severe illness, concentration camps and under persecution. How they heard God's voice through the biblical words was actually much too naive according to historical-critical understanding, but it "worked," has been source of strength to live, fight and die.

It Comes Down to Practice
April 24, 2014

Part 1

In a discussion group, the topic was "Love your enemies." Someone told a very concrete story from his everyday life. Immediately we were all filled with typical human anger, and not in short supply. Fortunately, it did not stop there. In the further conversation it became very clear to us: It is good that Jesus's love was unconditional. We live from this and we should remember this well and often; that Jesus gave himself for us, although he knew how difficult it would be for us to learn from him. So lonely, betrayed by friends, understood by no one, wanting and doing only good, condemned unjustly with lies—how will he have felt?—and he knew this from the beginning. And still he prayed for all and loved them until the end. And he knew, even after that, the great insight would not suddenly come immediately.

I thought about this again later:

When I ask now (which I often do) that Jesus transform me more and more into his image, well knowing that my own strength is too small, I should keep in mind what I often suppress in the process. The goal, and therefore of course the path to it, is not simply a steadily growing warm comforting feeling in the heart and that everything becomes easier as a result, but includes participation in the solitude of Jesus. (Mother Theresa comes to mind, who thought a lot about this). Yes, love sometimes causes love in return; however, this is not always to the same extent, and also often contrary to it rejection to an increasing extent or at least indifference. But the more I become capable to love and ready to bear injustice (which is actually a positive aspect), the more sensitivity grows, rejection hurts, one becomes even more sensitive to injustice, and so on, it makes one sad (which is a painful aspect of the matter). In some respects discipleship is and remains a path of suffering, even if it is overall and ultimately a path of healing and above all the one that connects us to Jesus like no other and enables experience of deep communion with him. This suffering is insofar a constructive one, ultimately. But: Do I really want that, not only with the head, but from the heart? Do I want to learn to love, even where it means learning to live patiently with rejection and without grumbling? Love is not a "method," not a patent key to the heart of all people. True love is an open-ended gift.

Part 2
In addition, the devil naturally wants to prevent me from all this with all his might—by not looking at Jesus, by not seeing the devil behind the person, but by "demonizing" the person himself, especially by resisting the training of my character, which is only possible in challenging situations (which I don't like), etc. Can't it just be a little easier? After all, I am not Jesus. Or if Jesus would finally change the other, then I wouldn't have to get so upset anymore.

An old American television series comes to mind once again. Jeannie only has to cross her arms, nod three times and then the wish is granted. That would be the best if the Holy Spirit answered our prayer for love so promptly and then we simply couldn't help but love. But he doesn't.

So to speak of the necessity of love, to be convinced of it, is one thing. To convert this into small coins, to really surrender my comfort, inertia, longing for inviolability, justice, being understood, recognition, etc., to surrender the inner "claim" to it, is another. And I sense how I am still very much in myself and my ideas of how life should go and how Jesus should work for justice and salvation at my side, instead of loving him and really leaving everything to him, no matter how crosswise I am in detail.

Saying it with these words helps me not to hide my poverty behind euphemistic or justifying thoughts. Of course, others do a lot of crap. Constantly. How could it be otherwise? But the way I react, my ability to love, my character is what I should take care of first. No matter how much sweat it takes. Dying to one's ego is the way to new life. Nobody really wants to die. Dying is scary, dying hurts. But Jesus says: Give me your ego, let it die. That is the way to life.

Honest self-assessment, good intentions and approaching them with positive conviction are first good steps, and supporting each other through honest sharing and prayer is another. And then it comes down to practice.

Higher-level Ethics
June 17, 2014

What helps or doesn't help sexual orientation? Problem statement.

Observation: There is a tendency in our society to assume more and more: My feelings are my identity.

But this can be very misleading and problematic, if only because of the changeability of feelings; in addition, the causes of feelings are complex and therefore not simply suitable as an orientation guide to truth (although the search for truth no longer seems to play a role in postmodernity anyway).

The reference to the fact that also in the animal world by no means only heterosexuality occurs and therefore other variants should be regarded as natural also for humans is also a very problematic train of thought. Many animals have changing partners. Or live polygamously. And some eat their partners or children. That is quite natural for them. But who would want to deduce from this that this is also completely okay for humans if it occurs to them? The example makes it clear: Ethics cannot simply be derived from what occurs factually; it needs higher-level standards.

Do I Really Have to Forgive?
July 17, 2014

The discussion group dealt with a hot issue—readiness to forgive. Actually, everyone knows that bearing grudges does not make anything better, but in some situations it seems to be unimaginable to pronounce forgiveness regardless of the behavior of the guilty party. Some afterthoughts on this.

The vocabulary is somehow treacherous. Again and again it is said: "I can't do that." Actually more correct would be (even if inability is a partial element in it): "I don't want to." (And there is also a certain defiant tone here).

Why is that so difficult? (Although people usually have more burden than relief from it). Is it to keep open a back door for revenge, if one day the possibility should arise?

Does a sense of justice militate against it? Does the inner upholding of the legal claim (the other person owes me something) at least give the *feeling* of being above the other, even if it comes to nothing, and on top of that is practically only possible at the high price of one's own bitterness?

A few more impulses to check yourself:

First of all: What exactly do I get out of resenting? What exactly is the counter-value of bearing grudges for me? In a short sentence to the point?

Only then consider the following thoughts further.

Can the fact not to want or not to be able to let go be an indication that I have not yet grasped God's other "righteousness" in depth? For example, do I still secretly make differences, live by comparing ("Okay, I certainly don't deserve God's love, so for sure I am grateful that he is merciful to me, but let's be honest: others deserve it even a little less")? Instead of living only to look to the cross and the certainty: If I were the only person on earth (of course, somewhat absurd idea, I know), Jesus would have died anyway—for me! My sins, my imperfection are sufficient reason for it! (This realization of his love should actually overwhelm me so much that out of gratitude I hardly know what to do and become ready to do everything for him.)

Do we perhaps *practically* think like this:

That God accepts me as I am I appreciate very much.

That he does not want to leave me as I am in some respect, but wants to change me for the better, is also fine with me.

And it's okay if that costs me—a little—effort.

But please, only in those respects that bother me, too.

Surely he cannot expect me to really give up *all* my rights to surrender them to him!

One thing is certain: Jesus says clearly (without exception and unconditionally): "Forgive. Forgive 7x77 times. Forgive your enemies (not only after they have become peaceful or even friends!). So I am, to you and to others; and so you shall be also. You cannot consciously or willingly reserve my love for yourselves without thereby turning your back on me."

Who am I, that I little human being want to negotiate with God what he can and cannot expect of me? What does that say about my willingness to obey?

And what does my refusal say about the measure of my trust in Jesus? I do not hand over the case to him because I think in some corner of my heart that it is in better hands with me; I fear, perhaps diffusely in my mind, but at any rate strongly emotionally, that he might somehow shortchange me, that he does not mean it as well with me as I mean it with myself.

Finally: A partly justified objection is that severely injured people are overwhelmed by this, and that such a proposal from the Christian side can therefore come across as uncharitable, inhuman, arrogant, etc.

It is true that we need help, but again: this is what Jesus promises.

And in this testimony that there is a way of healing, a way to peace, a way to new life despite past catastrophes, there is a huge opportunity for Christians—namely, to testify to the gospel and to invite to the healing and salutary discipleship of Jesus. Do we perhaps shy away from witnessing to Jesus's challenge not only because we worry about hurting the other person even more, but also because we do not dare to point so clearly to Jesus? Either because we ourselves are not sure of our faith or because we are ashamed?

Similarly one would have to ask oneself the questions really honestly, if one wants to get on the own track.

A Healing Atmosphere
October 5, 2014

This morning in the service I asked myself again what—especially older—people can actually comprehend of this liturgically and theologically so dense event, for instance, due to tiredness, shorter attention spans, etc. Then the first thing that came to my mind was the old story in which a woman describes her benefit from the service with a metaphor: "When water runs through a sieve, it doesn't stay in it, but the sieve becomes clean." I couldn't really put the image into concrete terms until now. What does *clean* mean? But then it crossed my mind, just the reassurance: "I am not alone with my basic faith" can already have a positive effect; but above all at the moment when I am in the service, I am not somewhere else, not in an environment that distracts me, that is clueless with regard to faith, etc.; I am in a healing atmosphere and at the same time I give God the opportunity to say something to me through various channels. The central point is not to understand everything or even as much as possible, but to be in a space where God can contact me. This can happen elsewhere, of course; but the fact is that, for example, when reading the Bible at home, we are usually the ones who determine the type and amount. Worship offers much more "surprise possibilities" from God, which are not pre-filtered by us.

Love Learning Program
November 16, 2014

"By this everyone will know that you are my disciples, if you love one another." (John 13:35)

Jesus stands for love, and this should also be reflected in us. We are to be recognized by this.

Scholarship, fighting spirit for the truth, etc., are anything but unimportant; nevertheless rather subordinate (while the content of love must be oriented to Jesus!).

The Song of Songs in 1 Corinthians 13 has a basis here. One cannot live love alone. Being a Christian therefore also is not lived alone, because this is the love learning program par excellence.

To Serve and Be Served
December 25, 2014

Daniel T. Niles, Ceylonese theologian on service and Jesus as a servant: "He was a true servant because he was dependent on those for whom he had come to serve ... This weakness of Jesus we must share as his followers. To serve from a position of power is in truth not service, but charity."[3]

Further, "The only way to ignite love between two people or two groups of people is to relate to each other in such a way that you need each other. The Christian community must serve. It must also be in a position where it needs service."[4]

K. Bailey comments: "Thus the cycle of pride in the giver and humiliation on the part of the receiver is broken."[5]

Finding the Positive Starting Point
April 13, 2015

I try to be very intentional during the day about imagining Jesus at my side (kind of like if the disciples were walking around with Jesus today and I was part of the group) and thinking about how he would see, hear, comment on what my eyes and ears would see and hear. The goal, among other things, is to get away from a one-sided negative view. An example: While shopping at a supermarket (where I am often struck by the dullness and emptiness of people) I saw from a distance —approaching the entrance—how people were getting shopping carts; a father was trying to maneuver his child into the cart, and there was laughter. I was struck (once again) by the thought: Many people obviously live a completely superficial life. Next thought: Superficial, yes, it may be, but it also reflects an unselfconsciousness for which we were actually intended. Spontaneous joy, living in the present, like dogs playing, just being there and frolicking, fun, enjoying little things, variety.

This somewhat more nuanced view is probably more in line with Jesus's merciful eyes than my first impression. And is definitely more helpful, creates a more positive starting point.

Under the Same Cross
July 7, 2015

At the interpersonal level, there is usually a spiral going on: Injury (whether objectively or felt subjectively, is secondary), reaction to it, etc.

As a Christian, I am challenged to a different possibility: Bring the woundedness (by all means complaining) to Jesus …

… forgive the other (regardless of his request)

… ask Jesus for help to bear the burden

… ask Jesus for help to repay evil with good

… try to approach the other person anew (1 Corinthians 13!), to become positively active as long as this is at all possible.

Extreme example: Jesus also washed Judas's feet, served him; that is our example. This is much more than not reacting negatively or neutrally.

Actually this is not an option, but a commandment. It applies regardless of the "(advance) payment" of the other. And if I have problems to let myself in for that, if my pride rebels against it, my pain, my self-pity, my sense of justice, my frustration, my escape reflex, my fear, my mistrust to fall short or whatever, this proves my own deficiency regarding trust in Jesus and ability to love. (This can be quite understandable from a purely human point of view, but that is not our standard.) And when I honestly face this deficiency, I recognize myself—once again—as standing next to the difficult fellow Christian or fellow human being under the same cross, on which our common Lord died, so that through his love we get other options for life. The other one acted wrongly, may be. He remained below his possibilities, may be. But under the cross my gaze should not go beside me, but up to Jesus. Every small or big *but* that stirs in me against it tells me: I need the doctor. Now. With top priority.

How I behave must feed on: What serves love, peace, togetherness, the other one, not: what serves me or what do I get along with best or what do I think I can handle? Because my well-being I have actually given into Jesus's hands. He is responsible for that.

1 Corinthians 13 is the way Jesus loves me, the kind of love I live by and which should ultimately run circles through me.

So my thoughts must revolve around the question: How can I win the other? With the readiness to endure the suffering if and as long as it does not succeed, and not to close down, as it would be humanly normal self-protection. I can and should pray for the other and for his change, but at the beginning there is the prayer for change for me—to become capable of such devotion that reflects Jesus's searching love and mercy.

All this may sound humanly crazy—exaggerated—but the decisive question is: Is this heavenly logic true or not? And if I think it is true, am I willing to put my faith in it, independent of short-term success experiences within reach, but simply for the sake of Jesus?

If I have answered the truth question positively, the only choice left is between obedience and disobedience.

For Christians, in any case, there is ultimately nothing to demand for oneself, but only to give oneself away; to raise one's voice for others, "the cause of the mute" (Proverbs 31:8) and to demand it is another matter.

Surrender, letting go. Once again. And at the same time, the secret of those whose love ultimately proved overcoming power.

Why Silence in Persecution?
October 7, 2015

Today "our" Syrian refugees asked us why the European churches had helped the Christians in the persecution so little—that they had stood up for the Yazidis, they have heard in Syria. But something comparable for the Christians—not.

This reminded me again of the comment of a dean from southern Germany, which I read some time ago in the info-sheet of the Westphalian pastor's association (June 2015):

> As a dean, one gets around in many services by virtue of one's office. What strikes me time and again in these months, especially in the intercessions: the comprehensive lack of mention of persecuted Christians in many oriental countries ... People from other church districts or even regional churches confirm this perception. ... We all know about it—and our church is more or less silent about it. In the case of natural disasters, escalations of

violence and wars ... they usually react quickly with collection announcements and templates for intercessions. This is often helpful. In the matter of Christian pogroms, I have waited in vain for something like this. More than a few weeks ago the somewhat dull headline "EKD is concerned about the situation in Mosul" I have not yet noticed officially in the church. ... Someone told me recently: Explicit intercession for the persecuted Christians is heard in our church as implicit criticism of Islam. That is why we prefer to remain silent, because we do not want to expose ourselves to the accusation of encouraging a criticism of Islam that is often carried out in a repugnant way in right-wing conservative circles. I am not at all sure that this fear is true. But it probably says something about a kind of interreligious correctness that is currently mainstream in our church. Whether this is helpful remains to be seen. ... Last but not least: It is a rather bitter irony that we, who today rightly lament the failure and silence of our church 70 years ago vis-à-vis the Shoa, now find it opportune to remain silent vis-à-vis another ethnic religiously motivated mass murder. Apparently because it concerns Christians.[6]

The dean named further motives; in my opinion they all point to an underlying fundamental identity crisis. Development aid, practical emergency aid—yes; help for spiritual life—no. Rather, bashful silence, or even publicity for an allegedly in essence peaceful Islam, all in the name of tolerance, and common mantras like as ultimately no one has the whole truth, and somehow we have (almost) the same God and so on. Interesting also: Even the feminist theologians practice restraint instead of offensively attacking the Koran's image of women.

Change: The Challenge of Discipleship
October 19, 2015

As a woman following Jesus, sometimes it is important to point out what is not said or which answer to a question cannot be true.

Nowhere in the Bible is it said: Become a better man, a better woman (which would require an ideal-type checklist across cultures and time). That would also be trying to get a hold of an amoeba. All are as Christians a new creation, are children of God and are to become Christ-like. *He* is the standard of comparison, not inner-worldly ideas and expectations. These can be helpful, can reflect correct hunches, but do not have to. *"Test ..."* (cf 1 Thessalonians 5:21, Philippians 1:9f, Ephesians 5:10)

To become like Jesus means to be rooted in the love and vocation of the Father; it means to learn to serve, to learn to give up caring for oneself and to be there for others, transversely to the usual standards of the world (prestige, power, self-interest). I don't need to be afraid of breaking a prong out of my crown because my crown is in heaven and well protected there. Therefore, there is something fundamentally wrong when people draw their sense of worth from their superiority over others, whether men or women. The moment I squint to the right or left or below myself, I no longer look upward, I am no longer Christ-focused.

To point out that this is something that lies deep within the human being is no different than saying that we are sinners and need healing. All of us. Galatians 3:28 (in Christ there is no longer Jew or Greek or free or slave or man or woman) is a reality that originates from the invisible dimension and should increasingly take shape in the visible one.

Jesus says nowhere: This and that would be actually right, but it is too difficult for you; therefore you can resign yourselves to the reality and need not strive for higher goals. No. "You shall be perfect." Double commandment of love: "With all your heart." "Love your enemies!" These are huge goals. Feelings of inferiority, whether male or female, are post-paradise and in need of healing by the Holy Spirit, not by avoidance strategies regarding stressful challenges. It can be more loving to refrain from false consideration and protection and so make way for growth.

Thought on the view often expressed in conservative circles that women should not push themselves to the fore: What specifically does that actually mean? At first it sounds as if it's about an inner attitude. But who can judge this apart from the person concerned? Or is it about certain activities that are basically labeled that way—as soon as they are performed by a woman?

In any case: Nobody should push oneself into the foreground. We should put Jesus into the foreground and point away from ourselves towards him. And therefore it is best to concentrate on the question of how this is best done and not on the (again self-centered) question of whether we are restraining ourselves enough, which can also again act as a diversionary tactic. That other motives can get mixed in is no question, but firstly it affects men as well as women and secondly it must not be an obstacle to testify to the truth. Otherwise we may have to be silent or hesitant until eternity. Philippians 1:15–18 helps. Truth remains truth, even if the witnesses of this truth remain imperfect. But everything that structurally amounts to witnessing the gospel less instead of more can only be wrong. It is always a matter of being ready to speak the salvific word at the right time—that is, to be fundamentally open to God's commission to witness.

Moreover, one should not lose sight of the possibility that people impute false motives in order to avoid their own changes, the challenges of discipleship.

For the tradition of interpretation of past centuries it seems to me meanwhile more profoundly effective than I have assessed so far that the disputed Bible passages on the role of women were usually read on the background of the firm conviction that the woman was fundamentally inferior by nature and less capable. Only the new evangelicals do not tire of emphasizing that the *equal value* is completely out of the question, that it is only about the *unequal ranking* (which makes the adherence to the restriction of women seem all the more random).

God Finds Us
April 14, 2016

Reading Joni Eareckson Tada's devotional "Who Helps the Most" in her book *Secret Strength: For Those Who Search*.

She cannot answer the question what helped her most after her accident and the following paraplegia with a reference to a person or a sentence or verse; what she initially sought and needed most was not knowledge, but love, attention. This means for those who want to help in similar situations: apart from 1 Corinthians 13, they need not bear in mind unusual requirements; no need for training, expertise, special talent, spiritual expertise. One brought envelopes and even stamps, another took care of nail care, etc., all the little things of everyday life, and thus these people were God's love in action.[7]

Taking her experience to heart can help not to despair of one's own feelings of powerlessness. Like when I think about the situation of a refugee family: The problems in their family, the problems with learning German, the reading blockades caused by depression, the limitations of cell phone use because of finances, the lack of media availability, the lack of familiarity with digital devices, all of which makes spiritual accompaniment even more difficult than it already is. Then I often choke on talking about trust in God.

The conclusion of Keller's book *Reason for God* keeps coming to mind and has become my prayer:

> During a dark time in her life, a woman in my congregation complained that she had prayed over and over, "God, help me to find you!" but it had been to no avail. A friend who was a Christian recommended her to change her prayer to "God, come and find me. After all, you are the Good Shepherd who goes in search of lost sheep." When she told me this, she ended, "The only reason I can tell you this story is: he did."[8]

On Being a Slave to All
August 27, 2016

Mark 10:35–45, "… be a slave of all."

A slave has practically no rights. His own needs are subordinate.

First thought: Doesn't this clearly contradict the modern attempts to tame the call to unconditional love and devotion by pointing out that only the one who loves himself and therefore can also set boundaries can love others?

Second thought: No one can be a slave to everyone. If, for example, parents and spouses make contradictory demands or even go against God's will, priorities must be set on one's own responsibility.

Third thought: It is about the inner attitude, the motivation; do I worry about losing face, that something could be "beneath my dignity"? Something like that must not be the guiding principle of my actions, because then I have not yet completely handed over the care for my life to God. If this question is clarified, however, further criteria can and will have to come into play, because as said, otherwise nobody can be slave of all; that is practically impossible. It cannot be about will-less obedience (that would be literally irresponsible). Also Jesus did not simply do everything others wanted. He asked for God's will.

Echoes of Compassion
November 15, 2016

While sitting in the airport, an image came to mind as I thought about prayer teamwork. Why is this so encouraging, when God definitely hears our silent sighs as well, and also certainly doesn't need a reminder of our needs? Nor does he first need to be made willing to care for us.

Already purely humanly not to be alone with our burdens is certainly one of the different factors here. Another, quite related one: Could it be that prayer companions are meant to serve in some way as God's more concrete "shoulders" that he deliberately offers to lean on by having us stand together? He knows how easily he can appear to us as hidden, which is adding to our need, and perhaps that is why he wants to assure us of his invisible presence through his visible human co-workers. "Your compassion is an echo of mine, even greater, be sure of it!"

Just a thought.

We See His Glory
February 4, 2017

Transfiguration of Jesus, Mark 9:2ff.

You can't hold on to the special moments, but you can't erase the fact that they were there either; they are starting points, equipment for the way through everyday life.

Why did Jesus take three men with him up on the mountain? Witnesses. They can later assure each other (and others), "We weren't fooling ourselves, you know it too, you were there!" (By the way: John begins his Gospel "We have seen his glory"; Peter refers to it in 2 Peter 1:18, John in 1 John 1:1ff.)

It also makes sense to share our personal mountains with others, for mutual reassurance when we are overcome by doubts.

Gifts Oblige
February 23, 2017

Somehow the question came to my mind: Am I okay, grateful, to be a woman? Am I happy about my mission to shape my piece of the world as a woman?

Unusual way to formulate the question. So the answers didn't exactly tumble spontaneously. To be allowed to give life, to care, to promote, to be hospitable, to care for relationships—all these are certainly things for which I am grateful.

Not new, but important to keep in mind: We have to take responsibility for our own lives, not pass on the processing of our inferiority complexes to our partners, for example, and expect them to provide the solution (receiving and accepting support is different from being dependent).

This is part of growing up. Women cannot be responsible for men's complexes (by holding back, making themselves small, etc., as it sometimes seems to be taught and lived in many evangelical churches, not only in America) and vice versa does not work either. The only meaningful and lasting source of identity is Jesus. Anything else will always lead to fearful comparison, not freedom.

In the context of "responsibility for gifts received," I continued to think of the parable of the entrusted pounds. Gifts oblige. Women are not exempted by Jesus.

Moreover, while thinking about how being a woman or man actually distinguishes us in concrete terms, I remembered God's self-introduction to Moses: "I am who I am." God's person remains something mysterious, despite his self-revelation, which cannot be captured in definitions. We are to some extent created in the image of God, reflecting something of him. So perhaps in this question, too, we would probably do well to preserve the element of mystery also with regard to our genders instead of designing role-casuistry. "Just be" and imitate Jesus and let him uncover and us discover who we are or are to become more and more instead of squinting to the right and left and man-made specifications! Seek first God's kingdom and rely that everything else necessary will be added. I cannot achieve happiness in a direct way. My personality is perhaps another example of something that unfolds and becomes more coherent when I don't try to work on it directly, but simply walk after Jesus.

Being Jesus's Shoulder
March 17, 2017

As we prayerfully reflect on the situation of the refugees, it gets under our skin what challenges they have to face, what they have had to leave behind, how difficult it is to get used to our culture, which is so completely different, despite all the help they receive, and so on. An American friend wrote about this, among other things: "Sometimes, I think Jesus allows us to feel the weight of the world, not because He is unjust or cruel but to dig our wells deeper. Like thirst draws us to drink, so this weight draws us into a deeper compassion."

My answer:

"You are right. The most intense prayers are when I am overwhelmed with wonder or need. When I *am* prayer, not just 'saying a prayer.' And there is another step to it, for me actually once again a step of repentance or conversion, in order to learn. If Jesus wants his followers to become like him, then our willingness to learn is challenged. Because love involves feeling compassion, which in turn involves accepting and enduring suffering (while my natural instinct is a longing to get rid of it). A few days ago, I was talking to a refugee about how helpless I often feel because I would love to help so much more effectively than I do. But I just can't. But what I will try to do is: at least not run away, but stay by their side. That's at least a small reflection of what Jesus does, too—he promised never to leave us alone, whether we feel it or not. So, whenever possible, I want to be 'Jesus's shoulder' for others to lean on at least for a moment of fellowship, even if it's nothing more than shared helplessness (that points to him, though). Better a moment than none. And I want to learn to accept and bear the grief of those masses of lonely sufferers in this world as part of our transformation into the image of Christ, the compassionate God who will one day wipe all tears from our faces and from the millions whose names only he knows."

Hard Forgiveness
September 2, 2019

Forgiveness. Reconciliation. Why is this so difficult?

For Jesus it seems to be rather very simple. "Do this. Again and again. Without accounting. And take the initiative. Don't be afraid to lose yourselves." Is he making it too simple? (A still open sub-question: Is processing of being hurt really only possible by working through completely or not perhaps also by leaving it behind? Are psychology and faith different in their available options?)

First of all: Attention, trap (always applies to all sides involved)! We should not expect our own peace from satisfying reactions of others. Biblically, it is rather a matter of letting go of expectations of the other in favor of one's own unconditional surrender. (Not to be confused with the kind of un-expectancy that is basically resignation or indifference, where one no longer cares about the other. Rather, I am just shifting the focus of my hope to our common heavenly instructor).

And: In the New Testament, the attitude of Christians seems to be not to avoid anyone in church, marriage, work relationship, if possible, but to stay at the side of people, even if their behavior or thinking is difficult; to actively try to overcome evil with good, to persistently and actively start peace initiatives.

The basis should be Jesus's teaching and example. Jesus also did not first send his disciples to days of reflection and give them a time-out until they learned their lesson (e.g., not to compete for places of honor, but to finally internalize service mentality and the reversal of culturally customary values).

"If we are faithless, he remains faithful." (2 Timothy 2:13)

Or am I wrong?

The only contrary example I can think of: If a village does not want to receive the disciples, they should move on. But this is a different context (mission strategy, not team behavior).

Of course, such faithfulness can theoretically be lived and maintained from a temporary distance. When people turned away, Jesus did not impose himself, although his stomach often turned and tears came in the face of the confused people around him who actually needed him so urgently.

But did he himself actively send anyone away? Not even Judas.

Doesn't that mean at least as a basic attitude this should be our role model? Colossians 3:13: "Forgive as the Lord forgave you."

I went searching for biblical foundations or examples:

Judas. Peter. Thomas. In general, the discipleship community (see, for instance, the discussion of places of honor just alluded to). And otherwise anyway, what conclusion do we draw from unconditional forgiveness of Jesus towards us? The parable of the "unmerciful servant" (Matthew 18:21ff).

One might object that would possibly amount to playing down, covering up or even factually confirming wrong behavior in this way, for lack of a harder stop sign. But it is not about saying nothing, rather about the how and about not complaining, but about leaving everything else to the work of the Holy Spirit. We are meant for each other as advising companions, but not as enforcing educators! (Possible special situation though: extreme cases of church discipline.)

I understand Jesus in such a way that in conflicts we are asked not to dwell on weighing the duties of the other, but to "simply" use everything that is possible for ourselves.

Then I listened to Michael Stahl on YouTube.[9]

Sounds crazy, radical, and yet at the same time triggers a sigh of relief, an inner agreement: Yes, that's how it is true, it can't be any other way. And it's what has always moved me, what "only" has become question-worthy to me recently. Here it is being lived. And it works. The circle to the beginning of the entry closes. The difficult thing about the gospel of grace is the simple. I spontaneously sense feeling at home, awakening joy.

Transcribed excerpt:
So I was standing in front of this door (of the Dad)
and all of a sudden I remember, in the Bible it says,
with my God I jump over walls. That was the biggest

wall in my life, to go to my tormentor and the one who degraded me, who hurt me. And then I went in. My father was standing inside. He used to weigh 130 kg, that day maybe 70, 75 kg. He wants to start screaming again or something, always had some reason. I said, 'Dad,' I waved him off, 'I just wanted to tell you … tell you that I love you. And I wanted to ask you to forgive me.' And for the first time in my whole life, there is silence.

How often do you think I said to my father: 'Stop drinking, you're a disgrace. Finally stop embarrassing yourself and all of us like this. With you, it's shameful. Change!' Again and again: 'Change yourself!' … 'I know only one person whom I can change, namely myself. And if you have made ten thousand mistakes and I have made one, then I ask you: forgive me this one mistake.' …

My mom lived above me, she sometimes beat me so much as a child that I couldn't breathe. I had then stopped breathing. Today I take her in my arms and kiss her. Not a week goes by where I don't take her in my arms and tell her that I love her.

I loved her well, my mother. It's been a lot of struggles. But love is awesome.

What about Women?
September 9, 2019

Topic: Women as teachers and leaders—allowed or not?

Among evangelicals there are, roughly speaking, two main groups. For the complementarians, the woman is subordinate support of the man due to creation, and there are different areas of responsibility corresponding to the nature, not the gifts, and the woman is not allowed to intervene in those of the man. For the egalitarians, both sexes were originally created equal and are supposed to complement each other in a gift-oriented way.

Both groups have a different basic attitude, a different attitude towards life.

Complementarians: They are convinced that there must be a casuistry rooted in the nature of gender, i.e., a kind of rulebook for situations that contains different commands and prohibitions depending on gender; but it cannot be looked up exactly anywhere; one must therefore always be on the lookout for possible rule violations.

Egalitarian: One simply only pays attention to servant attitude, respecting the other higher than oneself (and talents, of course), but this applies to everyone and everywhere.

To me, this seems to be significantly more constructive and less fear-driven.

Hint: Women, according to the New Testament, are supposed to learn and teach and lead—at least women and children; so the activity of teaching or leading in itself cannot be against identity of being female. But then for the modern complementarians, contrary to their protestations, the only conceivable reason for keeping the prohibition against teaching men remains that there is some kind of status difference; and this then becomes more important than contents and talents and is based on nothing else than gender, determined by God without communication of the reasons; for us this can ultimately only seem arbitrary. And it is misleading on top of that, because on the one hand to want to go against the class thinking of men (Galatians 3:28) and on the other hand to want to maintain structures in an area which confirm exactly this—what sense is this? And further, a reason is provided which offers a piously camouflaged hiding place for sinful male self-conceit. If this should make sense in God's eyes, as an ideal and not as an interim solution in need of overcoming for a time, then this would not exactly speak for reason as a characteristic of his being.

The whole topic is very existential for me even after more than 30 years, although I personally do not suffer from any disadvantages. One reason is certainly the following consideration: What do I testify as God's optimal conception in this area, if people ask me (even our grandchildren one day!), because I am his ambassador as a Christian? 1. I should not have to be evasive, but be certain and be able to give coherent and convincing information. 2. I should be able to identify with my Lord, to "make him strong," to admire and respect his wisdom over human piecemeal and thus be able to appear with a positive passionate charisma.

What, then, can ignite joy and admiration for God?

Certainly his genius as a creator. But this also includes his character and thus justice and that he deals better and fairer with people than people often do. His love becomes credible in the fact that he stands up for the weak; that each individual is important; that he does not exclude, and so on.

These are precisely the things that have motivated me since my youth. And this joy flares up even now when I read, for example, about Jesus's treatment of women. If there were something fundamentally wrong with my perspective, this could not remain without effect on my faith!

An attempt to make things vivid: Let us imagine two men.

Both have German citizenship and grew up here. Same education. But different skin color.

Example situations in which conflicts can arise:
- They are both theologians and are looking for housing.
- They are both retail salesmen and apply as store managers.
- They are both lawyers and apply as judges.

Would it be fair if candidates of color were sent back home from the start? Because skin color, not talent, is the top priority? Certainly not. There would immediately be talk of discrimination.

Why then is this different in the case of men and women in the teaching and leadership office, and on top of that, without the conservative as complementarians thinking men really feel the injustice and are honestly sad about the arising conflicts? Especially since the whole thing in the last consequence amounts to the fact that it is better to keep silent about God's word than that a woman passes it on (and thus, e.g., actually all missionary women have either talked themselves into their calling or are at best makeshift nails).

Causing Complexes
September 11, 2019

Topic of women in church continued—an observation on the behavior of complementarians:

Fathers, after all, simply tell their sons, for example, "Always do your best!" No one would tell them, "But be careful that you don't cause complexes in women by your ability."

Women, however, should additionally take care that men do not feel inferior if possible (at least this is subtly suggested by John Piper and other authors); women have to be careful not to get the label "career woman," etc. They may be made responsible for how men feel, have to be cautious or restrained instead of helping them, at least in the medium term, to deal with their own problems differently, to make self-worth not dependent on comparison and higher status than women, but on Jesus—that can't be healing!

Further hint of another (egalitarian thinking) author to Galatians 3:28:

As a slave one would possibly still have a chance to become free; as a Gentile a chance to become a Jew. As a woman, on the other hand, never a chance to come into freedom, without externally imposed restrictions simply to be what and how she is, if she were subordinated by creation.[10]

Prayer Pulses
November 2, 2019

A few days ago, I spontaneously sent the watchword of the day and a personal experience with it to a friend who lives far away. Now I suddenly had to pray for her again and again the night before. There was no specific occasion. So why? No idea. Imagination? My mind spinning? Purely inner-psychic late after-effect of the fact that I thought about it sometime days ago? Or does God use the latter and intensify it? I don't know.

Unable to shake off the thoughts, I asked myself: Should I tell her about this? Again: I don't know. I started a short message several times, but always discarded it. It could be a mistake; it could even come across as pomposity. (Though I also know from a few similar experiences in the past years that there can be more to it; and yet the skeptic in me still remained strong). In the end, before I went to sleep, I sent a late short hint before sleeping. That such an impulse returns so persistently can also be intended by Jesus—as an encouraging sign of his nearness, his hidden activity for both of us, which would strengthen hope. I had to get the back and forth out of my head to find sleep.

Today she wrote back. The email with the watchword (in my eyes completely unspectacular) must have been a direct hit in terms of content and timing. And my reference to the intercession impulse of the evening before as well. A difficult domestic situation had been tolerable during the week, but on the evening before it had become increasingly tense and hurtful. My friend, however, had somehow managed to remain calm, and the high tension slowly dissipated. This was more or less parallel in time to my prayer impulses. That blew me away. Crazy, and yet real. Heavenly network.

Love Counts
December 22, 2019

Biblical basis for the guiding principle: Love counts.

"The goal of this command is love, which comes from a pure heart and a good conscience and a sincere faith." (1 Timothy 1:5)

The double commandment of love:

"Love the Lord your God with all your heart and with all your soul and with all your strength and with all your mind"; and, "Love your neighbor as yourself." (Luke 10:27)

Different Sensitivities
March 8, 2020

1 Corinthians 12:17: The eye perceives the visible, but not the audible—to think that sounds do not exist would be fatal. The ear perceives audible, but not visible—same situation.

It is certainly a danger to overinterpret the picture. Nevertheless the question: Transferred to the worldwide community, perhaps differences in temperaments and emphases are also at least somewhat related to the fact that they reflect different sensitivities for areas that somehow all belong to our complex reality! So that highly liturgical congregations must not be played off against reformed ones or gospel music against chorales!

A Chosen Time
March 20, 2020

Many people find it not easy to read the Bible because it clearly comes from a different time, a different culture, a different linguistic and intellectual world. And that perhaps also brings with it the appearance of being outdated or even fairy tale-like. But we must consider: If it would have been written as it is familiar to us in the 21st century, it would have been difficult for the people at that time. God had to choose a time window that was conducive to the worldwide spread of the gospel, given the timeline of our history and the nature of salvation history and this was optimally true in many respects for the time when Jesus came and the first churches were formed.

Where Pride Lives
December 28, 2020

I'm reading *Your God Is Too Safe*, by Mark Buchanan. The subject of pride is on my mind: How do I discover pride, how do I track down its subtle manifestations?

Pride lives from comparison. That is, wherever I perceive my fellow human beings as different, the danger lurks of complacently elevating myself above them.

Furthermore, the author confirms a modern trap that I have also noticed several times: grace is seen as the opposite of effort. Grace, however, is not the opposite of effort, but of earning.[11]

Consider 2 Peter 1:3–8, where activity, training is unabashedly called for:

"For this very reason, *make every effort* to add to your faith goodness; and to goodness, knowledge; and to knowledge, self-control; and to self-control, perseverance; and to perseverance, godliness; and to godliness, mutual affection; and to mutual affection, love. For if you possess these qualities in increasing measure, they will keep you from being ineffective and unproductive in your knowledge of our Lord Jesus Christ."

Very good reference to how the ethics of the Pharisees and the ethics of Jesus differ: The Pharisees focus on avoidance, Jesus on involvement, participation ("ethics of avoidance" versus "ethics of involvement").[12]

This sums up very well why Jesus seems to be unafraid of contact, concerned about his reputation, etc.

To Speak or Not to Speak
February 20, 2021

"One of Crete's own prophets has said it: 'Cretans are always liars, evil brutes, lazy gluttons.' This saying is true." (Titus 1:12–13)

Are sweeping judgments, clichés, generalizations legitimate for a Christian, a "prudent" way of speaking that reflects Jesus? Hardly. We have become sensitive today to how inflammatory, condemning, disrespectful such language is and what dangerous potential it has (which is why it is deliberately used by the powerful of this world for brainwashing and propaganda purposes). It promotes feelings of superiority, appeals to base instincts instead of differentiated thinking, is a diabolical seed.

If we were to present the words that Paul chooses here, for example, in a seminar on the topic of "How Christians Should Speak or Not Speak" for evaluation, without naming him as the author (of course, there should be no Bible experts present …), then hopefully at least the vast majority would immediately react negatively.

But because it is Paul who expresses himself in this way, we are in danger of not wanting to see the forest for the trees, of excusing him, of looking for explanations that try to turn black into white.

Couldn't such misbehavior simply be the practical expression of the fact that he, too, is still a learner? That sometimes his temper still gets the better of him, too? And that God allows that something like this found its way into the canon as a negative example?

The alternative would be to take Paul as an example, and if you formulate it like this, it becomes clear how absurd that would be. Hmm, but all this could be thought too short; the matter is even more complicated. Jesus can also talk like this:

Hans Bürki writes in the *Wuppertal Study Bible*,

How can Paul adopt such a summary judgment and still affirm it? If such sentences were in a travelogue about Crete, they would be out of place, because they do not describe, but expose and accuse. Here, however, prophetic punishment and rebuke** is the determining background. One is reminded here of Jesus' woeings over the Pharisees. As a mere assertion, as an expression of personal or collective aggression against those who think differently, such sentences would, of course, be inadmissible and incomprehensible.

Only those who struggle and suffer for people in ultimate devotion, as Jesus, the prophets and apostles did, can so bluntly expose all that is rotten and wrong in order to awaken an individual, a circle, a congregation or a whole people and call them to repentance.

Paul writes "with weeping of the enemies of the cross (they are not his personal enemies) … whose God is their belly" (side note: Phil 3:18-19), and Jesus weeps over the inhabitants of Jerusalem who stoned the prophets and will also kill him.[13]

(See also footnotes from the *Wuppertal Study Bible*:
Footnote 22: Matthew 23:3, 15, 23, 25, 27, 29: hypocrites, blind teachers of the blind, whitewashed tombs, serpents, brood of vipers; likewise the Baptist to the crowd: you brood of vipers … (Luke 3:7–14). (Quotation does not end here yet). Footnote 24: Bürki quotes a modern scientist (anonymous) who describes his society as characterized by apathy, hypocrisy, petty bourgeois egoism, etc.)

In other words, it is not about "copyable" speech in general, but about expression of prophetic insight, which is however accompanied by inner suffering, motivated by the struggle for the people. Perhaps Spurgeon's reference fits here, who is supposed to have said that only he who can really weep over the lost is allowed to preach about hell.

Longing for Healing
April 11, 2021

Sermon today: Beginning of the Letter to the Philippians.

We all have construction sites.

Therefore: Pray for each other. Help to focus on Jesus.

In the conversation in the car I realize once again that on the one hand I have seen the church for a long time as a "mobile hospital on the way to eternity" (and therefore I breathed a sigh of relief when this view also shone through in the sermon today), but on the other hand somewhere in a corner of my heart I probably still have the opposing longing that the sick should actually be healed as quickly and permanently as possible and be made fit through health, not through weakness, for use for the sick "outside." The sick should actually only be "outside" the community.

Educated Parents
April 11, 2021

Education.

In the evening, retrospective general, basic reflections on parenting —what could or should I have done or said differently, where was I too naive, what did I overlook, etc.? (Questions that many ask themselves, as I know from many a conversation.) This just keeps popping into my mind and bothers me when I think of some of the children's "legacies." I realize in my head, of course, that I can't change anything anymore, but maybe I can then react more sensibly here and there at least with regard to the grandchildren one day.

Starting point: The fact is, we are passing on burdens and deficits to the next generation. The only way out, if you think it through to the end, would be not to have children.

In a certain way, marriage prepares the ground for educational failure.

Marriage means to want to bear the weaknesses of the other, those that the partner recognizes and tries to change as well as the others that he cannot, will not (yet) see. And which will have an effect in the next generation, simply by being like this. But we can't wait to start a family until we will be mature parents (when will we ever be?). So we as parents have to expose ourselves to our children as we as spouses have to do so to each other, too. (We have decided to do so voluntarily, but the future children are of course not asked about it ...)

Therefore a solution can only consist in conscious acceptance of this basic problem and in the attempt to compensate with regard to the children as well as possible whatever deficit one or the other parent or both become aware of. But to "educate" or blackmail the partner or even separate in favor of better chances for the children to develop their potential does not solve the problem in the end, and anyway separation can only be a very last means (in case of violence, for example).

There is no escape from this framework, which is given by our human imperfections and biographies. The very fact that we learn in the course of our life means that until then we live in each case with less insight, wisdom, or experience; we are marked by deficits and weaknesses. This is why we make mistakes. This is also what our loved ones around us have to pay for.

But how to deal with it without ending up in the dead ends of despair or stubbornness?

Realistically, the only thing left to do is to consciously accept this challenge every day anew: to somehow help our children to learn to live with the burdens and deficits that we mean for them, up to teaching them to see hidden chances in it (or to hope that others can manage to do that).

Driven by the desire for optimal promotion, we would like to spare them these burdens. But the negative parts of our ways of upbringing and our deficits belong to life, even more, according to God's will, they shall serve even as a means for the unfolding of potential; not only our good and positive contributions. (By the way, it will not happen differently to them one day with their children). This can make us more relaxed; it can make responsibility for the life entrusted to us bearable, acceptable, maintain hope, reduce paralyzing fear of making mistakes—at least for us as Christians. Because we know the Creator and Lord of our life, who loves us (and our children!) as exactly the special piecework that we are and wants to use us (up to the point that he makes us dependent on the help of others!); and this can save us from or help us out of the victim role, which otherwise ultimately slows us down, drives us into self-pity, frustrates us, possibly even makes us bitter in view of the more positive life possibilities that are withheld from us.

But isn't this rather pious whitewashing of what is nevertheless tangibly evil in our lives? An attempt to think positively, that the glass is half full instead of half empty? If you want to, you can of course categorize it that way. However, do not forget: it is not about just letting everything go uncritically and thoughtlessly, to justify clear mistakes simply by oneself, in order to get out of the problem! But this negative pigeonhole is not a really constructive alternative. And another, really constructive alternative to the Christian perspective I don't see (yet?).

The effort not to fail remains. So does the pain when you do fail. It is therefore a matter of seeking refuge from despair in grace. With the gracious One. And he is one or better *the* source of hope. The well-being of our children, "well-being" not filled according to our wishful dreams, but in the sense of what is realistically possible—ultimately does not depend on the degree of successful education according to our ideas, but on what they make with God's help out of what is given and given up and withheld from them, if they seek his help. When we as educators say the sentence, "We did our best," we must not continue, "… but it was not enough," but rather, "… this must and will be enough." Not measured by our dreams, but measured by God's thoughts.

Exceptional Women
July 13, 2021

Observation. In some conservative circles, women in the preaching ministry are accepted as an exception under certain conditions. Could I live well with that if at least I myself fell under the exception? No.

At first the label "exceptional woman" may seem more pleasant than, for example, being accepted only as a "stopgap" as long as there is a shortage of men (a theory by which some theologians accept women missionaries as a temporary solution outside the home country), but at closer look it remains very unpleasant. Being an exception sounds not like a satisfactory solution. It even would make me rather aggressive. Why actually?

It makes one insecure, possibly to be some kind of hybrid between man and woman. Aftertaste: in any case, somehow not being a normal or real woman.

It separates again, this time even more so within one's own gender. It reinforces the consciousness of loneliness.

Besides, this would actually (at least theoretically, if consistently applied) make necessary further corresponding fundamental preaching against women's service; which would be absolutely against my view, my conscience. If I didn't completely exclude the topic from my sermons, I would have to tell other women: "Yes, I am allowed, because I have exceptional qualities (who actually determines and judges them?), but *you* better stay away from it." If that doesn't sound arrogant ...

On top of that, it could promote envy and resentment, among other things.

Tired Rescues
February 19, 2022

So often I find my rescuer skills that are requested of me so painfully inadequate. As I think about this, I sink deeper into the image of the rescue team (mountain rescue, fire department, ambulance, etc.). Of course, the rescuers must be stronger than those in need. Otherwise they would not be able to help. But even rescuers can't do everything, and even rescuers get tired in the field, no matter how well trained they are. This is one of the reasons why usually teams are deployed. And sometimes rescues don't succeed even despite all efforts. And yet it remains a blessing when those who suffer are at least not alone. So Christians on this side of the "curtain" can at least be the visible embodiment of the Lord, who can only be invisibly present here, but who is visibly waiting on the other side. That is *not* little (especially since not even that is always possible), but much, as little it appears only if I measure it against my ideal of perfect and quick solution here. Tiredness is okay; longing for more fundamental changes for the better also; looking for energetic team reinforcement anyway; but giving up —not. I have to keep that in mind.

Women's Speech
March 2, 2022

Regarding the main New Testament passages foregrounded in the discussion of the role of women in the church, one thing is certain: The two Corinthians passages (1 Corinthians 11 and 1 Corinthians 14) are about order in the assembly, but the subject of teaching does not come up.

Also certain: Ephesians 5 is about relationship in marriage, not church ministries.

Of course, this does not necessarily mean that these passages do not have something to contribute to the topic, but it does mean that things are not as obvious as some people make them out to be.

Only 1 Timothy 2:12 pronounces keyword *teach*, but in a context that is very puzzling on several levels. And the fact of these as yet unsolvable puzzles is recognized by all theological schools.

The interpreters differ in dealing with the verses. Some consider it possible and appropriate to extract a few words that seem clear in themselves ("I do not allow women to teach") and make them the overriding key verse for the overall biblical interpretation. Others do not consider this possible because they think that these few words only *seem* clear, but in truth the content and meaning depends on the (just unfortunately puzzling) context.

So it is a perfectly reasonable thought experiment to consider which biblical statements might spontaneously lead an unbiased reader (e.g. one who is reading the Bible from cover to cover for the first time) to the statement: "Oh, it says here that women are excluded from the preaching ministry!" The result should make you think: Such unambiguous verses simply do not exist.

What is also certain: Women are to learn.

Women are supposed to teach children and other women; i.e., they are not regarded as in principle unsuitable for spiritual leadership. And this also means that teaching does not contradict the female identity or nature in principle.

And the word *teaching* is not more precisely filled with content or formally described, certainly not limited to pulpit speaking by an ordained or specially trained person. (The attempt of the American Wayne Grudem to draw up a casuistic list of permitted and forbidden types of speeches for women, containing 83 points, appears, soberly considered, as a very questionable, high-handed and fanciful enterprise).

Behaving Unpredictably
March 5, 2022

Jesus undermines honor-shame culture: He cultivates disreputable contacts without concern for his good reputation; he does not shy away from defilement (by the sick, women, social outlaws or people of other faiths), allows himself to be honored by people who are despicable in the eyes of the good, washes his disciples' feet—simply behaves unpredictably. At the same time, however, he does not pour his behavior into sets of rules. In *Icons of Christ*, Witt aptly calls this undermining of what "one" does, and what I have so far described for myself as "breaking up structures from within," "Christological subversion."[14] Paul was certainly very sensitive to this, both first as a very angry persecutor of Jesus for precisely this reason and then as a devoted follower and very conscious imitator of Jesus. Can it make sense to assume that he, contrary to this, makes an exception in one single area (relationship man-woman), sees *these* status-related male feelings of honor as permanently appropriate, "given by nature" and wants to cement them with his instructions? It seems to me very absurd to assume such an attitude, whatever else may have been in Paul's mind.

Tear Down the Walls
March 17, 2022

Jesus, after washing his disciples' feet (John 13:14 and following), explicitly asks them, "Do you understand what I have done for you?" He thus challenges, "Think deeply, consider this in your hearts!" This was certainly necessary and meaningful in view of the revolutionary behavior.

The *Lord* and *Teacher* serves as a slave—explicitly this "status," these roles or functions are mentioned, and explicitly not to maintain the demarcation we have been used to, but to break it; and this is to serve as an example, John 13:17: "Now that you know these things, you will be blessed if you do them." (In the Greek the word *know* resonates: "grasping with inner conviction," full meaning). The disciples owe it to each other to behave in this way. Status thinking, honor culture is turned on its head. Tear down the walls.

Should not what is true of the slavery issue also be true of the traditional role assignments of women?

The Goal of Jesus Takes Shape
March 19, 2022

"A new command I give you: love one another. As I have loved you, so you must love one another. By this everyone will know that you are my disciples, if you love one another. (John 13:34–35)

If this is the goal, that selfless, self-sacrificing love, not concerned with one's own right and status, will take visible shape, how will love be recognizable to society if care is taken to maintain boundaries and roles in the congregation? This goal implies a legitimate hermeneutical key for understanding the instructions of Paul and Peter to their congregations; they must be able to be understood and applied in such a way that the goal of Jesus takes shape.

This verse, which is practically a commentary on the washing of the feet beforehand, is also a helpful biblical proof of the quotation I had already placed at the beginning of my presentation on Paul some years ago:

> How convincingly do we embody the loving caring community of redeemed men and women that Christ established by his coming? The community of Christians is to serve as a visible sign of the reality of the 'kingship of God'—that future community we expect and will one day experience, and it is to form a community in which the structures of sin are not perpetuated. The challenge for Christians is to make Christ recognizable to the world; to do this, we must reflect his values, his vision, and his truth.[15]

The Do Nothing Job
March 21, 2022

Triggered by a phone call.

"Get used to different …" ("The Chosen") is also true on the following level: In the beginning we have to do more or less everything for our children.

On a more external organizational level: We learn to care, play, educate, teach, organize, etc. Some things we can do from the beginning, some things are easy to learn, some things take time, we have to train. And in any case, on top of that, we have to practice doing many things in parallel.

At some point, we'll be relatively fit.

And our children are grown up and have their center of life elsewhere.

And we realize that they have internalized some things. Some things, however, only for as long as they were with us.

With a trained eye, we quickly grasp what could be done better, faster, more effectively.

But we should better hold back in silence. Now our job is learning to "do nothing." Compared to the start of family life, it's exactly the opposite direction. Letting go. At first it can seem like living with the handbrake on.

And on a spiritual level, some things change, too. They continue to develop, weave their insights with their new experiences and encounters into a new whole—which we wish them from the bottom of our hearts, until we discover: That doesn't just come on top of the common foundation, like a roof extension or a balcony extension and the like, but also includes estrangements. Logically, actually. But just *actually* …

In the end, new buildings emerge, possibly with more or fewer familiar features, which still triggers the beautiful feeling of common origin in our encounters. But nevertheless also with other features, which can also cause us more or less trouble. Puberty is not simply a seizure that passes and then we return to familiar normality. We know this in our heads, especially since we are familiar with the differences in the personalities of our original children. And these differences are dear to us. At least as long as the children still more or less have their feet under our table and we can set certain limits to their acting out. But when that changes, we should be prepared for the fact that we may *not* be as prepared for the coming changes as we thought.

And then spouses come into play.

And then we ourselves may go on with a laughing eye, but also a crying eye.

And our children will feel the same way one day.

And now comes what is still more of a conjecture, because in this stage I am still only at the beginning:

And at some point they will begin to ask themselves: How did our parents manage this and that, cope with it, etc.?

And perhaps then, at the latest, some closeness that has been missed in the meantime will once again become possible on a deeper level.

Life remains adventurous. And adventure means a mixture of fascination, exciting discoveries, but also sweat and tears and much more.

But in the end there will be amazement for all of us, we can and must hold on to that, we can already look forward to that!

It is actually crazy that one has to make many important decisions in life phases in which one could actually make good use of the life experience that one has only gained through them in retrospect.

7
TRUSTING AS GUIDANCE ON TOUGH ROADS

Following Jesus changes our lives for the better in many ways. That is tangible reality. But Christians are not spared of the sufferings of life. Therefore disillusion is tangible reality as well. Yet, we are never alone on this way. Our companion is invisible, yes. But reliable, again yes. Therefore it is a way which in the end is worth all efforts.

~

Measure against the Mission
January 12, 2010

Dis-illusion.

We are no longer in paradise. Life is not simply about us, about our small or greater happiness, about holding on to "Shire flair" (as in Tolkien's novel *The Lord of the Rings*). So it was in the beginning, so it will be again in the end. But now, in the meantime, it's about struggle. We are in this world to do the right thing in a world that is in the process of destroying itself.

In other words, there are certainly again and again oases, and also there is often a satisfaction, which grows from the Christian lifestyle, but basically life is and remains a fight in this time. In most parts of humanity this is still the case anyway. In the western world, however, we are in danger, due to the media, of being persuaded that at least a small paradise is attainable for everyone and, above all, is their right.

If the world were as it should be, we would not need a savior, a redeemer, a renewer. Because the world is not as it should be, our life is a struggle with ourselves, with others, with problematic structures.

We have no choice whether we want this, only on which side we want to stand. The evil has leavened everything. Here in Germany this is often rather less obvious; here it appears often more in the way of superficiality, obtuseness, thoughtlessness, etc. Elsewhere it appears as blatant cruelty and injustice.

Our Lord has determined the time of our birth, the place of our life. He has complete control over the circumstances of our lives. He has a mission for us (the details of which are partly revealed to us little by little, but partly remain hidden). Not measured by the paradisiacal ideal, but measured by this mission, we get everything we need to live a meaningful and fulfilled life. For all that is beautiful, as for all that is difficult, all things must work together for good to those who love God (Romans 8:28).

In the case of the beautiful, it is easy for us to accept this; in the case of the difficult, it is usually not.

The trap we often fall into: We measure against the ideal, and therefore we feel the deficits, the negative all the more severely.

The task is to subordinate myself to the problematic circumstances, to fit myself into them, to affirm and to endure the tension. On the one hand to perceive the evil as evil, to fight against it and to suffer from it and on the other hand not to claim a perfection from the people for this time, which is not possible. It helps to hold the following perspective: Everything that I personally lack, measured against the ideal, and that wants to seduce me into grumbling and self-pity, is something that God builds into his life's mission for me and thus transforms into the best that is "gettable" for me out of this life.

Going forward in faith: On the basis of trustworthy information about our generous Lord

… often in the dark (normal, not alarming)

… bound to the word, not to the feeling

… giving up trying to understand the whole picture

… to take care of the part of the puzzle that represents our place in life and to prove oneself there as ambassadors of truth, trying to shake up, to awaken.

What Did You Miss?
January 13, 2011

Open and closed doors.

Sometimes in life one can have the impression of running against the same door again and again in vain. It remains closed. I came up with one conceivable reason through computer games. There are detective stories in which you have to collect clues, to solve tasks; this may also involve, for example, exploring a house to find an urgently needed object. So you go through the rooms bit by bit, finally find it—and have to realize you've rejoiced too soon. You can't click on it and take it with you. Programming error in the game? No. This happens when you have overlooked something in another room that you could and should have taken with you. So back to the previous rooms, take another close look. And indeed: There is something that you can take with you. Now back to the room where the other object could not be collected. And lo and behold, now it works.

Isn't it sometimes like that in life? The seemingly most urgent thing is not necessarily the most urgent thing from the point of view of our heavenly director.

Training Perception
January 14, 2011

Knowing God's will.

Trust is often initially more a decision and action than a feeling of security. The people of Israel certainly did not feel secure when they had the Egyptian horsemen behind them and the sea in front of them. But the clear instruction was: Get into the water!

From this it follows that in connection with the question of learning to trust, another question arises: How do I know the will of God?

A GPS reports when I am to leave road A, for example, but not every few meters as long as I am to simply continue driving on the current road. Readiness to listen, ability to hear, concentration is required; earplugs or continuous sound at disco volume would be unfavorable, for example.

What does listening to the heavenly GPS look like? What has God said about where and how he wants to make himself known?

- in Bible reading
- in sharing, asking and listening/waiting prayer, individually and together
- through sermons, worship, books, watchwords, etc.
- through conversations with other Christians
- through dreams (but very rarely).
- through circumstances (doors close or open more or less clearly)
- through inner certainty
- through a combination of several of these factors

If I don't get any special instruction, it is obviously enough to stick to what I can take from the biblical guidelines about how I should shape my life or to continue as before to the best of my knowledge and conscience. In any case, it is important that I train my ability to perceive, as far as that is possible. An essential difference to the GPS is finally that though God is different from humans he is nevertheless a person, who wants to be discovered, to be known, which needs time among other things.

The Promise of Perfection
January 15, 2011

"Be perfect, therefore, as your heavenly Father is perfect." (Matthew 5:48)

An acquaintance had problems with the idea: "When we die and wake up in eternity, we are free from our present imperfection practically from one second to the next." To him, therefore, the idea of various stages of heaven seemed somehow a more suitable transition, where one does not get the impression of suddenly being almost a completely different person. Question therefore: How is the promised perfection conceivable without us already feeling almost alien to ourselves?

Attempt to answer.

In the origin, sin is not only a certain deed, but mistrust that I might come up short, if I follow God's commandments; to miss something (in paradise the forbidden fruit). This mistrust leads to the attitude: I must regulate my life myself, get the best out of it, avoid problems if possible etc. And from this follows the further concrete sinful, i.e., thoughts and deeds detached from God. But when I stand before Jesus, exactly this basic problem will be tackled at the root. I will be overwhelmed by the reality of Jesus, by the truth of everything that I had suspected and hoped for until then, but could not know with absolute certainty. Even the enemies of Jesus will undoubtedly acknowledge their error and guilt. How much more, then, will we be filled with joy and unshakable confidence in his love. There remains only the astonished exclamation "My Lord and my God!," just as the initial doubter Thomas addresses Jesus when he encounters the Risen Lord (John 20); and his original desire to touch Jesus simply disappeared. But with this certainty, in turn, all breeding ground for sin is gone, and with it all further "training necessity" for our character, which is still imperfect according to present experience.

Therefore, in eternity unbroken fellowship with our Lord is possible for each of us in the same way.

Is God's Closeness Possible?
April 1, 2013

Friends are fighting serious health and other issues, here and overseas. And the news is full of negative stuff anyway, as usual. And it is Easter. Questions suggest themselves: What is really true? What is sustainable?

This question comes to mind when we have images of the insanity of this world before our eyes, but at the same time we know of credible people who testify to experiences of God's closeness in their suffering. How is this possible? Helpful framework: "We are not in the land of the living and going toward dying, but are in the land of the dying and going toward life" (quotation to this effect, author unknown to me).

This world is a battlefield. We don't need to sugarcoat that, even as Christians. And dying is often a long and arduous process. And it is not only dying at the end of our earthly time, but dying in the sense of letting go, saying goodbye, permeates the whole of life.

But: God accompanies us in it and gives us respite and prepares us for the new life. This perspective is sober, realistic, can save us from illusionary expectations and disappointments leading to doubts. Seen in this way, sorrowful experiences no longer automatically speak so simply against God, as it sometimes appears at first glance.

"Even though I walk through the valley of the shadow of death …" (Psalm 23:4)

The (In)Constancy of Moments
May 21, 2013

A friend's daughter finished school. It makes me aware that every past day, every past hour, every past minute is irretrievable. That seems to be a self-evident banality, we know that of course—somehow. But the fact is that we don't really face that in its full weight. The proof of this are transitions such as birthdays, school changes and graduations, career changes, family changes, retirement, etc. There really is absolutely nothing constant in life except the eternal Lord, a fact that can be comforting and frightening at the same time, depending on what or whom we set our eyes on. A realist is one who faces this fact and entrusts life to the Creator of this life and the life to come.

Good impulse: "How happy and wise is the man, who knows no other care but to live as he will wish to have lived when he dies!" (Thomas à Kempis, *Imitation of Christ*, 15th century)[1]

Longing for Explanations
July 28, 2013

Once again, I experience one shambles after another in the lives of the people around me. And I feel, right into the physical, the longing for explanations (although my head clearly knows about the futility): "Why, Lord, why don't you spare your children more of such painful experiences?"

But usually he doesn't give explanations. He has promised and vouched with his life: He is simply there. Always. He who himself struggled in Gethsemane and knows how we feel.

But it is like the lion Aslan, the king of Narnia, whom C. S. Lewis describes in his stories: Only sometimes he shows himself; for long stretches he hides himself. Nevertheless, it remains and becomes true again and again: he does not let anyone down; you can count on him.

Our lifelong training program is short and "simple"—always to trust. Being on the road together with others is an enormous help.

And perhaps also an observation made by Philip Yancey in *Disappointed with God*. Job did not get explanations for his experiences of misery, but Jeremiah did, and yet the laments are similar.[2] So it's not that simple that if we were just given explanations, then we would definitely be better able to deal with the emotions. This observation can help to focus on persevering and leave it to Jesus if and when he gives us more insight into the background.

"Now faith is confidence in what we hope for and assurance about what we do not see." (Hebrews 11:1) "Moses held on to the one he did not see as if he saw him." (Hebrews 11:27, LU84)

Counting Hair
September 13, 2013

Our hair is numbered (Luke 12:7). How many do we lose every day and we don't even realize it, but God does; who can imagine? I suspect that this is not meant literally; God surely has better things to do. The image is rather meant to be a hint so the sensation it triggers is definitely an appropriate pointer to God's infinite mindfulness. We can't begin to imagine the whole concept behind it (even less so when we try to understand the role of evil in it). But that makes it all the more important to keep consciously reminding ourselves of this in order to keep the big horizon of our lives in view, especially when we stumble across anything in front of our feet. We are such easily forgetful people.

Watchword today: "Only be careful, and watch yourselves closely so that you do not forget the things your eyes have seen or let them fade from your heart as long as you live." (Deuteronomy 4:9) This is a clear reinforcement in gathering signs of God's nearness; it makes sense, is even decreed: "I have delivered and will deliver, so open your eyes and ears!"

A Trusting Mouthpiece for God
October 16, 2013

There are times when nothing seems to move forward in a congregation, when all effort and talk end up in front of thick walls. What can help to deal with this?

A thought on this: Perhaps we are to be God's (and some others') mouthpiece with our insights, regardless of success, as if to keep a sore wound open until it is eventually cleaned. In any case, the task remains, wherever we are placed, to put everything at God's service and to let him use all our gifts. Not only if this is more or less quickly successful in our eyes. Simply out of love for him and trusting that he sees meaning where we do not (yet) see any. Sometimes we lose sight of this dimension too much. That the time may not yet be ripe for a solution, but that we are nevertheless working towards it if we remain faithful.

A Knife in the Jungle
November 11, 2013

There are hours in my life when I feel like I'm in some kind of inner jungle, having lost sight of the path or being in danger of doing so. Once again, I struggled through such a day. The jungle seemed to become more and more impenetrable and foggy. Finally, in the evening, I was able to sit down—praying, reflecting, determined to break God's positive perspective and mission in life down to a very few key words that I can keep handy in my head as a kind of iron ration and thus use as a "bushwhacking knife" when things get serious:

- Recognize Jesus's love even in the small things of everyday life.
- Perceive signs of his closeness.
- Put everything in relation to him, rejoice, marvel, learn to love, give thanks.
- Fight for him, not for a cause.
- Pass on his love.
- Save what can be saved. Every single person counts.
- Accept the small framework of life.

- Share experiences. Become a guide, an eye-opener (Colossians 1:28; Micah 6:8).

Then I just wanted to check something very briefly on Facebook, but got stuck on a friend's post that included Philippians 1:6—Paul's confidence that God, "who began a good work in you will carry it on to completion." One of the "red threads" of my life; and today was a confirmation and reinforcement of my thinking in more ways than one. Coincidence? I can't believe in that. Rather: Jesus is very creative in his ways of communication.

Training Hope
December 2, 2013

While searching for a particular text, I "accidentally" stumbled across a quote that I had found somewhere years ago and that has now engaged me anew:

> Shattered Dreams
> As kids bring their broken toys with tears to us
> that we may repair,
> so I brought my shattered dreams to God
> as He is my Father.
> But then, instead of going and leaving Him work alone with this
> I stayed and tried to help
> in a way that corresponded to my ideas.
> Finally I took them back and cried:
> "Why are you so slow?"
> "My child," He said, "what should I do …
> you never let loose."
>   —Lauretta Burns[3]
>   (my re-translation from German to English)

Spontaneous thoughts with corresponding memories of family (and also congregational) life coming up:

We want back the familiar and loved shape of the toy;

we are orientated backwards.
We like to repeat (good) experience.
It suggests some kind of safety and peace.
And absence of pain.
He may have in mind a new shape.
He is orientated forward.
We need to train hope.
That opens up new experience.
There is no life here without pain.
Safety and peace always lie in being close to *him*.
And in the end: there alone.
This is far from an attitude of resignation or fatalism.
It has something very active in it.

The Witch Doesn't Know Everything
January 8, 2014

Watchword: "Stand firm then, with the belt of truth buckled round your waist, with the breastplate of righteousness in place, and with your feet fitted with the readiness that comes from the gospel of peace. In addition to all this, take up the shield of faith, with which you can extinguish all the flaming arrows of the evil one. Take the helmet of salvation and the sword of the Spirit, which is the word of God." (Ephesians 6:14–17)

This day caused an inner earthquake. I have recorded it in more detail, because it shows some typical things with regard to what temptations do to us and what we can do with them.

We took a day trip to Chicago. The nice parts of it were seeing our kids' apartment, the college, and some beautiful places. But faced with masses of people, the so-familiar question popped into my mind once again: Where will they all end up? Would the world one day turn out to be an unimaginable mass grave filled with people with no future with Jesus because they never really got to know and love him? Horrible vision. A tour through the theological college fortunately pushed the thoughts and emotions soon more into the background again. Jesus's love is greater than mine, not smaller. And he obviously calls many more into his service, to reach many. He has the overview; I do not. And who, if not *he*, will be a just judge?

Then we made a short detour to the bookstore of the university—very short indeed, which had been completely clear from the start in view of the schedule. Nevertheless, I found it very difficult to leave and I also knew the deeper reason for it. It was not simply the shortness of the pleasure of diving into the world of books and into the thoughts and experiences of others that hurt me. It was the impression: Here is the equipment that I would have liked to have in my studies, but did not get and still do not have. But I long for it and think I need it so much. But it is crystal clear: A comprehensive access to it will remain denied to me already because of my life phase. Frustration.

My next thought gradually brought some peace: If Jesus had thought it necessary, he would have arranged the circumstances of my life differently. Many people have nothing but their Bibles. So I should rather face the obvious truth that I probably look too much for hope and certainty in other people's words and experiences instead of simply in Jesus himself. And so I had better consciously accept this challenge to focus on the source of it all, on him and his words. (This is of course not directed against book-reading in general, which has accompanied my whole life, but had to do with my specific situation here.)

Outside, shortly after, we saw a homeless woman begging in freezing sub-zero temperatures. Our son-in-law had just bought a water bottle and was holding it in his hand, and you could watch the water freeze. There are so many as poor as this woman. Another familiar question came to mind: What on earth are we usually busy with in our communities at home—so much, at times even most, seems downright grotesque and ridiculously trivial compared to such enormous needs?

Once again I could give myself the answer and become a little calmer again. Jesus alone knows where he puts us and where our place is in the big story in which all our little stories play.

At least the evening promised to be just relaxing; we watched the movie "Narnia" together, which I appreciate very much. But I hadn't thought about the scene where the lion Aslan (King of Narnia) is killed by the witch and Lucy desperately buries her head in his fur. That was the decisive jolt that made me lose my footing. The memories of our dog's death were back as vividly as if it had just happened. And what filled me was not only the longing that he would be alive again, but much more an immense aggression against death and transience, old age and illness. All the stressful impressions of the day suddenly condensed into a renewed general attack on my belief, thinking, feeling. This is simply not how things should be. And there it was again, the question of why, the question of theodicy.

It took time. But somehow I could start to think things through for the umpteenth time, as good or bad as it is possible (good that by now there are already quite well-trodden trails), to get God's human face before the eyes. He who lived and sacrificed his life for us. To come to rest under the cross and with the knowledge of Easter.

Conclusion of this day: I know that temptation will remain a part of our lives; and since our lives are very individual, I should expect that to be true of the corresponding struggles as well.

At the very end, I looked up the day's scripture once again. These verses are under the heading "the spiritual armor." Without being aware of it, it had been in use several times today. And it felt like Jesus was saying, "Okay, I've given you time to think about these things, to face things. Now it's time to move on. You have the equipment. Remember what I said. And feel free to think about Narnia. The witch thinks Aslan's death is her triumph. But that is not the end. The Witch doesn't know everything."

Life Is Not the Movies
January 11, 2014

Well-intentioned comparison: Being a Christian is a great adventure.

That's true in a way. But that is only part of the truth. The other part that is in front of my eyes is this:

Being a Christian is not an adventure like in a video game or a movie:

In the movies, the blood is ketchup; in life, it's real.

In the movies, the wounds and scars are painted on, in life, they are real and painful, and minutes and hours and days can feel like half an eternity.

In the movies, there are stuntmen; in life, you can't be represented.

In the movies, you can jump out of the script in an emergency; in life, you can't.

In the movies, the heroes always cope with their losses more or less well; in life, sometimes wounds remain agonizingly open.

In the movies, the dark valley is surrounded by spotlights; in life, it really is pitch black there.

And you don't know when and where it will end.

Therefore, it is no cause for shame to feel exhausted and tired from time to time. That has to do with reality and how we are made. But let us never forget:

In the movies, God is often a fairy tale or peripheral character or simply not there.

In the life of a Christian, he is and remains the central and ultimate power.

To Discover God's Plan
January 24, 2014

Questions for a self-check.

To discover God's plan, I need criteria by which I can recognize it as his, distinguish it from others. What are these criteria? Does it include that my desires and ideas fit into his plan as conflict-free as possible? So would that be God's plan, where his ideas and mine fit together perfectly? Rather unlikely. Or what else do I see as identifying marks to look for?

Another question: Am I willing to go any way or do I set conditions? We tend to see God as a helper of our self-realization (possibly even piously justified: He has created us as we are) and have more or less short-term concrete goals in mind that we would like to achieve (these can also be pious!), so that our life seems worth living and right. However: Things can even be fine in themselves; but God is not necessarily interested in us achieving certain goals or moral standards as effectively as possible, but primarily in our character—in learning to trust unconditionally, to give up control, to submit, fall in line, no matter what it takes. At least, this is the impression I get from the life stories handed down to us in the Bible.

Of course, that sounds a bit abstract; and getting to the bottom of myself is certainly only possible to a limited extent. Nevertheless, I have to ask myself the question: Is there anything that I "prescribe" to God? Conditions that I set, that must be met, so that I am willing to recognize a way, call as his? ("This and that are out of the question, ruled out from the start, cannot be God's will, because ...")

What Does Growing Spiritually Mean?
February 9, 2014

Yesterday evening I was leafing through my diary from my student days. The question came back to my mind: What does "growing spiritually" actually mean? When I look into the old records, also over the years, then the aspect of knowledge-growth, understanding in the mental sense, is certainly the clearly smaller part. It seems to be more about learning to live always the same very "simple" challenges to trust, to let go in all vicissitudes of life and everyday life. It is that "simple," and therefore intellectually quite simple people have exactly the same (or maybe even better?) chances to find a deep faith as much-thinkers. Fits to "the weak (according to worldly standards) God has chosen ..."

Normal Life Is Struggle
February 11, 2014

The complex hardship of loved ones drives me. Once again, emergency alarm.

During prayerful reflection, the psalmists come to my mind, who consciously recall and praise the great deeds of God and thus assure themselves of the unchanging faithful character of God; and specifically the exodus of Israel from Egypt. I realize again that the wonderful result of the Exodus permission was preceded by terrible plagues and quite a few apparent setbacks, and followed immediately by the next problems. Normal life is struggle.

But accepting that remains enormously challenging again and again. It all just looks so disproportionate, at least in my eyes (which is probably a fairly natural part of the fact that we are still on earth and therefore cannot yet see things from God's perspective). That there are no less painful and disturbing ways for an omnipotent God to bring us to this goal is beyond my imagination; I can only try to trust him, because anything else would be absolutely illogical and would not do justice to his character. But this is more a help on the rational level than on the emotional one.

Of some comfort: Even Jesus in Gethsemane did not get a reassuring explanation why there was no other way (at least as far as we know), but was simply confronted with the painful facts. And obviously he found peace and strength in obedience. Devotion: "During the days of Jesus' life on earth, he offered up prayers and petitions with fervent cries and tears to the one who could save him from death, and he was heard because of his reverent submission. Son though he was, he learned obedience from what he suffered and, once made perfect, he became the source of eternal salvation for all who obey him." (Hebrews 5:7–9)

Also impressive in this context: After the temptation story it says: "… angels came and attended him" (Matthew 4:11). And so Jesus also experienced it in Gethsemane (Luke 22:43); still in prayer, but after "not my will, but yours be done."

And apart from that: Everything that causes us distress and how we react to it is not just about us, we are part of a highly complex story. In some moments I still lose sight of that. But it is certainly a very important point of view in order not to get a distorted view of God and to prepare a breeding ground for doubts.

It is not pessimistic, but realistic and therefore helpful to keep all this in mind as "normal" also for a Christian life in this world (illusions only lead to disappointment). Only in eternity we will be able to look back in amazed praise on all that confuses us now because of our fragmentary perspective.

Until then, we need Hebrews 12:2 to keep us on track: "fixing our eyes on Jesus, the pioneer and perfecter of faith."

Unbelievables
February 20, 2014

A day full of alternating baths.

A friend who was already very shaken in health ended up in the hospital instead of on the planned and hoped-for walk. No stroke, but everything else still unclear. Sigh ...

I accompanied a refugee to the hospital for a pre-op examination. Papers were missing. "But you may come back." Immediately to the authorities. They reacted very quickly. After a few hours, back to the clinic. Forms, forms. Then finally an examination: No surgery necessary for the time being, the cyst has disappeared! Hallelujah!

I think of photos from the Hubble space satellite that someone recently posted on Facebook, and also my own collection of "unbelievables" in our world that we once put together for a service. How incomprehensible is this range between macrocosm and microcosm, and somewhere in between we are, and the Lord of the galaxies is counting our hair, our tears.

Holding Fast
March 8, 2014

In faith, too, there are often memory problems. I, anyway, frustratingly often find myself forgetting important insights and experiences. This is a cause for keyword search "hold fast," "stand fast" in the Old and New Testament, with an old concordance.

Notable results include altogether about 12 content-matching passages in the Old Testament.

"He is not strong who does not stand fast in troubles!" (Proverbs 24:10, LU84); helps to disillusioned self-assessment.

"I have the Lord before my eyes all the time; if he stands at my right hands, I will stand fast.. (Psalm 16:8, LU84); hint that steadfastness is not in me, but in teamwork.

The results included altogether about 23 content-matching passages in the New Testament, in terms of quantity a clear lead. There are eight of them in the letter to the Hebrews alone, which speaks into persecution situations.

"Stand fast therefore ..." The exhortation only makes sense if or because Christians must be prepared to be overthrown. The image of the armor Ephesians 6 fits into this context. The onslaught of hostile forces is to be expected and therefore all forces are required to keep balance and stay on their feet, to resist.

Jesus: "Hold fast to what you have until I come." (Revelation 2:25, LU84)

"... looking up to Jesus, the pioneer and perfecter of faith" (Hebrews 12:2, LU84). Psalm 16:8 (see above) corresponds here; there is no other way.

And: It is not just about holding on to just anything; it has to be *the* right one.

Puzzling Battles
April 2, 2014

Everyone can only fight his own battle, not that of others.

Everyone can at best puzzle together his own history from the events of his life a little or increasingly. Only our creator has the complete "bird's-eye view."

In other words, in the consequence: I cannot do that or only very limitedly representatively for others. But: I find myself taking this standpoint in the theodicy question (why does God allow this and that?) practically again and again, in order to wring solutions from God vicariously for others. I should not be surprised if I run again and again in front of impenetrable walls.

Let Go. Accept Limits.
April 3, 2014

Perceiving the suffering and evil in this world with open eyes and a compassionate heart is part of our new identity as Jesus's rescue team, but on the other hand it can also lead to paralyzing despair. It remains a challenging tightrope walk. Are there mental "protective fences," "tethers," that we can latch onto and keep ourselves from falling into dark holes ourselves? Yes:

- I cannot carry the weight of the world.
- I do not have to.

- I am not supposed to.

Isn't that an escape into one's own little happier world? It looks like it, feels like it.

But it is the only possible realistic and responsible attitude, which at least still maintains strength to act in my place—where it is difficult enough. To remain stuck in defiant anger, impotent despair would not change or improve anything either.

And neither would giving up faith.

The fact is those who live in faith usually have better chances of overcoming crises than non-believers.

And my concern in phases of doubt, to possibly only produce new disappointments with defiant holding on, does not hit the whole reality either. I should then actually at least also think that even placebos—to assume the theoretically worst possibility—are sometimes helpful. From this point of view, it makes sense to fight to fade out to some extent the suffering that I cannot change, because otherwise I am paralyzed with regard to where I can do something.

Globalization overwhelms us; the information flood as well.

Let go. Accept the limits. Don't try to be God.

Hope Needs a Long Breath
April 5, 2014

"It is impossible to imagine what God can do with the fragments of our lives if we leave them entirely to Him." (Blaise Pascal)[4]

Surrendering is not a backdoor method through which you can achieve with certainty what you would like to achieve, if only you can get "it" or "this lesson" "right." The challenge is to learn to let go in a truly open-ended way. It is a piece of dying. Surrendering our lives to God and trusting that he, as Creator, can and will make something out of the dying grain of wheat that we will marvel at—one day. But we don't know how long the time will be until then, nor what the result will be. And the process of dying is not pleasant and cannot be shortened. Everything in us actually resists dying. Hope needs a long breath. Eternity perspective.

Held by His Hand
April 6, 2014

Married 33 years. A miracle in so many ways. Where has the time gone?

During the prayer time in the evening service, a few scenes from the years suddenly passed me by as if in fast motion.

There were times when many others in my situation would have lost the ground under their feet long ago (which I would not have seen or assessed at that time), but where I was still on my feet, held by Jesus's hand.

There were times when I subjectively lost the ground under my feet in a way that not everyone experiences, but I remained objectively held by his hand.

At the moment I am getting firmer ground under my feet again, I am more or less on my feet again, although sometimes still stumbling —but very obviously still held by his hand.

Often, but not always, I have felt his hand in the various situations. But surely it has always been there. Otherwise I would not be where I am. He has kept his promise: "Nothing and no one will snatch you out of my hand." (see John 10). How good that he is so faithful and patient.

Keep Climbing
April 11, 2014

I am once again reading *Keep Climbing*. Some notes.

From François Fenélon:
> If there is anything that is capable of setting the soul in a large place, it is absolute abandonment to God.[5]

And from Oswald Chambers:
> There is only one thing that God wants of us, and that is our unconditional surrender ... [Have] simple perfect trust in God, such trust that we no longer want God's blessings, but only want Himself. Have we come to the place where God can withdraw His blessings and it does not affect our trust in Him?[6]

My spontaneous reaction: Isn't that completely unrealistic? Superhuman? Can't God alone love so selflessly? That's how it seems to us. But the fact is: The first commandment demands exactly this. And if it is about the restoration of the true humanity, for which Jesus is the prototype, then it cannot be about less, actually. But that is exactly why we need him in us. And that, in turn, is what Jesus offers us—to dwell in us. The one who makes the demand is also the one who wants to bring it to fulfillment in us. What comes to mind is what I wrote down recently on Luke 9:57ff (April 8, 2014). Jesus offers nothing. Rather, we will have to let go in discipleship. But that is a prediction rather than a precondition. And what follows letting go remains at first obscure to us. The experience of his nearness is not something that can be tested in advance "on trial" whether it is worth the losses to you.

Gail MacDonald in *Keep Climbing*:
> I believe Thomas à Kempis was correct when he said, "Two things increase temptation's hold on you—*an indecisive mind* (emphasis mine) and little confidence in God." I have come to embrace the truth behind the following story. Charles Spurgeon once traveled to the countryside to visit a friend who was building a new barn. On the roof was a weather vane with the text "God is love". Spurgeon asked if the man meant God is as changeable as the weather.
>
> "No!" the man exclaimed. "I mean it to say that God is love no matter which way the wind blows."[7]

Gail then tells of a couple who worked as missionaries in Kabul and eventually built a beautiful new building there with their church. Political circumstances forced the couple to return to the States one day. Shortly thereafter, the congregation was informed they should vacate the building; it would be razed to the ground. A worldwide prayer campaign began. But the day came when the military arrived with bulldozers and flattened everything. The couple learned of this through a telegram. The missionary fell to his knees and gave thanks. Why? His community had learned to say yes to everything God allowed. The Christians provided tea and pastries for the soldiers during the demolition:

> I am impressed that the Wilsons and the Afghan Christians did not whine or cry "foul" when God did not choose to answer their prayers to save the building. Theirs was a faith built on no false illusion. They believed that God was love no matter which way the wind blew. Their concern was to obey God and even to love their enemies. Serving them—even refreshing them—was more important than crying in protest when something special of theirs was taken away. Their behavior was a miracle, I think—a miracle according to God's script, not ours."[8]

In the end it is actually an over-sharpened formulation to say that one should act obediently completely independent of the thought of God's blessing. In his nature it is already founded that in the end there will be something good and meaningful. It is rather about giving up one's own dreams; about desires that take on the character of conditions; but the radical expression or flinching may help one to discover where one is fooling oneself.

Gail again:

> When you affirm that God is indeed in control, you no longer have to pin your life to artificial and sometimes inaccurate conceptions of who God is and what he may or may not do.
>
> This is a much harder affirmation than any of us imagine, and one needs to be careful before issuing a glib positive response. For it is not unusual for us to experience many noes on the way to the ultimate yes.[9] (examples of Carey, Corrie ten Boom, Joni and others follow.)
>
> When we are tied to the initial noes rather than the ultimate yes, it is usually because we have put conditions upon God as I did. Our misbeliefs, our illusions, our preconditions are all constraints we try to place on our Father. They must go.[10]

And finally Amy Carmichael:[11]
> "Anything but that, Lord," had been your earnest prayer. And then, perhaps quite suddenly, you found your feet set on that way. Do you still hold fast to your faith that he makes your way perfect? It does not look perfect. It looks like a road that has lost its sense of direction; a broken road, a wandering road, a strange mistake. And yet, either it is perfect or all you have believed crumbles like a rope of sand in your hands. There is no middle choice between faith and despair. Life is a journey; it is a climb; it is also a war!

"Lord, Anything, But Not ..."
May 1, 2014

More than once in my life I have said (and my family knows some of this): "Lord, anything, but not ..." I suppose on various occasions this seems to have been a kind of invitation to Jesus to lead me into exactly this kind of situation, but not to show me who is the big boss here or to make things particularly difficult for me, but to open my eyes to things or potentialities or solutions that until then I simply could not imagine and sometimes did not want to imagine (which was the natural reason for my fear).

I should have learned my lesson by now, but I admit that I still tend to get weak in the knees when I have to face a new variation of what is somehow a familiar experience; but it helps me to remember again his actions in the past and his patience, and that I need not fear reproach because he understands human nature. When I try to imagine the scene of the Exodus—Israel walking through the walls of water of the Red Sea on the right and on the left—I suspect that their feelings were far from those of a relaxed walk. But God brought them through to his destination. *He* who began the good work in us will finish it. (Philippians 1:6) So good to know!

Detour the Best Way
May 21, 2014

Late afternoon, long conversation with someone. Problems at work, catfight, illogic, unfair behavior, etc. I had to think of the Passion story

—everything human occurs in it. Jesus endured it. Modeled what it means to suffer injustice without striking back, what it means to go the second mile, to wash feet instead of heads, etc. We pray to become more like Jesus, but rarely realize that this means sharing in his suffering. We prefer to relate this to "being able to do good" rather than "being able to suffer evil," to share in not being understood and unfairly insinuated, etc., to suffer unjustly and to respond to it by "going the second mile."

I remember a friend who was actually "part of the inventory" of her company and a few years before retirement faced the choice of unemployment or a move to a distant location. During our telephone conversation the verse came to my mind: "Vengeance is mine, says the Lord" (Romans 12:19), and I just couldn't get it out of my head, resisting for a long time saying it because I felt it was an imposition and so inappropriate. Finally, however, I passed it on, and in retrospect it turned out to be very helpful. We cannot and should not regulate many things alone, but "by above" and what seems to be a detour is probably often the best way.

We still wonder how sick the world is and in what illusions about this state. Yet the cross was necessary precisely because of this; we should actually be the ones who are least surprised. And yet we are again and again.

What to Make of Healings
May 28 and June 4, 2014

After listening to several tapes of a healing conference and taking notes on them, the following will continue to stick with me:

Jesus healed immediately. So did the apostles. Examples that people should consider themselves healed, even if they do not notice it for a long time, are not found in the New Testament.

"All who turned to Jesus were healed.": Yes. But also: Jesus approached the one sick person at the pool of Bethesda (John 5) on his own initiative, the sick man had not asked Jesus. It is not said whether more people were healed, but if the whole pond had been closed for lack of patients, this would have been noted at least with high probability. And Mark 1:31: Jesus moves on, away from Capernaum, leaving behind disappointed people.

It is very strange, to say the least, that much is said on this subject and the role and nature of the faith necessary for it at such events, but so little is said in the New Testament.

Jesus gives us a lot of promises—his love, care, assistance in persecution, eternal life, forgiveness, and we can and should nail him down on that—but nowhere is there even a single clear reference to some kind of right to integrity already in this transitory world that we simply have to claim. So there seems to be some disparity in the weighting of some of our needs.

In all of this, I'm concerned about the conflation of right, wrong, and crooked; the fact that some things may be perfectly fine is not enough for me to encourage people to get involved with these teachers, because I fear self-dynamics that could backfire. On the other hand, it's not easy to warn against them in a fair way.

Open question with need for research: What is behind the healing experiences? Why do some types of diseases seem not to be healed or almost never healed?

Attempt of a catchy short formula for difference between New Testament and healing movement:

New Testament—I believe that God is good, although I experience my reality as bad (which he can and will change in his time).

Healing Movement—I believe that my reality is good, even though I experience it as bad (which will change as soon as I believe perfectly enough).

Live Consciously
June 23, 2014

Consciously live your normal everyday life. Some quotes:

Let the way you live,
be a constant going out—trusting in God—
and an unspeakable magic
will be over your life.
 —Oswald Chambers[12]

Never let the thought arise, "Oh, I cannot be of use where I am," because you certainly cannot be of use where you are not. Pray where God has just placed you; call upon him continually.
—Unknown

When the steps become firmer,
when someone can overcome the obstacles of life, then the blessing of God,
that is upon that person, emerges.
—Unknown

Via Ferrata
June 26, 2014

Our journey of faith resembles a via ferrata in some respects. In some sections, it makes sense to simply fix our gaze "only" on the next steps while climbing forward and not to want to see too far ahead. Out of trust. In what? In the professional who has prepared the way well. At the first moment, we may sometimes not be able to imagine how we are supposed to manage the next step; how the strength is supposed to be sufficient, when there is already hardly anything left of it anyway, but there is still two-thirds of the way ahead of us and we actually don't want to go one step further, but just sit, etc.

Admittedly, the paths in life are much longer (compared to via ferrata), and so are the times of exhaustion, fear, and so on. But I think the basic principles in terms of continuing remain the same. And in both contexts there are a few breaks and bivouacs. Rarely when you crave them more than anything else, but still timely.

Feet on Wide Space
July 21, 2014

Nothing repeats itself exactly. Sounds like a truism, and in a way it is, actually. But we unfortunately tend to repress it, to forget it. And then looking back on difficult experiences in the past becomes a source of negative pre-feelings, pre-judgments, worries. "Oh no, not again …"

Jesus, on the other hand, is forward-orientated, future-oriented.

He says to me, so to speak: "Whatever frightens you, unsettles you, triggers anger—leave it to me. Neither situations nor people are your true enemies. The true enemy sits in your own thinking and feeling. In my hand, all disturbances become a tool to learn the great 'nevertheless.'"

Nevertheless:
- I always stay with Jesus.
- I want to leave my security, my need for protection to him again and again.
- I will again and again put aside my wishes, rights and desires and wait for his time and way of fulfillment.
- I want to meet everyone again and again with love.
- I want to serve again and again without reservation.
- I want to take pain and disappointment again and again without reproach because I know that Jesus only allows what I can bear and what he wants to use for some reason, for whomever he wants to use it.

This does not mean: If I try to decide on such an attitude, then the next time a situation will surely be fine, which has caused me problems many times before (because I have already learned crucial lessons, at least theoretically). No, it's not that simple. But I make myself aware: I do not already know how it will be. I can never include Jesus's intervention beforehand, nor which elements will be different this time —but which will make a difference and which I don't want to overlook. Perhaps even a decisive one.

I can't safeguard myself. I do not have to hedge.

I can afford to put aside my previous patterns of interpretation for situations and people, up to and including my own behaviors, and engage with the current reality.

I concentrate on the question: How can I hold on to Jesus now, in this moment?

Through this, let *him* grow in me.

Living moment by moment in what is, not in what supposedly could be, because it was already so.

Thus he places "in a spacious place." (Psalm 31:9)

Training Camp for Faith
August 5, 2014

What value do we place on faith in our minds?

Many think religion is a hobby like sport, politics, healthy nutrition, or fashion. Others are already looking more consciously or existentially for an explanation of the world, often primarily on a rational level. Theories are compared, new drafts are made and put up for discussion. Basically it's "talk show" compatible, so to speak.

In the New Testament we get a different picture: God's self-revelation is not debatable, but predetermined. Faith means to go to a training camp for followers. There necessary information and proven insight is passed on and this is to be practiced; whether and how far this corresponds to the personal taste is irrelevant. How far the trainee completely understands this is also irrelevant. Many things only become clear in practice. Therefore, it is about encouragement and admonition, rebuke, adherence, obedience to truth—and this does not always taste immediately well to our rather anti-authoritarian democratic sentiments.

Postage Stamp Sticking
August 14, 2014

Protracted conflicts. I catch myself: In some corners of my heart I still dream of peace also in the sense of absence of stress, although it is clear to me from the head that this life is fighting time.

Little by little, several ideas come to me.

One is the urgent call to await God, Psalm 42:12. For me, awaiting (German word: *harren*) is connected with intense, tense expectation, looking out; much stronger than waiting. God's action is promised; it is only a question of time until we recognize and experience it. There is no other way. This is biblical realism.

The other is the Greek word for patience: *hypomone* = "staying under." Staying under the "yoke," trusting that he is by your side. I'd rather get out; just cut through tricky Gordian knots once and for all. Better short-term effort with all my might and then finally be able to check off than long-term permanent strain with an unforeseeable end. And then, of course, also clearly more modest sounding sentences shoot through my head: "If only at least ... then"—as if then the next challenge would not come.

The prophet Hosea comes to mind, whose marriage and family was supposed to depict the disturbed relationship between God and Israel. What a frustrating perspective for a family life; destined for unhappiness, at least permanent stress! Or Jeremiah, who gets the information right at the beginning of his ministry that he will preach and run against walls nearly all his life. Or Elijah. And many others.

Nevertheless, "Wait for God, for I will give thanks to him" was already a well-founded confidence in their times, without people knowing about the kind of closeness that Jesus promises us. And nevertheless it is always so difficult, in the face of long-term difficult situations, not to withdraw grumpily or resignedly into the snail shell, at best now and then stealthily sticking out one's head to see if there is not in the meantime a way of escape, rather than to really actively bear the problem, so to speak, trustingly, hopefully, no matter how confusing the road is.

So what can help to bring about a constructive change of perspective?

Keeping Jesus's nature and will in mind and that his love is there not only for me, but also for all people he has involved in my life.
- Letting go of my dreams and exchanging them for openness to his plans and goals.
- Not: He *will* intervene at some point; he *is* already at work all the time.
- Therefore, consciously decide against grumbling and impatience. And consciously express that in prayer.

Short list of keywords that are always important:
- turn around
- devote, let go (this sounds more positive than surrender)
- humbly accept one's own limits with open hands, not with clenched fists
- stand firmly by the decision
- trust
- endure and persevere
- maintain amazement

Watchword: Philippians 4:4, "Rejoice in the Lord always. I will say it again: rejoice!"

Don't forget: Even if the basic mood in the lives of the prophets mentioned was dark, there will also have been signs of God's nearness and small and greater joys in their lives. God does not lock any of his people permanently in a windowless prison of dark feelings; to think such a thing is once again devilish constriction!

For smiling, yet profound: Phil Callaway writes in his book *What's the Skunk Doing in the Trunk?*: "You just have to do it like the postage stamp: You just have to keep at it until you get there."[13]

Heavenly Logistics
September 15, 2014

Autumn mission convention in Bad Liebenzell.

The exchange of experiences is an enormous spiritual refueling station. God has somehow become more objective, more concrete, through the broadening of horizons, the many experiences that were shared during these days. Many a time our eyes have become moist.

I would like to note only three points here.

Starting from the sermon on Psalm 23, it went through my mind: Just as this shepherd has me in mind, so also everyone else. I may be temporarily assigned as an under-shepherd, for example with the children, and feel the responsibility accordingly, but on a higher level I am sheep like all the others and *he* is the one ultimately responsible. This helps to let go, to entrust. He finds his people.

Besides, sheep sometimes seem to find the grass greener in the neighboring pasture. It is up to the shepherd to choose the pasture; and he has his good reasons, and we can save ourselves from squinting.

An essential thread throughout all the events: God is there and is still acting today, in ways that simply do not fit into any pigeonhole, and which definitely could not be explained with wishful thinking or other alternatives. God acts in ways that sometimes also reflect his humor, and in any case also his patience. And this is immensely moving and encouraging and motivating to want to practice the long breath to endure even the difficult stretches of the way (of which also much has been told). Faithfulness, following the instructions, no matter how inconspicuous they may be, seeking his closeness—that's what matters, and everything else is subordinate to that. One must know that one is in the right place, whereby "right" cannot be measured and recognized by "success." The certainty of vocation must be independent of this, and the ways in which God expresses himself are very different.

There is another thread that runs through missionary work and Christian witness ministry wherever it happens: Many, many difficulties, headwinds; which spontaneously often triggers the naturally futile question "Why can't it be easier?" But also, again and again, the experience that God is there, in everything; often hidden for a longer or even despairingly long time. But sooner or later always come the days when one can look back overwhelmed by his incredible logistics, which triggers the amazement: Speechless—except: "Hallelujah!"). We can only live forward, but often see him only in retrospect. But every experience of this kind makes the foundation stronger, on which we can continue to build in confidence and hope, despite the headwind. For he does not change. We build on his character, his work, on reality.

So what remains—very briefly? He is there. Always. He gets his people. Stay put until he calls for departure. Heavenly logistics work.

Life before and with God
September 30, 2014

What actually is spiritual life?

Seeking God's face—what does that mean? How can that look practically? A few thoughts in rough.

Obvious pious activities, permanent stay in the "quiet chamber," withdrawal from normal life into prayer can certainly not be the point; my spiritual life does not begin the moment I open the Bible and ends when I close it and turn to "normal" life. That would mean permanent division, a "double life," not wholeness.

Spiritual life can actually be nothing else than life before and with God, in everything, as he has designed the possibilities and necessities of our lives up to the most banal things like dozing, cleaning up and garbage disposal. It seems to have been like that in paradise. It has something to do with the larger horizon in which we as Christians can see or suspect our lives embedded—where and as long as I live in this horizon, I live spiritually. The comparison to the animal world comes to mind. A dog is where it is and what it is. This instinctive wholeness has something of the originality in paradise; Adam and Eve had a simple experience of creation in relation to God and one another. As post-Paradise people, in our experience of sin, our ability to reflect on ourselves leads to dividedness and diversity, to stepping out of the present and out of directly experiencing and accepting what is at hand; ironing and plucking weeds appear as less "actual" life, appear more as means to an end than as life already full in itself, as part of God's design; as opposed to some obviously pious activity, as if we were closer to God there. Instinctively, we do not make quality of life dependent on the consciousness of God's nearness (which we also do not experience in a paradisiacal way), not on the giver, but on the kind of gifts and tasks. One day this split will be eliminated—the "simple life" plus the "awareness of God's nearness" will again come together completely: simply living in and from and before God.

My prayer:
Help me to live *now*
that I may rejoice with an undivided heart in what is beautiful;
that I may do with a determined heart what is due,
that I bear with a trusting heart what I cannot change.
And that I learn to keep *you* in view in everything.

Suffering and Character
October 3, 2014

In what way exactly can pain and suffering actually build character?

The thesis comes up here and there in Christian testimonies; but apart from the experience of the deeper dependence on God, it is not described in much more concrete terms.

My guess:

The natural reactions to stress and pain tend to be mostly negative. Trust in God and in hidden meaning, however, can help to fight self-pity and self-centeredness, can help to try to continue to love and be patient instead of becoming embittered, can help to become more merciful to others out of one's own experience. So, from trust in God, positive behaviors toward him and toward fellow human beings can follow, which are trained to an unusual degree. Times of suffering are intensive training camps for strength of character, which also benefits oneself and others afterwards. And furthermore, these times help to recognize what is essential, what counts and remains:

Good find: Jim Elliot. He demonstrates enjoyable realism in the face of the term "surrender of life" (which is not used like that in the New Testament!):

> One does not surrender life in an instant. That which is lifelong can only be surrendered in a lifetime. Nor is surrender to the will of God (per se) adequate to fulness of power in Christ. Maturity is the accomplishment of years, and I can only surrender to the will of God as I know what that will is. Hence, the fulness of the Spirit is not instantaneous but progressive, as I attain fulness of the Word, which reveals the Will. (Jim Elliot)[14]

Choosing Trust
November 4, 2014

Once again I witness how in the life of a close person one crisis follows the next instead of the tide finally turning.

Why does God sometimes take away all the supports which, of course, are ultimately illusions, but which nevertheless reassure us and help us not to live constantly in a state of extreme alarm?

Why does he unabashedly hold up before our eyes our total dependence? Does he need to show us that he is the big boss? That would be an absurd insinuation.

"The truth will set you free." (John 8:32) This actually seems to me to be the only tangible meaning that we can discover at this time. He wants to save us from deceptions; save us from the fear of the breaking of the supports, which can't keep what they promise anyway, because he is the only one who can (and will!) keep what he promises.

Sometimes letting go, giving up, is not really a choice, but an inevitable imposition; whether I react to it with bitterness or trust, however, is my choice. But I need reasons to choose trust; why should I believe in love behind agonizingly terrible experiences and hold on to that? In what sense can these be an expression that he really wants the best for us? I need reassurance that behind such moments there is not the grimace of Satan, but the loving, compassionate and perhaps even tearful gaze of Jesus (cf. John 11:35).

Here it has an effect, how far I have used the calmer times of my life to strike deep roots in God's revelation of his being, whether I have formed "iron rations," therefore can assure myself more or less immediately of the elemental in acute emergency and thus oppose the inner negative spiral. For example by remembering that it is not only about my little life; we are part of a much bigger story.

Remember Omnipotence
November 7, 2014

I remembered (prompted by the urgent prayer requests around us) a pastors' meeting where God's omnipotence was practically abandoned in favor of God's solidarity in suffering with people. Where is the consolation in this? Certainly, it has become clear to me more than once how essential it is to know oneself not be alone; this is unquestionably one of the primal needs of man, if not *the* primal need. But as a rule, it is connected with the longing to have someone at one's side who is stronger, especially in times of need and one's own weakness; who is reliable reassurance in person that the situation will not get out of control, will remain controllable—if possible, even who can ensure exactly that. Children find security with parents through the hierarchical gradient—"my parents are bigger, more experienced, they can manage that we get through together." But if even God, the creator of the universe, is powerless at the mercy of the overpowering evil destroyers of life? Somehow this is not thought through to the end. Perhaps well-intentioned, but in the result more horror than comfort.

Standing by Our Side
November 16, 2014

"Peace I leave with you; my peace I give to you. I do not give to you as the world gives. Do not let your hearts be troubled and do not be afraid." (John 14:27)

Peace: a pleasant feeling? More likely not.

But at least in the first place: the objectively established and lasting reconciled fellowship with Jesus.

He never withdraws from us again, does not terminate the fellowship. See also John 16:33: In him peace, at the same time in the world affliction— so it cannot be a peace that simply eliminates the pain of affliction, gives us pure feeling of well-being, or eliminates the affliction, but it must have something to do with a superior fact; and we are to be sure that the situation never gets out of control. Affliction is not accidental, but announced part of the fellowship with Jesus; but in everything Jesus just stands by our side, is our friend, does not withdraw or even become an enemy. His peace = peace from his side = his nearness. Of course, this can also result in inner rest.

In the service I was moved by Jesus's words: "I am the life"—either Jesus is speaking as a megalomaniac or it is the truth. It sounds so fairytale-like. But who knows—maybe we should question our view of fairy tales, broaden it. They also reflect insights, experiences; maybe the fairy tales are given to us as cross-cultural indicators of greater realities.

Big Shoes, Little Feet
January 13, 2015

"Take my life, take it entirely." In some songs there are very strong, all-encompassing words of devotion. And I always ask myself then: Can I really pray all this honestly, undividedly? Honest answer: No.

And I would also prefer to have the result without the way to get there. Does it still make sense to pray like this? Yes.

Sure, the shoes of these words are way too big for my little feet of faith.

But my Creator can and will let me grow into them, according to his timing. I cannot overtake myself (inner postscript admitted: unfortunately.).

Can I at least ask for far lesser goals at the same time, probably even more honestly? Might be less spiritual though. And perhaps amount to contradictory prayers. But that is not the essential point.

He has made us human. So he knows.

We need both the big goals and the little burgers or pizzas or sushi or oases of whatever kind along the way—and the Holy Spirit, whom the Father himself sent to translate the sighs of our hearts. (Romans 8:26)

The Promise Remains
January 27, 2015

Thought while praying, in the closing words of my prayer, "Lord, you have given me my life, …"

Keep me from imputing to you,
what is in truth diabolical.
Your motives are always positive.
In you there is light and no darkness.
Please remind me of this again and again so that I can remain faithful to you.

This time is the time that God takes to give priority to the courtship of love over the enforcement of justice and the overcoming of evil. That is, as a rule, conscious preference for the path of suffering. For me, it is helpful to consciously keep this underlying positive motivation in mind and to express it and not to stop at the superficial fact that God just tolerates some things.

Note under the watchword: Psalm 142:8, 2 Corinthians 3:17.

"Lord Jesus Christ, you were poor and miserable, imprisoned and abandoned like me. You know all the needs of men, you stay with me when no man stands by me, you do not forget me and seek me. Lord, whatever this day brings, your name be praised!" (D. Bonhoeffer)

My thoughts: The prayer triggers association: Jesus is in Gethsemane alone; even he longs for fellowship, but the most faithful friends fall asleep. He knows what being alone means, is a "compassionate high priest." He will never abandon us.

The greatest freedom is the dependence on him.

Later I read Psalm 142 as a whole. Context: David in the cave (I had not been aware of that; but in some respects it's a kind of Gethsemane situation!). The persecutors seem overpowering, and are—humanly speaking; but even for that, he "knows our path" (v. 4). The Savior will come, one way or another, no matter how many hours and days have to be endured in the cave. I think this can be transferred. Whatever "persecutes" us, inwardly or outwardly, and seems overpowering, the promise remains valid. It is sealed with his blood, his experience and his ultimate triumph.

Flee and Draw Near
January 28, 2015

"The fear of the Lord is to hate evil." (Proverbs 8:13)

"Flee the devil and draw near to God" (cf. James 4:7–8) is a similar double movement. We are not only to be for God, but also clearly against the devil.

Is this not automatically the case? Yes and no.

What is evil? That which I intuitively or spontaneously recognize as such? Possibly; because with the conscience a kind of compass is built into us according to creation. But not necessarily, because this device must be calibrated to the standard of God; and if it is merely calibrated to the social consensus or an ideology, the conscience is not a reliable guide.

In the reverence of the Lord, I come to know what he rejects and why.

Hate: to have conscious, active aversion to something. And to name it, expose it, make it knowable, for myself and others, consciously decide against it.

It is too little to focus on the good and hope that the rejection of evil will automatically follow without addressing it.

I am thinking, among other things, of preaching. It is too much to expect people to be able to recognize and draw the consequences of the good put before their eyes and ears right away and, on top of that, to have the opposite automatically before their eyes. The most dangerous evil is the rather veiled, not so obvious one—and one must talk about it, also to counteract trivialization. For example, it is quite easy to talk about the value of fidelity in general; but if you expose sexual "permissiveness" as self-centeredness, sin, that is guaranteed to be another matter for the listeners. Standing up for life is one thing; opposing abortion is another. And so on.

Later, I turned to today's page in a devotional book on the watchwords, and "by chance" this devotional confirmed my impression of this morning. One prefers to concentrate on the presentation of the positive in today's preaching and rather to leave the transfer and drawing of the counter-pole consequences to the listeners.

Inner Peace, Outer Discord?
January 29, 2015

Jesus sees the whole, people only a part. This truism also means that he also sees good yet and already in situations where my gaze is completely captivated by evil. Reality is greater than our little insight. This knowledge must be proven again and again:

"Even though I walk through the valley of the shadow of death, I will fear no evil, for you are with me; your rod and your staff, they comfort me." (Psalm 23:4)

"We are afflicted in every way, but not crushed; perplexed, but not driven to despair; persecuted, but not forsaken; struck down, but not destroyed." (2 Corinthians 4:8–9, ESV)

What juxtapositions:

Afflicted—*that is the painful foreground part of reality*

but not crushed—*background reality: the invisible Lord at our side will make sure for ways where our feet can go (P. Gerhardt hymn, "Thy Way and All Thy Sorrows")*

Perplexed—*that is objective fact believers are not spared of*
but not driven to despair—*background reality: with the invisible Lord at our side there are no hopeless cases*

Persecuted—*that is inescapable hardship*
but not forsaken—*background reality: the invisible Lord at our side sealed his promised of lasting nearness (Matthew 28:20; John 10:28) with his blood.*

Those who find faith find inner peace, but often end up in outer discord. Experiences of inner plus outer peace are rather occasional foretastes of eternity, especially seen worldwide. This has been the inescapable experience of Christians from the beginning. And Jesus himself experienced and predicted it—"Do you think I came to bring peace on earth? No, I tell you, but division" (Luke 12:51); the natural interpersonal bonds become problematic.

Praying, Praising, Giving Thanks
January 30, 2015

Reflections on the day's watchword.

Three times a day Daniel "got down on his knees and prayed, giving thanks to his God, just as he had done before." (Daniel 6:10)

Pray three times: Good habits (not empty rituals) can help not to be overwhelmed by distracting influences; can help to live instead of "being lived."

"Be joyful in hope, patient in affliction, faithful in prayer." (Romans 12:12)

Joyful in hope: Attitude of anticipation—the road is often rough, even sometimes marked by loss, but in the end there will be joy.

Patient: Tribulation is limited. Our Father does not sleep, so does not fail to recognize when we run out of strength.

Persevering: Not many words are needed, not even a correct persuasion strategy. The Creator of our hearts knows about their fears, longings, pains—from experience. The point is to keep "eye-contact" and thus remain open to God, so that he can remind us of the truth about the otherwise hidden aspects of our reality.

Satan wants us to lose sight of all this and discourage and paralyze us. We should expect his attempts to prevent prayerful eye-contact as much as possible.

Between the Green Pastures
April 20, 2015

Even with very familiar texts, surprises can still be waiting. I felt this way with a hint of our guest preacher on Psalm 23. In our country we take it for granted that there are always lush green pastures and that it is therefore quite easy to move from one green pasture to the next. But in Israel, purely because of the landscape and the season, there can be arid and arduous stretches between pastures. Because the animals travel under the reliable protection of the shepherd, when the animals arrive they will find enough to eat, but that still does not mean that it is comparable to Bavarian or Irish meadows.

I have actually only ever seen the valley of the shadow of death as a symbol for hard times—happens, but rarely. And the green pasture seemed to me to stand for the normal experience, which does not really correspond to our experience. And this gap between word and experience sometimes makes me rebel: "Lord, you make too big words. You raise expectations that you don't fulfill. Our pastures are far more often barren than green."

The misunderstanding was probably on my side.

The Whole World a Shire
April 21, 2015

Sabine Naegeli's prayer under the day's watchword from Job gives food for thought.

"Painfully I lack what you have taken from me, God. But I no longer rise up against you. Still I weep, but I feel it becomes calmer in me. Though I may remain a wounded one, I believe that one day I will outgrow the lament."[15]

There is a meaning in everything, even if it is often beyond our imagination, which makes it so difficult for us. Not to trust in a sense is senseless in view of the way our universe is shaped. It occurs to me: (author forgotten; Amy Carmichael perhaps?): "Why does God expect from us to go through this or that? Answer: he gives us credit for that." So there is, in addition to the assurance of getting through, a kind of honor in that. But since I don't have an innate desire for heroism, I would still rather live peacefully as a hobbit in the Shire. The whole world should be like Shire.

Vain Struggles
May 12, 2015

Again and again these days, but especially at night, when I woke up, I had the impression of somehow running against an immense steel door, although it no longer makes sense, because it has fallen into the lock, to struggle in vain and yet ceaselessly against the inescapability of transience, against powerlessness in the face of the finality of mortality, against the irretrievability of past moments. There was still so much left fragmentary or undone, but the hourglass is inexorably ticking away. Difficult to grasp. In any case, connected with the knowledge that we know all this for sure, but not if and what comes after.

This one seems real, the "land" behind the death line unreal, despite all the arguments I've gone through x times. So it's really just a feeling, I know. Nevertheless, I feel this sometimes as a tons-heavy weight on the soul, sometimes as—in an uncanny sense—almost self-evident insight.

But, think to the end! Because: If there is a God who loves us, would it really be conceivable that he would leave it on his part with our fragmentary recognition? That our life and love would remain here without completion? See watchword: 1 Corinthians 13:12: "For now we see in a mirror dimly, but then face to face. Now I know in part; then I shall know fully, even as I have been fully known." (ESV) This actually corresponds to an inner logic that death cannot be the end. Otherwise the world history would be like a colossal mass grave of destroyed hopes, an immeasurably huge accumulation of aborted drafts of biographies with which God would not have reached the goal—provided, of course, that he had such a goal with it. But a God with a throwaway mentality would be a very strange idea. This world in any case cries out for completion. I stumbled over Isaiah 65:20–23, which fits to it: "Never again will there be in it an infant who lives but a few days, or an old man who does not live out his years ... They will not labour in vain, nor will they bear children doomed to misfortune." Here indeed the visions of earthly and eternal renewal are still mixed, but God's will for completion and his unwillingness to accept fragments is clear.

Peace begins to spread, the hereafter begins to gain weight and reality. May it also encompass the night.

Growing in Dark Phases
July 3, 2015

Temptations are regular companions of believers in the Bible, whether we like it or not, whether we understand the reasons or not. We have to come to terms with them. What can help us to do this?

During the mountain tour yesterday, the thought came to me: How do people overcome the fear of heights or narrow paths? By consciously exposing themselves to such opportunities to a gradually increasing degree. Slowly one gets used to it, and the experience "I will get out of this scary situation" sinks deeper into the heart (even if, of course, individually different limits remain in this training). Maybe something similar is the background of my dark phases, seen from God's perspective; teaching me that it is temporary (for whatever reason it happens in the first place) and that in a way I should not take it too seriously and be very careful to draw conclusions about reality in general from such momentary experiences, at least while I am still in such a phase.

Faith probation makes patience grow. (James 1:2–3)

Second: Most of our gifts come with stressful aspects. Having a thick skin helps to move forward in challenging situations, but can be an agonizing source of hurt toward others in relationships (so one must learn in this area). Again, being sensitive can be a help in relationships, but a burden when faced with the inability to effectively do something about the pain of others (so one must learn in this area).

To pray, "Lord, see to it that I am no longer overwhelmed by what I see happening in other people's lives," must not be accompanied by the subliminal false expectation that there must be a discomfort-free version of the gift of sensitivity. That would amount to hoping for or claiming a change of personality.

Third: When we pray to be transformed into the image of Jesus, to become like him, this includes not only aspects such as his patience, longsuffering, understanding, etc., but also his deep aversion to evil; he is not passionless in this, but passionately engaged. So when I long for freedom from the emotional and almost physical pain caused by, for example, news of Christian girls raped (by IS) and burned alive, I am basically longing for freedom from sharing his holy sadness and rejection of evil. Of course, I am a fragile human being and cannot deal with these challenges as God can, which makes my sighs understandable (and mixed with sinful elements); but the question still remains: Do I want to share his love and suffering of this fallen creation, at least to some extent, or would I rather be spared this element of solidarity and communion with him? (Whether in this direction went what Mother Theresa often felt when she suffered from God's silence?) And, in a way, my rebellion against some outbreaks of evil is even a hint to him, yes, it is not as it should be, it is a reminder that God himself feels this far more than I will ever be able to do, and for whatever reason he does not crack down on it as I so intensely long for.

Fourth: Why is it often so difficult to perceive Jesus's presence and speaking—although he is in us, very close? Especially in John's Gospel there are enormously strong words, which can tend to raise unrealistic expectations! Wouldn't something like a pen-pal relationship under the conditions of pre-industrial times be a more appropriate description? Yes, from the subjective perception, the metaphor would make some sense. But: We must keep apart, how the things present themselves out of God's dimension and how in contrast in ours and from our subjective perception possibilities (and also consider our perception does not determine what carries us deeply!) The reality viewed out of

God's dimension (which encompasses ours) is more complex than we can guess with our pictures, which is why we need several, even if we cannot bring them to coincide. That I do not always feel God's nearness can have several reasons (including guilt), except for the one that God is not there. This reason drops out.

Do not forget: Even Paul, who certainly had special encounters with Jesus, still feels the clear disparity in the relationship when he points out in 1 Corinthians 13 that for us "to know as we are known" is still pending as the perfection of blessedness in eternity.

Beware the Traps
July 11, 2015

Revelation of John 11 and the following chapters on the Antichrist.

The question came to me while reading: Why is it actually so bad to worship the Antichrist? How would one explain this to the people? Isn't it just a harmless ceremony for someone who does a lot of good after all? Is God jealous? In any case, the submission seems to be useful, the refusal leads to disproportionate suffering.

The trap is that evil never fully reveals its true motives. Evil is insatiable. Power wants to be increased more and more, wealth, reputation etc. as well; there is no limit to immoderateness (Scrooge McDuck's avarice unfortunately reflects deep realism!) People are only a means to an end. (One has seen that with the Nazis; still today some point to the highway construction as a good idea and on top of that was a job creation measure and fade out that the real goals were not the welfare of the people but the preparation for war). The subjects are only granted as much good and for as long as it benefits evil's own goals. Those who allow themselves to be blinded by the seemingly harmless beginnings, who play down the claim to totality in them, will one day experience a rude awakening.

Bishop Lilje writes about this in his commentary:[16]

> The unfolding of power does not repel at all, but exerts a mysterious charm. Power has its fascinosum, its mysterious attraction. As there is an intoxication of power, so there is also a worship of power. For great, truly great power always reaches beyond human

measure; and still in the usurped and abused power lies the memory that all earthly power has its origin in God's omnipotence. But this origin is forgotten and denied here. But the world, which never gives much thought and as a whole is always devoid of principles, sinks into adoring amazement at the revelation of such earthly power. Nothing convinces so much as the success. ... The blasphemies of the people are only surpassed by the blasphemies of the beast itself. It has no own message, it can only blaspheme. It also has no own positive historical mission, it can only destroy. Therefore, war is as indispensable to it as blasphemous speech as a means of effectiveness.

Goodness Is Real
July 12, 2015

The series "The Pacific" gives impressions of the war between Americans and Japanese in Micronesia during World War II. One scene that haunts me:

A Japanese woman was initially able to hide during an attack, but is then found. The American, Eugene, first wants to shoot her, but doesn't; she wants him to shoot her, but he doesn't either. He holds her head while she dies. Humanity in final boundary experience. "Useless," even dangerous humanity (when the woman has died, her hand opens, from which falls a hand grenade not yet detonated; a danger of which Eugene was aware when he entered the cabin). Where does this humanity come from, if not from God? It is rather contrary to nature.

The war brings evil to light, but also the knowledge: This is not how it should be actually.

Even the crying of a baby or child still penetrates through the jaded hearts of the soldiers (not always though; in other countries today child soldiers are raised by adults!).

Even in the SS, the good could not be eradicated. In their own families, the same men could be caring fathers who acted out like maniacs while on duty.

Goodness is real.

Hollywood would not exist if it did not address what is embedded in the heart.

The moments of immediate joy point beyond themselves; in them shines briefly what is supposed to be. This world is not the first and not the last. The actual, most beautiful is yet to come (again).

We go towards *him*, from whom all good comes.

Decisive Direction in View
November 10, 2015

Our refugees: A lot of problems need to be handled. Stressful, though also surprising support happens here and there, too. Makes me think.

So much depends on an action that is inconspicuous at first as the alignment of our (inner) eyes. It remains a constant struggle to keep our eyes focused on Jesus and to resist the devilish attempts to distract our eyes. And physically tired eyes are especially prone to infecting our inner ones.

For example: Do we try to look into the future and imagine how impossible it will be to deal with all the familiar problems before us? Or do we look to the past and how God has brought us through past "impossible" problems and how he has proven his faithfulness in them, and do we accept the challenge therein to draw confidence and hope from them?

Do we look at our weakness and allow ourselves to become paralyzed, or do we look at the bigger picture, that we and our problems are in the hands of our brilliant and powerful Creator and Savior? For Peter in the stormy waters, the wrong focus led to mortal danger (Matthew 14:27ff.) The only thing left for the men at Jesus's side on Calvary on their crosses was to turn their eyes toward him or away from him; to admit their longing and neediness or to remain alone with it. And what a difference it made.

Walking through Darkness
April 16, 2016

In an email, sharing a bit of her book project (dealing with grief), a friend mentioned the expression "passion to live." The words stuck with me. Because I definitely lack that. We agreed to read Hebrews during the next days.

Hebrews 11–13: To bring the whole train of thought back to memory, I first read the chapters again completely.

What struck me especially and first of all: The more or less long waiting periods between promise and fulfillment. Our ancestors must have known the feelings of intense longing, painful "thirst" (reminds me of the Beatitude Matthew 5:6, by the way), existential distress, maybe also of doubts, and none of it is pleasant; it would be naive to assume that they would have been stoic or happy people throughout. And we know from the Old Testament about some situations where they were definitely not stoic. At least we are in good company when we suffer from a situation that is not yet as it should be. Here lies a literally diabolical spiritual trap: Giving in to cunningly formulated half-truths that want to creep into our hearts, such as "A true Christian should be characterized by an unshakable trust, that is a sure mark from which one can deduce that faith is rooted in reality." My mind knows this, of course. But there is also such a thing as "amnesia, memory loss of the heart." Encouraging, challenging to trust: Yes. However, a despairing person should not on top be burdened with a bad conscience, the feeling of failure.

What does it mean that Moses (Hebrews 11:27) held on to the one he did not see as if he saw him (according to the Luther 1984 translation)? In what way did Moses not see him? Had he not seen God and his mighty acts more clearly than many other people? Perhaps this statement contains a hidden hint that it would be an illusion to believe that Moses always "saw" God. Apart from the fact that there is no experience in this world that would be exempt per se from the possibility of being doubted, after all, in retrospect, (I know only too well what I am talking about), I find it hard to imagine that Moses was completely different from C. S. Lewis, Mother Theresa, many famous and many nameless Christians through all the centuries who knew not only something of God's speaking, but also of his agonizing silence. But certainly Moses was a model in his tenacity not to give up until he was granted a new encounter with his Lord.

John Ortberg came to mind again: "Sometimes faith means walking through the darkness and refusing to give up. Sometimes faith means just going on. Faith that makes it possible for us to be changed by suffering and darkness, is not to be confused with doubtless certainty. It is only stubborn obedience."[17]

The Right Battle
April 17, 2016

Hebrews 11:34: "… became strong in battle …" Actually one becomes rather weak there, apart from the initial adrenaline rush perhaps. So: One of the paradoxical regularities or possibilities in God's kingdom. And it is certainly not simply to be equated with the experience of growing beyond oneself against one's own expectations; at least not in the sense that outwardly, visibly everything turns out well after all. If one looks at the whole chapter 11, it becomes clear how often the strength proves to be in the way of suffering.

However, in order to go into battle at all, one needs the certainty of fighting the right battle, for the right commander, the right cause. And that it is worthwhile, that it changes something.

Why Evil? Why Good?
May 7, 2016

Psychiatrist M. Scott Peck offers a thought-provoking reflection in *People of the Lie*.

> It is a strange thing. Dozens of time I have been asked by patients or acquaintances: 'Dr. Peck, why is there evil in the world?' Yet no one has ever asked me in all these years: 'Why is there good in the world?' It is as if we automatically assume this is a naturally good world that has somehow been contaminated by evil. In terms of what we know of science, however, it is actually easier to explain evil. That things decay is quite explainable in accord with the natural law of physics. That life should evolve into more and more complex forms is not so easily understandable. That children generally lie and steal and cheat is routinely

observable. The fact that sometimes they grow up to become truly honest adults is what seems the more remarkable. Laziness is more rule than diligence. If we seriously think about it, it probably makes more sense to assume this is a naturally evil world that has somehow been mysteriously 'contaminated' by goodness, rather than the other way round.[18]

One Who Knows
September 26, 2016

"Blessed are those who hunger and thirst for righteousness, for they will be filled." (Matthew 5:6)

Who says these words?

One who knows what he is talking about.

One who knows the history of his people: the injustice within the nation and the oppression from without; he was very familiar with the passionate and longing descriptions of the prophets.

One who knew both from experience, during his own lifetime. Oppression, injustice and suffering were definitely associated with faces and names for him, not abstract concepts.

Hunger, thirst: This is more than a little appetite for some nice food. Those who have experienced war can tell about how painful hunger is. I myself do not know it. But I at least know a little of the pains of the soul and heart in a world that is on fire in more places than ever before.

Satisfaction is promised: It inspires hope, which is an essential, necessary driving force to go on living.

But since fulfillment refers to the future, at least as far as perfect degree is concerned, it also means that while we are still on the way, the experience of pain will remain a companion. We must learn to live with it. But in it we also have fellowship with our Lord.

I remember again an entry recently that fits with this: See chapter 1, August 12, 2016.

Glimpses of Glory
February 11, 2017

Watchword: "The Word became flesh and made his dwelling among us. We have seen his glory." (John 1:14) The apostle John got a few special brief glimpses regarding the glory of Jesus during his lifetime and his companionship with him; the most mysterious and impressive one on the Mount of Transfiguration (Matthew 17:1ff), to which John probably alludes in this verse. Unforgettable moments. Encouraging, reassuring, essential experiences. However, such peak experiences remain the exception. If we compare the times we may spend on summits with those we spend walking uphill and downhill and through the valleys, no doubt: there is a certain disproportionality.

So we will have to accept that is part of the realism of discipleship. But we certainly need and may therefore pray for encouraging peaks, unforgettable impressions of eternity, which make us strong for service in the normal regions of daily life and able to pass on grace and truth as much as possible.

The Victory of Truth
February 13, 2017

Sometimes we chafe at the fact that evil is allowed to spread for so long, well camouflaged, insidiously and yet with literally uncanny determination, that it is not nipped in the bud but can still do so much harm. For those of us who have open eyes and a fine sense, it is difficult to endure seeing something like this and yet not being able to stop it. Perhaps it helps for patience to realize: Evil must often mature, first take off its mask, reveal its destructive traits. In a certain sense, this is part of the victory of truth.

Strengthened in Suffering
February 15, 2017

In what way does Jesus strengthen the "weak" in suffering?

They overcome evil, even if the suffering does not (yet) amount to the complete destruction of evil. Example: non-violent resistance that is shot down: physical death is not synonymous with defeat, but rather with victory—even if perhaps inconspicuous at first—because people refuse to turn away from what is good and true. They withstand the seductive drug of evil.

What Is That to You?
May 4, 2017

John 21 is one of the most moving chapters, I always fine.

Jesus to Peter (vv.18ff.): "Very truly I tell you, when you were younger you dressed yourself and went where you wanted; but when you are old you will stretch out your hands, and someone else will dress you and lead you *where you do not want to go.*

Jesus said this to indicate the kind of death by which Peter would glorify God. Then he said to him, 'Follow me!'.

Peter turned and saw that the disciple whom Jesus loved was following them. (This was the one who had leaned back against Jesus at the supper and had said, 'Lord, who is going to betray you?')

When Peter saw him, he asked, "Lord, what about him?" Jesus answered, "If I want him to remain alive until I return, what is that to you? You must follow me."

Verse 18 is noteworthy in the literal sense: "you will stretch out"/" where you do not want to go"—it is a strange mix of promise and imposition. "Peter, you will become more mature" (positively compared to youth); however, this does not show up in other-worldly enthusiasm about martyrdom and being unassailable by pain, but in not trying to escape from it. Jesus knows again (as with the denial) already beforehand: the inner resistance against Jesus's leadership will probably be there, and Jesus will again not spare Peter this conflict simply with some anesthetic at the push of a button. Jesus also already predicts to him: stronger than the resistance will be the consent. So Jesus knows about the conflict and leads Peter into a situation where he is practically under *zugzwang*, takes away the decision in a certain sense. Peter doesn't have to be more of a hero than he is; in a way he does not really have to choose but rather to nod toward.

When I think about some of the developments of the past few months, I know that I would have liked to have avoided some situations, wished they had never happened (and future situations are already in front of my eyes, where I already feel reluctance). And because guilt also plays a part in these situations, there is also something legitimate in the wish that they had not happened. But that is only one side. Nevertheless, Jesus made something of it—used it to open my eyes about myself, my weak roots, crutches, powerlessness, etc., like a doctor who talks straight, destroys illusions, not to get one down, but in order to focus on how one's situation really is and what really helps. We prefer to avoid surgery as long as possible, and if rehabilitation is unavoidable, then at least it should go as quickly as possible. There are areas where I have to let things take their course. That is very difficult for me. Surrender.

But if we let ourselves in on this perspective, we can let that be transformed into something greater, what, from a human point of view, may at first look like defeat, and then we can ultimately become more authentic, more coherent in our faith and love and trust. This is only possible when we do not look to the side to see what more or less rapid effect this has on the others (that would be like sowing grass and immediately plucking the first stalks to measure the size of the root), but look to Jesus, when we stretch out our hands and let ourselves be led, at *his* pace, where we actually do not want to go. (Ultimately of course we want to go, just not actually at *any* price, but on a more comfortable path, which however does not exist). He who gives receives; he who lets go of his life will gain it; the grain of wheat that dies brings new life. We have to go through the process, there is no other way. We are naturally afraid of weakness. But the mystery is 2 Corinthians 12:9: in our weakness God's power comes to its aim, and we all felt something of that over the weekend. I suspect more and more strongly, the physical process of dying one day will bring all these things to the fore once again on another, the last earthly level (the increasing and consciously perceived weakness is, after all, often very difficult for dying people to bear).

Afterthought to the question, "How far is it legitimate to set boundaries for the purpose of self-protection?" This became acute now with different people in the community. It is not about never or always setting boundaries, but about the basic attitude and how far my behavior is more characterized by fear for myself and the need for control than by trust in my heavenly protector, whose protective power gives me greater freedom than is available to a non-Christian. The latter is a crucial point.

Holding On to Trust
July 30, 2017

We are made for fellowship, we need it, we long for it. But we are often deprived of it in part and sometimes for the most part—and on top of that, just when we miss it most.

I think of a woman who, like many others, faithfully and conscientiously brought her children through the difficult post-war period. And now—so much is broken. What a strange kind of heavenly care is this? Why? As usual, we don't get an answer to that. How then can we go on without ending up in resignation or bitterness? I am trying to formulate what attitude I would like for myself.

"The path was sometimes beautiful, even if it was mostly difficult. Now it is almost only difficult. But I will remain faithful over the last stage, if that is to be part of my divine assignment. And in this way, in my inconspicuous place, I will contribute to the victory over all evil intentions. I will still finish the last meters, even if it is desert stage, for whatever reason. Even if my life here rather smolders out than that I can still arrange it somehow. Then my last fight is just to let it happen, to wait for the goal, holding on to trust against all seeing, instead of slipping into bitterness or resignation. The Diabolos will not get me only just at the end to the prey. I will not engage in self-doubt and self-accusation."

But whether I will be able to put this into practice one day, and whether it will stand the test of time, my own age will have to show.

Afterthought to Trinity: After all, we know the experience that we can relate to ourselves, ask ourselves, hate ourselves, do good, talk to ourselves in inner self-talk.

Eternity in Views
September 9, 2017

The natural disasters don't let go of me. In Florida, there are faces associated with them. Not so with the tens of millions in Asia. That does not diminish the horror. I alternate between praying and trying to keep my eyes on beautiful things nevertheless and even more so, but it is very difficult, just feels terribly wrong. Of course there is no alternative. Our daughter is happy about unexpected three minutes of rain in California, I'm annoyed by the typical German gray continuous rain, and elsewhere there are countless life stories literally flooded—all in the same world. Under the eyes of the one Creator. Life is so unfair.

For so many people, joy in life as the common thread of their journey is largely out of reach, and even the gospel cannot change that. At best, it can try to bring eternity into view as a source of hope and of the will to live—and in doing so, more for the future than for the earthly life. Is that too little? At first glance: Yes; because it seems so little tangible in the face of such tangible misery. But then: No; because it releases forces without which everything would be much more difficult. And it mobilizes solidarity that goes beyond normal boundaries.

Thinking about Doubt
September 15, 2017

Temptation is not an uncommon theme in the New Testament; as Christians, we should reckon with such things in order to be able to defend ourselves. But I must state: in my consciousness, the subject is largely absent. This leads, among other things, to seeing doubt neutrally, purely factually. Behind this, of course, there is also a certain logic. If thoughts of doubt attack the foundation, then not only the existence of this God, but also that of his opponent. To unmask a "dark cloud" as a devilish attack and to be able to reject it more easily presupposes certainty concerning the basic principles of the Christian faith. But at least whenever this is given, it is worthwhile to look at the enemy in the background as a possible source of insecurity. Thomas à Kempis is right: "Two things strengthen temptation's grip on you—an indecisive mind and little trust in God."

Break the Tip of Evil
October 18, 2017

On the phone, someone shared their totally understandable frustration. There are already enough serious challenges to deal with, and then stuff is added that seems so completely random and unnecessary. Anger comes up in me, too. But still, at some point I try to get my act together and look to Jesus for something constructive in all of this, a way out of the emotional downward spiral. General direction: "Don't let yourself be overcome by evil, but overcome evil with good." In retrospect, the conversation once again passes by my inner ear. Doesn't this seem almost ridiculous, or at least unworldly, what I have tried to say? At the same time, I know of no alternative. Either we break off the tip of evil by turning it into character training, or we allow ourselves to be infected by abandoning the paradigm of "grace" and "trust."

We all face this fundamental question again and again: Do I have enough conviction to do the right thing simply because it is the right thing to do, and that means even when it achieves little or even faces headwinds? Or do I still depend on success?

Grumbling and Buts
January 26, 2018

Certain challenges in ministry have been strength-sapping for days. Very much. And seemingly so unnecessary.

An almost perfect time in the sense of unclouded perfection does not exist on this side of paradise. To get involved in the devilish illusory whispering that we might have this possibility here after all or even a right to it, means that we make ourselves producers of our own disappointments. Perfect in the sense of expedient is only to perceive beautiful and difficult, good and bad, funny and sad—everything as something that we can and should use in different ways as a bridge into the hidden eternal dimension of our life. There the house of our life is built, which will shine in perfect beauty one day.

Grumbling.

Diabolos wants to make us grumble and keep us in it. Because that paralyzes us. And for this he likes to foist thoughts on us like:

"Always this stupid 'try to see the positive in it,'—that's just window dressing, doesn't take my (surely justified) pain seriously, belittles it, makes it sound good, but I'm angry and I have a right to be!"

"At least that should be ... "

"Why this again and again in my life, in XY's life?"

"Why can't everything run without a glitch at least once?" (So we take this "once" seriously ourselves—that we would like to have this wish fulfilled only once in our life?)

"Does it never end?"

The nasty: A grain of truth is mixed in everywhere and thus contributes to the camouflage of the actually diabolical stench.

Basically, there are only two ways in which we use the little word *but*:

1. We describe the positive part of a situation and attach the (usually stronger) negative *but*.
2. We describe the negative part of a situation and attach the (usually stronger) positive *but*.

Emotionally, what comes after the *but* usually has the greater weight.

The decision for the (of course still correctable) choice of the version is usually made within seconds, has to do with our basic attitude, worldview; whether we can see beyond the situation and, if so, into which larger picture we place it. Therefore, it makes sense to preventively prepare ourselves for stressful situations and to consciously condition ourselves to the basic direction for which we have—hopefully—decided for good reasons (or otherwise should urgently make up for it. A diver who already reflexively knows how to cope with failures of his breathing apparatus in emergency situations is not naïve, but well-prepared, realistic, and only then can he act appropriately. Reacting quickly to stressful situations with "positive thinking" can therefore be very helpful in regaining balance and the ability to act more quickly.

In my eyes, the decisive factor is whether "positive thinking" is rooted in a Christian, biblical, sober worldview, in God's truth, or whether it is filtering wishful thinking, somehow differently founded ideology, but then ultimately rather ostrich politics or Münchhausen tactics, trying to pull oneself out of the swamp by one's own hair. (Baron of Münchhausen is a famous German fairy tale figure.)

Listen, Trust, Obey
February 25, 2018

The gospel is simple in the sense of plain, straightforward. Jesus prompts, challenges—doesn't send his followers first to church-building seminars, motivational courses, or burnout prevention. All this is not bad in itself, but not the first or most important thing. If discipleship is not to be the luxury of theological or other specialists, but in principle possible for every simple person everywhere and at any time, then the essentials must be able to take place in a very simple, plain way—listen, trust, obey. Just as the encounters with Jesus took place during his lifetime. Decisions must be made, not avoided by endless differentiations and considerations and postponed until the last day.

What of Judas?
March 29, 2018

Passion Story.

Critical comment on the insinuation often made by preachers that there is a Judas in all of us, and if we were honest, we would have to admit it. (Converse: if we are not, we are not honest or insightful enough.)

I cannot understand this undifferentiated reflex of interpretation, that we have to identify ourselves that way with the biblical persons, especially the "bad ones," because we are all sinners in the same way. That seems to me much too detached from concrete everyday life. And most people don't think in terms of lengthy theological labyrinths. Of course we are all sinners. Of course we are capable of much more evil than we often want to admit, depending on our biography and our concrete circumstances. Of course, we should not think to be better than others who, in the end, simply have different weaknesses than we do. But the possibility of identification depends on the recognition of the concrete, therefore, precisely because of the differences in the concrete, it does not make sense to claim that in each of the Twelve there was a Judas, and they would have suspected it, because they asked, "Is it I?" However, the betrayal of Peter was different from that of Judas. Peter acted against his actual intentions, Judas according to his intentions. Possible background of the question of the other disciples: they perhaps feared to play into the hands of the enemies of Jesus by thoughtless behavior—contrary to their actual intentions. Cowardice is also a sin. But a different one than, say, treacherousness. No more and no less.

Was Judas treacherous at all? Fact is, we do not know what was going on inside him. Yes, at some point he was also accused of love of money. But who knows if he had not already overcome this phase at the time of the betrayal and had other motives than to get hold of the 30 pieces of silver? For example, to put Jesus under pressure to act? And therefore it is nonsense—based on perhaps completely wrong speculation—to simply claim that Judas is in each of us. We don't know. Let's better compare ourselves with those of whom we know more.

And what struck me once again: Even with the Protestant emphasis that we can't do anything on our own anyway, that only God can change us, I don't get along with this one-sidedness. That also seems to me to be much too detached and in need of explanation—and immediately triggers the next question: If only God can change anyway, why doesn't he? Surely there is no simpler way to raise the question of theodicy. In other words practically, one tries (in passing, which is already a problem in itself anyway) to ward off a problem, namely the exaggerated self-assessment of people; but one overlooks that one initiates at least equally big problems with it. In talking about this, someone said, of course, we also need to ask God to change us. I continue to think: Okay, I'll do it, partly pleading intensely. But if I expected this request to be heard immediately, reality catches up with me very quickly. How nice it would be if we could get out of sinful habits so easily.

The Practical Difference of Easter
April 2, 2018

Easter. From year to year fewer people are attending. Now they are hardly more than on a normal Sunday. Tempting thought: Evidence of the practical irrelevance of the Good News? I try to sum up what we can hold against this temptation, by asking: What practical difference does it make whether Easter determines my life or not?

No one can live without meaning, but inner-worldly meaning is always transitory. As a Christian, my life has imperishable meaning.

No one can live without hope, but inner-worldly fulfillment remains a gamble. As a Christian, I have a well-founded hope.

No one gets through life without guilt. As a Christian, I know where I can go with it.

No one can actively and effectively stand by family or friends in the long run. As a Christian, I can pray—and that goes much further.

No one can do without orientation, values, guidelines. As a Christian, I have more knowledge of the origin and goal of the whole and of wholesome ways to get there than anyone else.

No one gets away without making mistakes. As a Christian, I know that they cannot destroy me. (Romans 8:28)

No one can avoid death. As a Christian I know it is new beginning, completion.

If I am really sure of my Christian faith, it makes a practical difference in everyday life.

Life Should Be Fairer
April 15, 2018

Decision asked.

"One should not sit down and breed feelings, but one should ask oneself how one would act if one could really love God. When you have come to terms with yourself about this, you are to go and put your findings into action." (C. S. Lewis)[19]

"When something bad happens to you, you have three choices: You can let it define you; let it destroy you; or let it strengthen you." (Unknown)

"You have three choices in life: give up, give in, or give everything you have." —(U. S. Navy elite unit)[20]

I continue to think.

"Life should be different!"

"Life should be fairer!"

Such and similar outbursts are understandable. But they are pointless. It is what it is. And it won't change because of our anger or disappointment. The only meaningful question is how best to get through if we don't want to commit mental or physical suicide. How best to help our children get through. And our friends.

Is it easier without God, without faith? Better? Neither easier nor better. Christian faith has not made the world whole. But clearly more whole.

And yet it focuses on the perspective of eternity, which makes us realistic about earthly time and gives us hope that can protect us from despair. It helps to appreciate the beauty as a foretaste and yet to let go when the day comes when it becomes inevitable to do so. It helps not to despair of the bad. That, too, is limited.

The Limits of Despair
November 28, 2018

On the plane I saw the movie: "First Reformed." It is about a pastor who writes a diary for a year. At one point it says: "Despair is a well-disguised form of pride."

Reasoning:

Despair seeks security, places its own limited understanding above trust in a God with unlimited possibilities. It is unwilling to accept the possibility that there could be a God whose creativity in his dealings with the world is beyond what I can imagine. My lips may say otherwise, but practically I make my limited insight the measure of reality: "When I see no more reason for hope, there is none." Thought-provoking observation.

Passion for the Fight
February 15, 2019

A good doctor needs a lot of empathy, and passion to fight disease with all means and to develop ideas instead of settling for symptom relief at best. On the other hand, as a technician, a doctor must at times be at a sufficient distance to be able to apply these techniques, especially as a surgeon. The film about the American doctor Ben Carson came to my mind, which illustrates these two sides very well.

In terms of faith, I increasingly think that the reluctance to evil, the sensitivity to it, is part of sanctification, an aspect of "becoming more like Jesus," a little idea of how he is doing, who suffers from this world in such a way that he suffered *for* it and certainly, in a different way, of course, continues to suffer *with* it. And we also need this passion, as motivation for the fight. On the other hand, we are not yet the healed kind of "new Adam," as Paul puts it, who would be able to join all of this in a balanced way; and accordingly we are in danger to let ourselves be paralyzed and blinded by the Diabolos, the "muddler." All the more we need each other in this struggle to stay in the saddle.

Degrees of Anguish
June 22, 2019

Good find and a perspective worth considering when feelings of failure and guilt become tormenting because joy is not the basic tenor of life (consider the easily stress-causing sentence of the philosopher Nietzsche: "The Christians should look more redeemed to me!"):

> As I noted in *The Road Less Travelled*, it is often the spiritual healthy and advanced among us who are called on to suffer in ways more agonizing than anything experienced by the more ordinary. Great leaders, when wise and well, are likely to endure degrees of anguish unknown to the common man. Conversely it is the unwillingness to suffer emotional pain that usually lies at the very root of emotional illness. Those who fully experience depression, doubt, confusion, and despair may be infinitely more healthy than those who are generally certain, complacent and self-satisfied. The denial of suffering is, in fact, a better definition of illness than its acceptance.[21]

Below the Surface
September 24, 2019

On Facebook, I came across a striking photo montage of a woman who does prison chaplaincy. The image shows a view of the surface of the water in the ocean with a shark fin sticking out of it, but the body underneath is that of a goldfish.

It's an apt image not only for rebellious teenagers going through puberty, but also for many aggressive adults who want to make an impression. We usually see only what is in front of our eyes. Jesus teaches us to see deeper and to look for the lost child.

Another way of trying to make an impression: On the homepage of a news channel, there was a report on the German talk show "Hart aber fair" on the topic of cosmetic surgery. The quote at the end of the frightening article: "Cosmetic surgery is the clinical thermometer of our facade society, which is suffering from narcissism."[22]

One of the results of a society that no longer knows God and grace and unconditional love.

Do We Join?
October 2, 2019

We have the best news in the world! Why?
  There is reason for hope.
  Our longing does not run into emptiness.
  There is a workable concept of life.
  There is still justice. At the latest at the end of time.
  The individual counts—but so does the community.
  God interferes.
  Do we join in?

War in Peacetime
October 23, 2019

We live in a war—always, even in peacetime. But we have a problem of sight. If this war were characterized by destroyed everyday life, bleeding and dying bodies, it would hardly be a question that one simply has to get down to it. And the one would appear very obviously as selfish and irresponsible, who instead would rather continue to strive for a private island, as beautiful as possible, at least as long as one's own life is not endangered. But this war, which fundamentally shapes the biblical understanding of the world, is different—more veiled, more under the surface—which often makes it difficult to perceive its meaning and effect and one's responsibility in it; but it is real nonetheless. It is a battle for hearts, for souls. People hurt and are hurt, but seek healing in the wrong places and through ineffective means. People lose themselves and their future because they put their faith in the perishable instead of the imperishable; in their own spirit, the spirit of the times or other spirits, but not in the Holy Spirit.

Wherever senselessness, indifference, dullness, greed, envy, hatred, coldness, mercilessness, egocentricity, and bitterness, are sown, tolerated or developed, there are also devilish powers at work in the background. The followers of Jesus, like him, should stand up to them.

"Repent!"
December 15, 2019

Advent. Time to reflect on John the Baptist. "Repent!" Guilt—is that really still the key question today?

For a long time, it seemed to me that this question, which very much characterizes the church liturgy, for example, was rather remote from everyday life. And in people's minds, too, other questions seem to be in the foreground; above all: Why does God allow so much suffering? But haven't we perhaps simply lost the view of interrelationships that our ancestors still had? What is the basis of the increasing coldness, narcissism and aggressiveness in our society and worldwide? Evil does not depend only on the few "big ones" at the levers of power. It is also the many "little ones" who have given up, who join in, who do not resist, who look for their salvation in the wrong places and do not want to start counteracting before "the others" effectively get their act together. The "big" sins of the "big ones" are weighted much higher than the mostly "harmless" small ones of our own—a fatal misjudgment. The climate in our society, which many now experience as so oppressive, has not experienced a "temperature drop" from one day to the next. Cohesion was not broken up with a jackhammer, but slowly began to crumble. Something wasn't just imposed on us from the outside; rather, there are countless insidious little developments and decisions that have led to this over the years. Many wrong or not taken decisions of many individuals have become attitudes—and are now shaping the next generations.

And when I see that even there, where for example climate protection is finally increasingly recognized as actually necessary, it should still happen in such a way that we, please, do not have to change our lifestyle, then guilt is still partly responsible for the misery of the world.

On the internet I just came across a "small" example of how we owe our apparently quite harmless joy to the exploitation of others: Christmas star growing in Uganda. Also, the description of garbage people in the slums of Manila in the book I am reading is just creepy. This is not a natural disaster. There's greed, thoughtlessness, lack of respect, at work. Yes, repent.

A Faith Infection
March 30, 2020

Experience: It makes a difference whether I think about Jesus or in front of him, in conversation with him; whether I formulate something as concise lecture sentences or the same contents as a prayer.

What exactly can "speaking hope into" mean in situations like Bergamo, Italy, where one cannot keep up with the burial of those who died of coronavirus? Or in the hopelessly overcrowded refugee camps on Lesbos? That suddenly everything will be fine? No.

Protection from collapse? From contagion? None of this is known.

But: not being alone; that it's not the end; not out of control, even if it looks otherwise. This life is not everything.

Therefore, infect as many as possible with faith, love, hope—as far as the feet carry. This is not in vain.

Low-threshold invitations to faith that first off minimize the importance of worship and congregation in order to prevent reflexive defensive reactions ("I'm not a churchgoer") are not helpful. Church is a chance to encounter this God, on several levels. It would be better to communicate this. Life in the congregation is not a luxury, but necessary, among other things because God also wants to speak in this process and through the people in whom God lives—not necessarily in the sense of sermons or prophetic words, but also through what is initiated in these processes.

Hope in the biblical sense: Not to suppose, to consider possible or probable, but to reckon with God's action and therefore even now willingly to abandon myself and my fear; anticipating, inaugurating the future, so to speak, by concentrating on the present. That is freedom.

All Remains Grace
April 25, 2020

The current coronavirus crisis shows us how little we have under control and how many things are now so interconnected, even globally, that they inevitably follow the domino principle. That alone is a challenge. Enemy No. 1: It makes a difference whether I, as a coastal dweller, see a storm tide coming towards me or a tsunami. No wonder it is frightening.

"Nothing will be the same again," the new time calculation: before coronavirus/after coronavirus—all this is deeply unsettling. And we can't distract ourselves, but are constantly pushed by the quarantine on all levels to the changed reality, which at the same time outwardly seems so contradictorily unchanged. There is no debris around us as after a bombing, no fallen trees and covered houses as after a tornado, no overflowing cellars as after a heavy rain. The enemy that is causing all this is tiny and invisible. But highly effective. Insane.

So all this is in itself a completely understandable and justified reason for a comprehensive destabilization.

But I believe that for us as Christians there can be added another important point.

The degree of this insecurity is in itself another source of insecurity. We realize how little we can trust in our trust. We would not be so deeply insecure if our trust in God were really as unshakeable as we feel and imagine in better times—when medical care functions normally, the social network can be regarded as reliably financed, unemployment affects relatively few, economic slumps are not immediately existence-threatening, and on and on and on.

So basically, it is now becoming clearer what our trust is actually based on (namely, the visible "tangible" human safeguards, the number of available intensive care beds, etc.), even if our pious wish still says otherwise. And this self-awareness can give us a good shake. Because this is actually red alert; after all, our faith is actually our life's foundation, anchor, which should be able to carry us through. But the truth is: Often we do not believe, but believe in our faith. We *want* to believe.

Admitting to myself that my faith is wavering (or more accurately, proving not to be as firmly internalized and fleshed out as I wish and hoped) is appropriately frightening. This is enemy No. 2, and one that is generally little talked about, especially in our more pious circles, and which we are correspondingly little practiced in dealing with. And that's why we tend to close our eyes to it and not deal with it. Of course, we assure each other how good it is to know that God does not lose control; how good it is to be able to pray, and the like. But where and who can we share without shame and "just" bear with each other that these thoughts, as right as they are, still don't even work like a chill pill that takes away or, more accurately, numbs the fears? And that this is scary and needs treatment and healing—but however and whenever that might be going on? All of which many feel more than they can think or express, I think.

But the chance is that it is ultimately Jesus who reveals this truth to us. The chance is to learn to recognize that in the deepest sense it is not our faith that saves us (in the sense of a certain quality or intensity), but Jesus. It all remains grace.

Among other things, there is a deep comfort for me in Jesus's promise to Peter after Easter: "When you were younger … but when you are old you will stretch out your hands, and someone else will dress you and lead you *where you do not want to go.*" (John 21:18) That is, Jesus predicts to him that Peter will agree to a way with which, at the same time, he will struggle inwardly even then. And this is not a disappointment for Jesus. Jesus will bring him through.

A Candle in Deep Darkness
May 3, 2020

Inspired by a Facebook post.

"God is still in control!"

This is what Christians around the world are remembering in these difficult times. But some also react to it with very mixed feelings; because the sentence somehow sounds too full-bodied; or because it remains unclear what that means in terms of content, when pain and death obviously cannot simply be "believed away," "prayed away" by it; or because it almost inevitably brings the next (and very difficult) problem to the foreground: If this is so, but God obviously does not eliminate suffering, although he could—then the question arises what is meant by God's love.

I can therefore understand very well when resistance arises against such strong words. And for a long time I have therefore often hesitated to speak them. But more and more I try to concentrate on the biblical view instead of the possible misunderstandings and wrong conclusions. The sentence makes sense, even if the details are still hidden for us, nevertheless it is rooted in reality. At present, it is true, we know better what it does not mean than what it does mean; and that is why it is important to point this out explicitly in pastoral contexts, so as not to provoke expressed or tacit cynical reactions and also to counteract from the outset possible false expectations and corresponding disappointments. God's ways remain mysterious and often very painful. Most of us know this more than we would like.

But still, I try to hold on to the phrase; as a deliberately stubborn, defiant commitment to truth in the face of the forces of chaos and evil, grounded in the character and promises of God. The day will come when we will recognize how the Almighty has woven good out of evil, and when we will all celebrate that it is not chaos that will have the last word, but will turn out to be the loser. And in experiences with myself as well as others, this perspective has often proven to be a source of hope, or at least a help in not losing hope completely in life circumstances that are just truly exasperating and leave us with overwhelming feelings of helplessness. Just yesterday again I was talking to someone in such a situation, and it was helpful to reassure each other of this truth.

This is far from a button to turn off the pain. But it is a candle in deep darkness that helps to go on—step by step.

Biblical Realism and Jesus's Promise
May 27, 2020

The Bible says Jesus loves me.

And I know that. But he is silent.

He accepts me; I know that too; but he doesn't seem to change me fundamentally anymore, to work on my negative side.

He sees my longing and helplessness, but shows no steps, perspectives.

What should I do with it? How to find peace? Is my lack of peace perhaps an indication that I have seen or overlooked something fundamentally wrong so far, that I have lost my way and am therefore searching in the wrong directions? I don't know.

In any case it makes me ragged to have the impression that I'm predominantly killing time somehow (with simultaneous fear of activities that involve confession, testimony, taking responsibility).

After I wrote down these thoughts of last night and tonight here, I spontaneously called up the website of the parish of Hille; someone had told me the day before that daily short impulses can be found there as well, better and richer in content than the version of the church district. I open the first video; someone from the congregation has chosen as the text basis his wedding-verse, Psalm 119:105. God will give light, even if we are perhaps in a tunnel.

Someone else was still talking today, using concrete examples, about how in some situations it's just not possible to "think positively"; it just sucks. This is exactly biblical realism. In the dark valley, the sun is not simply turned on for Christians. Moving from pasture to pasture doesn't suddenly become a wellness experience at some point with a comfortable luxury van. The promise to Paul to survive the shipwreck does not spare him storm, waves, wetness, cold, and fear. There cannot arise joy, light-heartedness, ease. It can only and must be endured.

Is the call to give thanks in such situations then exposed? Or cynicism? Probably not. But what does it serve then?

And what helps to bear?

In any case, there is always one point: Jesus's promise never to leave us alone.

Faithfully Letting Go
June 23, 2020

"Letting go" is an expression that at first sounds rather negative: more like "giving up" out of resignation and pressure than voluntarily "devoting"; more like being defeated than being convinced, more like surrender than agreement; more like clenched fists or clenched teeth than actively extended hands.

Consciously adding the concept of faithfulness could therefore be helpful as a motivation to persevere and endure. In this way, I can better orient myself to God's example, who remains faithful to us in patience, who tirelessly continues to stay by our side even when we make him tired, who turns to us even when we keep turning and turning away, who pursues us even when we fall short of how we should live. God also sighs ("How much longer?" How many times have I ...?). But he remains faithful.

This is what I want to try to hold up to my tiredness and when I am fed up with life. And to do this, I will consciously look for words and stories that reflect this faithfulness and that can be memorized ("He loved them to the end" is also one of them, cf. ch.1, April 13, 2015).

"Lord, help me to faithfully embody what I am convinced of, even and especially when I miss it in others."

Longing Grows
August 18, 2020

Growing spiritually—what can that mean? (Prompted by thinking about possible topics for sermon in autumn.)

What would I be able to say? What would people possibly expect?

I have studied

I am over 60, so I have reached senior age

Certainly, I know by now a bit how to become an adult.
Really? No, it's not that simple.
Or exactly that—very simple?
Namely: Sharing life, joy and hardship with Jesus, as if I see the one at my side that I don't see.

In which areas is growth even possible?

Knowledge, recognition of connections, wrong ways, helpful strategies. Bible knowledge.

Love, more permanent or deeper awareness of Jesus's nearness; living within the larger horizon.

Trust.

Internalizing his character, radiating himself.

More quickly and routinely perceive pitfalls, make decisions.

Become more sensitive, compassionate (which is exhausting!).

However, challenges remain!

Mountain and valley hike (peaks are the rarer part), not continuous ridgeway!

And strength decreases. This can also make it more difficult to cope with the challenges.

So be realistically prepared for the fact that the problems do not simply become less or easier with higher age!

But longing grows.

Help Is Reliable
September 5, 2020

Again and again I am overcome by insecurity, paralysis, with what right can I talk to others about faith if I have to struggle so much in my own life to find a foothold in it? (A variation on the question of how I can preach when I myself have doubts, where Hans Peter Royer counters: The truth does not become true only through my faith, and it will prove itself in the lives of those who engage in it.)[23] Once again via ferrata: the ropes, tread nails, ladders are firm, reliable, yet I need strength to hold on to them. If this is difficult for me, for whatever reason, it doesn't mean that others have to feel the same way. In any case, the aids exist and remain reliable, and I can give information about that.

Expect Lifelong Sensitivity
November 11, 2020

Our body has individual weak points.

So does our soul.

This means: We must expect lifelong sensitivity in these areas. And they are the gateway for temptations. Paul's "thorn in the flesh" (2 Corinthians 12:7) could fit here.

The Basics Again and Again
November 21, 2020

Bible reading yesterday: Beginning with 2 Peter 1:5: "make every effort," then enumeration: virtue, knowledge, self-control or continence, perseverance, fear of God, brotherly love, charity.

Reflection: To formulate short impulses on virtues!

They don't come upon us like soothing summer rainstorms. Need of training. Struggle.

And not a kind of voluntary exercise, but obedience. Loyalty.

Doesn't that quickly amount to legalism, righteousness because of works?

No. Not already the call for effort or exertion is "unevangelical"—that would be the wrong label.

Whether something is legalistic or not depends on the motivation.

This becomes clear again and again in all the epistles. The apostles are not afraid of imperatives. From the repeatedly mentioned basis of salvation, the logical consequence arises again and again to now lead a holy life with all one's strength.

More examples of possible "label fraud" or language confusion in order to avoid arguments:

- legalistic
- intolerant
- phobic

Peter repeats himself consciously, knows about the necessity of remembering, even if it is about what is actually known. This reminds me of the experience of the past months, how quickly (sometimes already on the same day!) we forget in the meantime what someone has said in a sermon. Rather, the overall impressions remain, but rarely more. However, from this should not be deduced that the effort of sermons could be more or less futile; rather one should consciously and without shyness include the basics in sermons again and again.

Fight *for* Jesus
November 25, 2020

Two calls from people who have to cope with really heavy things and share this as a prayer request, so as not to be overwhelmed by it.

I realize that when I pray against bitterness, anger, despair or whatever pain I throw at Jesus's feet, I am still very much occupied with it, my gaze is focused on it, and I am often paralyzed, tied up by it. Therefore, I must also look beyond all that at Jesus's character, at his nature, at his love, his grace, his power, at the way he actually intended the world (and how I would like it to be). I need a positive counterweight, so that I do not only pray against something in me or the other, but fight *for* Jesus.

The following questions can also help: What hurts Jesus in this or that situation? Am I willing to share his pain as long as no other clear mandate arises? It may sound strange, but I have noticed with myself that it somehow makes a difference whether I ask Jesus to carry my pain or whether I tell him that I am willing to carry his. Mathematically it comes to the same result: two carry together; and yet it feels different. I then see myself more as someone who submits to Jesus's big plan with less clenched teeth and less clenched fists.

Grace and Knowledge
November 26, 2020

Grow: It's formulated as a call in 2 Peter 3:14–18. (see the previous entry!). The imperative makes it clear that one's own effort is part of it, and does not happen automatically, passively so to speak, as in organic growth. We are involved in the process through healthy nutrition, e.g., 1 Peter 2:1.

Grow in what? "In the grace and knowledge of our Lord and Savior Jesus Christ," 3:18; and 1:2, "Grace and peace ... through the knowledge of God and of Jesus our Lord"; likewise 1:3, everything necessary for life given through knowledge of Jesus; knowledge is proved by holy life (1:8). Looking to Jesus is the source of life.

Verse 13: Righteousness is not a characteristic of this world, but only of the new one. Interesting: The conclusion from this, however, is not passive waiting, but already actively adjusting to it in one's own life, practicing it.

"Immaculate"—how much do small stains on our clothes already annoy us. What about our soul?

Knowledge: There is the useless knowledge, empty theories, and in contrast to it the knowledge of Jesus, which has to do with personal encounter, lives from it.

Growing in Honesty
December 11, 2020

In the aftermath of a pastoral counseling conversation: Growing in faith—what comes to mind, what do I associate with it? Brainstorming:

- John the Baptist on Jesus: "He must become greater; I must become less." (John 3:30)
- Tree: grows stronger, bigger, bears more fruit if all goes well. So it is with the branches on the vine and the ears of corn in the field.
- The mustard seed shall become a tree.
- Our knowledge should increase; babies in faith should grow into adults with the appropriate foresight and depth, who can tolerate not only beginner's food, but solid food.
- Our hearts are to become firmer, less and less fickle and ambivalent.
- The disciples were fickle and sometimes cowardly, yes, but after Pentecost everything was different; they were even ready for martyrdom.

So this is how it should be in the life of a Christian. Going upward. Forward. And that is what we long for, at least in our good moments and phases.

In addition, the older we get, the more we have read the Bible, listened to sermons, heard about the experiences of other Christians, and exchanged ideas with brothers and sisters in the faith.

So our life of faith should actually become better, firmer, easier with time? And if it is not so or if we still stumble unexpectedly and badly in corresponding challenges, then it is a bit embarrassing. Or very embarrassing. And also frightening. What if things seem to be getting harder rather than better for us, even though we have actually been Christians for 60, 70 years or more? What if, when we read the Bible, not everything becomes more and more familiar and understandable to us, but if we make strange discoveries that rub us the wrong way, that raise questions, that drive us around and perhaps lead us into doubt? And what if we are gripped by the fear that this might not get better in time before we die?

What if we sit in worship, in full-bodied praise, and find ourselves thinking that the fire of our beginning faith has actually become a smoldering pile of ashes, and faith more routine than enthusiasm?

And then the question arises: How are the others doing? We are used to sharing prayer requests regarding problems in daily life like illnesses, job, etc.; maybe also positive experiences here and there—but crises of faith? Rather not.

Conclusion: We need honest exchange among ourselves. An atmosphere in which people dare to be weak (because that's how it is in real life) and help each other.

God's Maturing Times
December 29, 2020

I think about the hymn of praise of Simeon and Hannah, Luke 2:25–38.

At the beginning of the birth story there was the angel with statements about the glorious ruler; now at the end here, statements foreshadow that there will be complications, that it will get hard, connected with seemingly deadly pain for Mary. How this is to be brought in line (Mary could ask herself, for example, whether Simeon might not have been mistaken?)—Mary will not be able to make sense of it. Only in retrospect can it become clear that we are dealing here with two poles of an ellipse. Mary receives the prediction and the blessing as a kind of preparation; also the confirmation of Simeon by Hannah will be a help (two witnesses, biblical principle: Deuteronomy

19:15). But for a time that does not begin until 30 years later, when Mary is probably between 45 and 50 years old.

Long times of waiting. From God's perspective: maturing times. Again and again. For individuals as well as for nations.

And aids for waiting. But they are very strange. Literally noteworthy; yet so unimpressive. Only words. (Even the blessing, in its manifestation, is at first only words). But words that will prove true when the time is right. And Hannah is a model of faithful eager expectation—to the ripe old age of 84 she serves God "day and night"; lives in the present with all hope of the future. For most of her life she has had no sign of the coming of him for whom she waits.

Jesus in the Everyday
January 10, 2021

I ask myself: In what way exactly does the relationship with Jesus make everyday life, as it is, worth living or "satisfying"?

One help could be to imagine as concretely as possible what exactly would change in eating, drinking, working, marriage, free time, friends, if Jesus were a figment of our imagination? Go through a concrete day of the week.

If we do not find Jesus in the very everyday life we experience, then we would most likely not find him in the everyday life we dream of. This is likely to be illusion.

If we do not find Jesus in our difficult and adverse life circumstances, then we would have even more difficulties to find him when things were going smoothly and we were doing well. (In any case, experience shows that in such good times we tend to drift through our life rather than that the good things bring us into all the more intense relationship with Jesus.) He wants to be with the lonely, the imprisoned, the sick, those who are brokenhearted, those who need him—both those who know and long for it and those who do not yet know it; and thus also with us when life becomes difficult for us or others make it difficult for us.

In addition: The only time we can shape is the present. We can do this by learning to relate everything to the Lord of our lives and to this given time. Aldous Huxley said, "Experience is not what happens to you. Experience is what you make of what happens to you." Someone else has said, in the context of the coronavirus period, "Fear asks, 'How can I get out of here?' Love asks, 'How can I be a light here in this situation?'"

But what does that look like in concrete terms: Wanting to find Jesus in my everyday life? It can really only mean wanting to learn to look at every situation from God's point of view and to respond to it as best we can according to his will.

If we are not at peace, "in agreement" with our life, in our eyes it is usually the fault of other people or circumstances; and if what we think we can legitimately claim, we think it is legitimate to bathe in self-pity (often disguised as "simply justified anger about impossible conditions" or the like). In actual fact, this is ultimately unbelief and ingratitude, nothing else.

Because: For followers life worth living does not mean a life free of suffering. If this longing paralyzes us instead of motivating us, this can be a traitorous indication that we have not given up our self-determination after all, that we do not subordinate ourselves to a placement from God, but want to have more the bodyguard than the master.

Israel grumbled, disciples grumbled, Jews grumbled. All had their reasons. (In the German fairy tale of the fisherman and his wife, having reached one goal does not bring satisfaction but triggers next longing.) Jesus, would have had every reason to grumble, too. About people, about the disciples, about loneliness, about the lack of understanding of the family, of the neighbors.

But he did not grumble.

Some passages on grumbling:
- Exodus 16
- Genesis 14:27, 36
- Deuteronomy 17:20–25
- Isaiah 29:24 (opposite of grumbling: accept instruction!)
- John 6:41–61
- Philippians 2:14
- 1 Peter 4:9
- Jude 1:16

On grumbling see also already: January 16, 2018 in this chapter.

To pick up on the church father Brother Lawrence regarding the attitude to his workplace and to transfer this to my housework, which is often perceived as annoying and troublesome:

To possess something (and even more so: so much!) is challenge to gratitude. And to marvel at the diversity of human ideas.

To "have" to care for possessions is a thought-provoking impulse anchored in everyday life and a challenge to reflect on the ability to care—what our body can do. So an impulse to give thanks.

So really everything even seemingly inconspicuous or even annoying can become a conversation starter with our Creator.

Repetition: Paradise: joy in God and the world. Through the fall (at least) two things have fundamentally changed. God's nearness can no longer be experienced so immediately and unclouded; and we are challenged to share not only his joy, but also his suffering and struggle for this world and us as part of it.

Daily Dependency
February 13, 2021

Emotionally stable feels different than the last two days and nights. Quite a few ups and downs; at least I slept reasonably peacefully again last night.

While looking for strategies to deal with this, I realize: On the one hand, it is helpful and necessary to be able to recall clear decisions regarding useless, unhealthy mind games (in the sense of: "Wait a minute, we've been through this before; don't get involved if possible, don't question everything again!"). But on the other hand, it is an illusion to conclude from this that there might even be sentences or insights that, if I found them, would be effective once-for-all weapons of destruction. There's no point in deluding ourselves; we can't get out of daily dependency, and the greater security is not in having seemingly final clarity, but in the experience of being guided through the struggles, of being able to emerge again when I get caught by an inner vortex.

Tempted as We Are
February 17, 2021

"We have ... a high priest ... who has been tempted in every way, just as we are—yet he did not sin.." (Hebrews 4:15)

No, actually Jesus was tempted even more. In his case the angels came only afterwards. In our case he himself is always there. Our temptations are always accompanied by his support. Temptation is always about different kinds of trust: What counts for living and dying? Who is reliable? Who can provide? Who is in charge?

Worth It for Eternity
April 2, 2021

Good Friday. How would I have reacted under the cross? Knowing me, I would probably have given up in despair in the face of the superiority of evil.

What helped Mary not to give up? The words at the birth of Jesus ("a sword will also pierce through your heart," Luke 2:35) were far from unambiguous, but on the other hand pointed the direction enough not to be caught completely unaware.

The disciples did have Jesus announcements of suffering; but how completely different resurrection would reach into their reality this time was beyond imagination. And apparently they dared to inquire of Jesus after that only to a limited extent.

Jesus had in mind all his life what would happen—disappointment, incomprehension, betrayal, loneliness, torture, baseless slander. He persevered—also for me. Also for our loved ones. And ultimately for the whole world. We were worth it to him. We *are* worth it to him. Worth it for an eternity together. He has put in so much—and sometimes life becomes too tedious for me, for others, for the congregation, for Christianity in general, because things don't work out the way I dreamed they would? Rebellion can also be disguised piously, and still rebellion and mistrust remain. The original sin. Somehow I cannot, will not, believe him in the end that my life makes sense, just because I don't see that right now! This is the trap: Only through my point of view waiting becomes an imposition, namely, when I lose sight of what it has cost Jesus. For this blindness works against the trust that he cannot be indifferent to what hurts me and all of us, to what is lacking, takes away strength and courage or whatever burdens us—because that is exactly why he went this way, to declare war on evil.

An earlier entry keeps coming back to my mind, which was about the challenge:
- to believe in meaning where none is (yet!) to be seen
- to hold on to hope where all circumstances speak against it for a long and indefinite time
- to believe in his nearness, even when nothing can be felt
- to actively count on his truth, even if almost the whole world is against it—not knowing what it wants instead, but very sure that it does *not* want *this* truth.

And finally, a missionary newsletter also came today, with a devotional along the same lines. Heavenly nudging.

Mystery, Certainty, Knowledge
April 5, 2021

I started reading the Gospel of Luke with the commentary of A. Schlatter beside it; then turned briefly to his book *Hülfe in Bibelnot*, to the section on the Christmas story. In his typical way, Schlatter writes about the mystery that characterizes the work of God:

God's creation always proceeds in silence, so that no eye penetrates into the miracle of becoming. This was as certain to the evangelists as it is to us. That is why both Gospels are completely clean of pert theories about the way in which Jesus came into being in Mary. They speak of the miracle in the birth of Jesus in the same way as Jesus himself spoke of the miraculous nature of his life. When he spoke of his Father, he did not explain the way in which his life had its origin in God; therefore, however, his unity with God was not for him a dark mystery, not something he merely thought, wished, and hoped for, but with luminous certainty he knew that his life had its ground in God. The miracle that created him was evident to him in the fact of his life.[24]

What struck me about it is that the word *mystery* is associated with the word *certainty*, not with *knowledge* (which is analytically gained and can be expounded). Which, yes, usually upsets me, because I would like to know—as precisely as possible. But I become aware: Certainty can be the more adequate experience of reality, because reality is larger than our ability to know, which is limited to this dimension. Certainty can be based on wishful thinking, imagination, but it can also be based on reality. And then it provides a larger, more stable foundation than knowledge. Knowledge can have its justification and meaning as a subset of certainty; but certainty can be the more reliable concept, not less, can grasp more of reality, not less.

With regard to the prophecies of the prophets and the poetic element in them, Schlatter pursued a similarly helpful approach to thinking:

> We must get used to the fact—and this is no loss—that God is concerned with our heart, with the decisive central process of our life; he wants to give you and me a hope, not a theory. ... A thought that reaches into the future inevitably transcends the conditions of our cognition. Our cognition is necessarily bound to the state of life prepared for us, to that which flows to us as experience. But we can think beyond these limits of our knowledge, and we should. All that which we call poetry detaches itself from perception, transcends the state of consciousness and life that is factually given to us, looks out to the future and lets a promise shine before us. ... The prophet becomes a poet, and he must be, because he looks into the future.[25]

This helps me to make sense of the confusion of biblical prophecy that usually frustrates me so much.

Only in Crises
April 10, 2021

A shock news from yesterday still sits in my bones. (A case of child cancer, in the same family, though now in the next generation.)

Do I believe God's love, even if I cannot yet understand his self-restraint, which often appears as powerlessness, as part of his love? Do I trust his character, his word? Only in crises will be revealed what is going on in the depths of my heart and mind, only in situations that provoke my reluctance and thus challenge my decisions. I can wish as much as I want that it should work differently. But this is theory, not reality. Reality, the reality of experience, is that crises can do us this service rather than positive experiences. That is and remains very painful. But in this way we can at least gain something helpful from even agonizing situations and the resulting, but unsolvable questions.

Course Corrections
April 13, 2021

I think again about an impulse regarding Abraham and Isaac from a conversation yesterday, and go along biblical persons; a red thread: God gives someone his word, by it meets or awakens expectations and ideas, but then regularly thwarts them through the concrete course of life, corrects them. "First, things turn out differently, second, from what you think ..." (German idiom). Examples abound, with regard to individuals as well as the whole people (Israel, for example, had certainly imagined life differently after the Exodus).

And: Abraham is not the only parent who is explicitly entrusted with children and yet is also in some ways deprived of them. Isaac certainly had other hopes for his family life than strife and deceit. The same with Jacob—how he got his wives, what became of his children and so on. David certainly did not imagine the way to kingship as a 25-year struggle, and he certainly did not want his family life to develop the way it did, marked by deadly quarrels. Elizabeth and Zacharias, parents of John the Baptist. (Not sure if they lived to see their son's execution.) And Mary.

To name but a few.

We remain, in a sense, "surrogate parents"—preparing children for a life journey of which we ultimately know very little. We remain confronted throughout life with the tension of loving with all our heart (and therefore longing for closeness and understanding) and yet, for that very reason, truly letting go.

This reflects somewhat how God deals with us; he gives his life for us, and yet he leaves us free space, does not, as a rule, simply force us irresistibly into his plans.

From Pasture to Pasture
July 20, 2021

After a night emergency phone call, Psalm 23 crossed my mind as I searched for something encouraging: "I shall not want." That is something of a heading, after all. (Keeping in mind: it's all about the necessities of life when it comes to grazing.)

But: David *knew* lack. He was not naive.

It took 25 (!) years after God's first call to kingship, that is, after David's anointing by the prophet Samuel, before he actually became king—years filled with persecution, intrigue, loneliness, struggles.

His family later developed into a catastrophe; women's problems; sons who were bitterly at odds with each other over the succession to the throne, up to fratricide; who tried to overthrow the father; and much more.

So what could he have meant by "not want" or "no lack"?

A pastor's advice a few years ago was helpful. *When we* move sheep from pasture to pasture, we move the fence to the neighboring area next to the grazed one or put the animals in a trailer and move them to the next pasture. (Both happened regularly in Minden on the pasture next to our property.) This is done quickly and with little stress. However, when pastures are changed in Israel, this often means longer strenuous hikes through arid terrain ("valley of the shadow of death" is very realistic!), because green areas are not the normal landscape, but rather the exception.

In other words, a good shepherd was not someone who managed to spare his animals the experience of difficulties completely, but someone who could be relied upon to know his way around and, if necessary at the risk of his own life, would spare no effort and danger to lead his animals safely from one place to another. But it was clear that along the way there would be many a thirsty stretch and danger and possibly also accidents or illnesses to get through. And many an animal would also have to be carried at times.

This is how the psalm makes sense to me. David *has* experienced that God has kept his word and remained faithful through all the ups and downs of his life (which David certainly did not imagine at the beginning). And we too can count on this experience with our good shepherd, Jesus. He will bring us to the goal of eternity. The fact that the paths from pasture to pasture are often very arduous until then does not speak against the Good Shepherd. Our hope in him is justified; he has already proven it by the risk of his life. And the view of his character, his love and faithfulness is therefore the source from which our hope can be fed with good reason.

A Backpack of Promise
September 8, 2021

What does Jesus promise? "I am with you." Not, "I will solve all your problems …"

Tears will be counted and wiped away in eternity (Revelation 21)—then in person, but not before.

Andreas told me that he was looking for a vivid image of what Jesus's help can look like when heavy burdens weigh us down; a backpack came to his mind: "Jesus holds his hand under it, invisible but supporting, carrying."

I have continued to think about it and find the image very realistic. It picks up that I continue to feel the weight, which makes the question possible and understandable whether Jesus is really there and helps. But it also means: how heavy the load really is, I would only know if the hand was pulled off. Strictly speaking, therefore, I often do not *experience* the support; only when a burden unexpectedly becomes lighter or heavier for me, although it has remained the same in itself. A third possible case: If the load actually becomes bigger, but this bigger is absorbed in parallel by likewise growing invisible support, I do not recognize the intervention at all. I do not *experience* the help in the sense of noticeable relief. To interpret correctly what I experience is not as easy as it may seem at first sight. Jesus's action takes place on levels which are not directly visible, tangible for me, but hidden, invisible. therefore it is factually completely appropriate, unavoidable that we are challenged to (possible) trust in Jesus's promise and not to the (ultimately impossible) analysis of how he implements his help in detail.

Staying Under during Normality
October 16, 2021

Kind of a bad day. Sometimes it's just like an inevitable giant wave suddenly crashes over me.

But: The problems that trouble me—they are actually nothing unusual. They are rather those that most people have to deal with, "normality" (here and even more so worldwide), even if it is rarely talked about openly. Anything even remotely completely healed is the exception.

To what extent can faith help me at all?

Not through stoic calm.

Not by providing effective tools or methods that can make a change and be called up at any time.

Not by superpowers, supernatural know-how.

Prayer is not a shortcut either.

But: Through hope in a greater Lord and his will and his possibilities to work on others and on me.

Through strength and motivation to refrain from manipulation and bitterness and fighting back until then.

Through endurance. (The Greek word *hypomone* = patience = "staying under.")

None of this works every time or consistently. But sometimes, anyway.

And that's actually a lot. Because every time it succeeds, further land gains of the evil one are prevented. But it's no wonder that this also makes you tired. It feels as if you're fighting with all your might from the inside against the gate of a castle, which is being worked on from the outside by enemies with a battering ram.

Loosening the Fingers
October 17, 2021

Continuation from yesterday: today's watchword fits the theme of resisting, enduring.

"He was oppressed and afflicted, yet he did not open his mouth; he was led like a lamb to the slaughter, and as a sheep before its shearers is silent, so he did not open his mouth." (Isaiah 53:7)

"When they hurled their insults at him, he did not retaliate; when he suffered, he made no threats. Instead, he entrusted himself to him who judges justly." (1 Peter 2:23)

I may and must let go of the fear of wrong perspectives, decisions, resulting attitudes into Jesus's hands. Many things in life can be revised (even if not made up for); wrong interpretations can be corrected; mistakes—if they really are—do not inevitably have to mean only disastrous catastrophes.

Everyone is bound to make mistakes; we can't escape it. So it applies to me, too.

Waiting time is perhaps also time in which Jesus gently tries to loosen the fingers that are trying to hold on to something inappropriately. The devil, on the contrary, tries everything to prevent exactly that by endless evil variants of "head cinema."

Happiness, Waiting and Watching
November 7, 2021

At the beginning of the service, the Beatitudes were read. Once again I noticed:

Happiness here is understood *very* differently than our normal spontaneous ideas, once again "Get used to different" (the German subtitle of the new American series of Jesus's life, "The Chosen").

It is predominantly in the future; experiences of lack are described as given, partly even reinforced by faith as justified longing; relief is only promised for the future. Until then the challenge is to persevere faithfully.

What vision do we have or do we present to others when it comes to invitation to turn and join God's kingdom? Something like Tolkien's

Shire in times of peace (*Lord of the Rings* novel trilogy)? Or something else?

What went through my mind during Lord's Supper:

Jesus abstains from wine until the reunion with his disciples.

He is filled with anticipation, longing.

This will not be different for us. It connects us with Jesus.

A feeling of faith, of life without these elements would, on the other hand, deny this part of his participation in the suffering of this world to a certain degree, would want to avoid it.

Once again the old terms of the reformers: Jesus stands for the theology of the cross, enthusiasts for the theology of glory; they want more than is now possible and good: to bring perfection into this time already ahead of time.

The word *faithfulness* keeps me thinking. Faithfulness means to keep hope and longing alive, and at the same time to renounce pressure—like the waiting and watching father in Luke 15.

Overcome Evil with Good?

December 22, 2021

"Overcome evil with good" (Romans 12:21).

This attitude implies the possibility of winning over evil, of moving it over to the good side. But this can also subconsciously give rise to a false expectation that this *will* work sooner or later. Because that *can* happen, to be sure. Example Zacchaeus (Luke 19:1–10) and others.

But it can also mean: Simply to stubbornly resist the attempts of the evil one (who is ultimately behind the hostile person) who tempts us to evil reactions and thereby wants to drag us over to the opposite side; and not to fall for this tactic, that too is already a victory! And to unmask, to expose, to highlight the evil in any case.

But both can also cost the price of self-sacrifice (up to martyrdom) and thus—purely humanly seen—look like failure, like *not* overcoming the evil.

"If only I behave well enough, if I am as good an example as possible, then sooner or later I will win over the opponent" is in any case a devilish trap that loads more responsibility on us than we have and can bear. Even Jesus did not win them all.

This is especially important when it comes to relationships, where the hope of success and healing and the longing for togetherness fuel our motivation all the more and thus, in parallel, make our feeling of powerlessness more bearable. But we have the task of acting, but not of success; conversely, we cannot simply infer our failure where success is absent—that would be a misleading simplification. We are sinners, unlike Jesus, so certainly complicity can also play a role in our case; but nevertheless, the trap described remains a trap.

Longing for Well-being
January 22, 2022

Yesterday, a visit to a retirement home.

Very old, on the way to 100. "I always said, 'God, do what you want with me, but please don't let me go blind.'" But that's exactly what it gradually came to. Sun, the beauties of nature, the birthday flowers on the table in the room—everything is now in the dark.

How would I deal with such a situation? Joy is a basic need of life, but how is it still possible in such a phase of life (apart from the joy of unexpected visitors, like us, which is absolutely rare)? Especially since most of the houses of life from one's own age group have long since been demolished around you and you can see from the younger generations how many houses are cracking and crumbling.

The longing for well-being, for beauty is there after all. But the experience of it seems to lie in more or less distant past. Unless I can take these memories as a pledge for what the future still holds in store, and then, moreover, finally in the longed-for perfection. But for this I must be certain enough of the presence of my invisible counterpart and Lord—that his eyes will remain lovingly, attentively and caringly fixed on me even in this transitional phase which seems so long, impoverished and arduous.

This relationship is and remains the vital artery, it must remain the center of my life or become that anew again and again. And even if I can no longer see, I can usually still hear (or vice versa), and still fill my soul with good stories and impulses. It makes sense to train appropriate routines consciously and in time. How many people, for example, have been blessed by the Christian radio broadcast! Hearing about present experiences of others helps not to doubt one's own past experiences, but to keep the sense of reality—which includes more than what is just happening or missing in one's own life.

I remember what I photographed at the U. S. Olympic and Paralympics Museum in Colorado Springs: "We're all only able-bodied temporarily. Sooner or later everyone's body breaks down. That puts me ahead of the game because I already know how to live with part of me being out of order." (Candace Cable)

Clarity on the Time Line
February 2, 2022

Question: What distinguishes Christian letting go from fatalism and resignation? Response:

I still hold on to a Lord superior to us humans, whose love and wealth of ideas are infinite and dynamic, which is why a basic expectant attitude makes sense; hope for a future that is still open. I try to give up too concrete or fixed ideas about it; but my hope is still directed to experience sooner or later the positive attention of this Lord, which is just not dependent on the details of my limited dreams, but can turn out to be different and nevertheless real.

Fatalism, on the other hand, doesn't really dare to hope, and resignation is backwards anyway.

On Bonhoeffer in general: With the audio book of Metaxas's Bonhoeffer biography, it became clear to me how ready for print Bonhoeffer usually expressed himself, but also how he sometimes thought off the top of his head, still in a fragmentary way—and yet already aloud, in order to stimulate joint reflection, to put others on a track. Both have their justification. Particularly since not even what appears clear to *us* at a certain moment on the time line and therefore ripe for the public, is also objectively so or is also so clear to others, and possibly is even questioned by ourselves at a later time.

Actually I can *always* only be a witness with the reservation "according to the present best knowledge and conscience"—but that *I should* be. And leave the rest to Jesus. Otherwise, waiting for the right time can also lead to the cowardly shirking and waiting for the day of never-never—piously disguised by the reference to the not-yet ripe time.

Loosening the Mortar
February 12, 2022

In a conversation someone told how he often feels standing in front of a huge wall, without any idea how to get over it and what is behind it. The image triggered the idea in me: Perhaps God is already in the process of loosening the mortar around individual stones (perhaps the doctor's talks that have begun will also serve this purpose!) and thus, through the gaps, transform the wall into a climbing wall with steps that can be climbed little by little. That, at any rate, is the longing; and the hope.

Growing in faith: As strength wanes, we should expect that, despite life experience, not everything will be easier for us—especially as the nature of challenges and needs changes and you can't just recall and transfer what you've learned so far as if you were fighting the umpteenth flu.

Trust and Obey
February 13, 2022

In the service, the thought came to me:

A small child first trusts, predominantly instinctively; and then it increasingly learns some self-control over his or her world. In old age, the process is reversed: control decreases or must be consciously relinquished. This process teaches and demands trust on a new, namely this time, conscious level in view of the knowledge of how uncertain our life is (which is not yet so clear to the small child). What superficially can easily be perceived as a regression, and therefore be evaluated negatively, is actually a challenge for further development, for growing strength through growing weakness, as paradoxical as that may sound.

The service was about Jesus's obedience (Hebrews 5). My further thought: In the New Testament we are also often called to obedience. The advantage of obedience: Action is already possible, while trust as an attitude still has to grow afterwards.

Raise Up Your Heads
March 6, 2022

Word for the week: The reason the Son of God appeared was to destroy the devil's work. (1 John 3:8)

What are the works of the devil?

They begin by sowing evil seeds in hearts—mistrust, fear, envy, covetousness, etc.; and where these seeds sprout and the weeds are not fought, there will eventually be visible consequences.

Jesus came to expose this and make new beginnings possible through transformation in communion with him. He also sows.

Why doesn't Jesus just destroy the destructive power, when that is actually his goal?

It is a struggle for hearts in which we are and should remain involved; they are processes. From both sides, switches are not simply flipped, plugs not pulled or the like.

Jesus does not simply end the war, even if a heart attack for Putin certainly seems to us a desirable intervention by him.

This view probably oversimplifies things far too much. We tend to see ourselves more as victims with regard to the evil in us, more passively as seduced, and more actively with regard to the good. But no war falls from the sky. Not even Russia's war on Ukraine. It has a complicated history, in which also a lot of turning a blind eye, fading out, indifference, tolerated or advocated wrong values play a role, on an individual as well as on a social level; in which not only short-term but also long-term course settings have an effect. (There are, however, not only more or less obvious continuous developments in the "maturation" of evil, but also downright quantum leaps that defy any insight on our part; to leave that out would also be another version of simplification.) We ignore all such things when we concentrate only on the last explosion of evil and then, of course, in the face of the shambles, desperately want to claim Jesus's intervention and clamp down. How many of us (everywhere) who are now crying out for help have sought Jesus's counsel in similar intensity before, personally and in community, and might have been able to influence course-setting by doing so? Not that I want to say that Putin is now simply God's punishment for such failures—such a thought would also fall far too short; especially since we know that Jesus really suffers in and with his creation. And of course at least the little children who are dying now have no active part in all the misery anyway, but are really just victims. And of course Putin's actions cannot be justified by anything, rather he will have to justify himself before his creator and judge at some point. But the words *turning point* and *waking up* that have been used so often in the last few weeks and the lightbulb moments of our politicians make it somewhat clear that good and evil, right and wrong, truth and lies are not quite as easy to divide up as black and white.

The weekly verse remains true, even if we now only think to see the works of the devil and their now so longed-for destruction does not seem equally obvious.

And then suddenly it came to my mind: When you see these things happening (it is only natural to hang your heads or to bury them deep in the sand, but ...) *raise your heads*, because your redemption is near. (Luke 21:28) No idea, again, in what stage of history we are, and that "near" in Jesus's understanding of time can be very different from how we feel, I am also very aware. Nevertheless: The present disillusionments and fundamental shocks—first by coronavirus (how little is our life at our disposal!), now war (how naive we were towards the possibility of undisguised evil!)—can well be counted among the omens of coming redemption, however bad the way may still become for many until the end. And these shocks of our self-assurances and self-evident facts can at least lead to the insight into our limits—and can drive us into the arms of him, with whom alone in the end the security is to be found, which we long for and which no man can give us and guarantee.

Yesterday a psychologist from Hamburg confirmed the increasingly insecure feeling of many people in life, their fear of losing control; he sees demonstrations as a helpful way of not remaining alone with this and with the feeling of powerlessness. For us as Christians, there are even more alternatives to powerlessness: Helping people to become realistic and showing them and building bridges to our Lord as well as possible that continues to make sense and now more than evere.

Even evil still tries to maintain the appearance of good. The mendacity of war propaganda is so obvious and absurd, but still it is tried, and some even still fall for it, though surely at least partly because of brainwashing and lack of other sources of information.

Sea and Fog, Land and Light
March 12, 2022

Bible reading today: John 12:34–36. These verses seem unwieldy. On the one hand is the invitation to seek or enter the light while it is still possible, and then "When he had finished speaking, Jesus left and hid himself from them." He does not make it easy for people. Perhaps, among other things, so that they recognize whether they are serious enough to invest time in the search for truth?

"Believe in the light"—isn't light, when it is present, unmistakable? There is certainly such light, for example daylight. But if I am walking in the dark at night, perhaps in the forest, and then see a glow of light somewhere, I may well ask myself whether it is trustworthy, whether I should go in that direction or not. A mountain hut or lighthouse would be similar images for a light that demands a directional decision.

Someone once said, "Trust does not at all mean that you always feel safe. It means that you keep going."

An emergency phone call came in the evening; I continued to think about the words from the morning that go with it: Sometimes we feel like we're on a big sea in a small boat and it's dark and foggy and we have no idea where the land is, where we're going. And then every now and then a light flashes in the distance. A lighthouse. And every time we see the light flashing, we can try to steer there, correct our direction if necessary. Then suddenly fog comes again and we see nothing flashing. But the lighthouse is still there. So we keep our eyes open until the fog lifts again. And then we aim at the direction again, row a bit closer to it.

The picture of the boat in the dark is quite realistic, I think; it also makes it clear how much strength it costs us and how much we have to do and that all this can frighten us. And it points out to us that the darkness is not the only thing, not even the sea, but there *is* land and light. And the hours when things are better also point to that.

Today Is Today
March 14, 2022

Today, after a long time, I looked through older entries again—and I'm shocked at how much I've already forgotten in such a short time. That makes me restless; it's annoying. And I ask myself what I should think of this experience, which I have already made so often. My hope, my expectation, that I could or must be able to store and recall important things better, is obviously unrealistic. Although it would be actually so necessary and meaningful for spiritual stability! Certainly, not everything is important every day with the same urgency. So maybe it has to do with the fact that each day has its own priorities, for me as well as for those around me. To have everything in view at some point is not possible anyway. And probably not necessary. No driver takes always his complete workshop with him on his trips "just in case." Then good tools would become ballast. So maybe my longing reflects some counterproductive need for security, security from crises and in crises by "knowledge accumulation" instead of dependence?

The manna in the desert was also given only in daily rations. And if I feel the hand and closeness of the giver in my respective "ration," which does me good at that moment, leaves an imprint on me, shouldn't that be enough? For today and also as a reason of hope for the coming day? (especially since I have the comfortable possibility of the keyword search in my digital diary permanently, so in the end nothing really disappears anyway, in contrast to the options of our ancestors ...) Relying on possessions instead of the giver is probably not only tempting in the material, a trap, but also in the spiritual realm. "Blessed are the poor ... " The Holy Spirit has enough ways to remind me in due time of what is then necessary. Thinking these thoughts relieves and liberates. Today is today. That is enough.

Run, Stumble or Crawl
March 18, 2022

Bible reading today: Jesus was shaken (John 13:21): The events, the betrayal, the imminent loneliness—this does not leave him cold, even if he himself has planned everything consciously; to live through it is something else again than to plan it. "He loved to the end" (John 13:1), including Judas, presumably.

On this background and thinking of the life-threatening hardship of friends the following went through my mind:

Every crisis ultimately involves the same simple challenge—to trust that God's love is reliable, that his grace is sufficient, that his promise of salvation is sincere, that his mercy and patience are never at an end, that he will bring us to our eternal home—certainly not by sparing us problems, but by being with us when we go through them.

Ultimately, the decisive question is only whether we long for him, are at peace with him. That is what we should concentrate on therefore, not on what frightens us. Because then Jesus, our Good Shepherd, takes responsibility for our lives. In his arms we are ultimately safe, no matter what may threaten us. If we "fear" (in the sense of reverence) him more than anything else, we need not fear anything else. (I know, weak as we are, we still often do, yet we have a greater truth to cling to, and we can learn.) Not sickness, not loneliness, not weakness, not brokenness, not guilt, and finally not death will be the end. Rather, eternal fellowship will be the end, with our heavenly Father and Jesus, our brother, in our eternal home. *That* is the truth. That is the framework that gives a stable frame to the picture of our lives. We can trust our God. So will we? Do we long to turn to him, day by day, hour by hour? That is the question that every crisis asks us. And the important point is: We don't have to have strong faith to do this. We can run into his arms, but we can also stumble or crawl, again and again, like a little child learning to use his legs.

He knows the longing of our heart. He is a merciful God. And his arms are a kind of mobile refuge that nothing can destroy.

The Gospel for Powerlessness
March 22, 2022

n-tv.de interview with crisis researcher S. Grünewald:

We have identified six coping strategies that people use to get out of their powerlessness. The first is constant updating of the news situation in the hope that the redeeming news of the end of the war will come. But this drags people down even more, since the good news fails to materialize. The second strategy is to conjure up normality, including diversionary tactics: people throw themselves into work or go shopping or hiking to clear their heads. The third strategy is to help by donating money, packing packages or providing housing for refugees. ...

The fourth is to show solidarity through actions, in conversations or demonstrations. In this way, one feels a sense of solidarity and has the feeling that the masses can make a difference that the individual cannot. Thoughts of escape are the fifth coping strategy. Some have already packed their bags or are at least thinking about where they would emigrate. I already mentioned the sixth possibility: hoping for higher help. And if that doesn't work, that is, if China or the Russian people don't help, then you at least help yourself by hoarding food and equipping yourself for emergencies.

The six coping strategies have different track records. You can also get drunk every day to cope with something bad. But that's not sustainable, nor does it work long-term. Reading news every minute drags you down deeper and deeper. You hope and hope for a turnaround, but there's always more horrible news. It's hard on the mind.[26]

None of the six strategies can place the experience in a larger horizon, all of them are purely inner-worldly.

Fear cannot be given the prospect of protection, there is no real hope for justice and healing at the end of the tunnel; evil remains a barely endurable and successfully destructive superiority. Without a perspective of eternity, only shades of darkness actually remain.

The world desperately needs the *whole* gospel.

PARTING PERSPECTIVE

To end with this may seem strangely abrupt, but that is the nature of things—life and faith are not yet finished. The summit is still ahead of us. I hope that this book helps us to go on, encourages us, raises our anticipation and strengthens us. The apostle Paul found impressive words for this path (1 Corinthians 13:12–13, ESV):

> For now we see in a mirror dimly,
> but then face to face.
> Now I know in part;
> then I shall know fully,
> even as I have been fully known.
> So now faith, hope, and love abide,
> these three;
> but the greatest of these is love.

FOOTNOTES

Chapter 1: Living with the One Who Is Different
1. Eldredge, J. (2013). Der ungezähmte Messias. (English title: Beautiful Outlaw.) Asslar: Gerth Medien GmbH, 190ff.
2. Blatt, H. (2006). Josua. Marburg: Francke-Buchhandlung GmbH, 18.
3. Reeves, M. (2012). Delighting in the Trinity. Downers Grove, IL, USA: InterVarsity Press.
4. Ibid., 16f.
5. Zink, J. (1979). Was bleibt, stiften die Liebenden. ("What abides the Loving Brings About.") 2.Aufl.1979. Stuttgart: Kreuz-Verlag.
6. http://leben-und-spiritualität.de/die-bettlerin-und-die-rose. ("The Beggar and the Rose.") (accessed March 24, 20220)

Chapter 2: Communicating with the Different One
1. Elliot, E. (1979). Shadow of the Almighty. Bromley, Kent, England: Send the Light Trust, 81.
2. Tozer, A. W. (1994). The Best of A. W. Tozer. Grand Rapids, MI: Baker Book House, 218.
3. Wells, T. (1985). A Vision For Missions. Edinburgh: The Banner of T ruth Trust, 23.
4. Redman, M. No other source information available.
5. Lewis, C. S. (1959). Das Gespräch mit Gott. (English title: Reflections on the Psalms.) Einsiedeln: Benziger, 132.
6. Yancey, P. (2003). Sehnsucht nach dem Unsichtbaren. (English title: Reaching for the Invisible God.) Asslar: Gerth Medien, 119.
7. Watson, T. https://biblesnet.com/Thomas%20Watson%20Man%20s%20Chief%20End%20is%20to%20Glorify%20God.pdf (accessed March 16, 2021)
8. Trueman, C. (2013). Tragic Worship. https://www.firstthings.com/article/2013/06/tragic-worship (accessed March 16, 2021)
9. Pruitt, T. Is Your Church Worship More Pagan Than Christian https://www.christianity.com/church/worship-and-hymns/is-your-church-worship-more-pagan-than-christian.html (accessed March 16, 2021)
10. Kopfermann, A. (January 25, 2019) Gott ist nicht mein Kumpel. https://www.pro-medienmagazin.de/gesellschaft/menschen/2019/01/25/gott-ist-nicht-mein-kumpel ("God is not my buddy.") (accessed March 16, 2021)

Chapter 3: Existing in a Search for Meaning
1. See chapter 1, note 6.
2. See chapter 1, note 6.

3. Brother Andrew. No other source information available.

4. Ortberg, J. (2002). The Life You've Always Wanted. Grand Rapids, MI: Zondervan, 212.

5. Schnepel, E. Das Buch mit den sieben Siegeln. ("The Book with the Seven Seals.") No date. Bad Liebenzell: Verlag der Liebenzeller Mission, 53.

6. Ibid., 103.
7. Lilje, H. (1940). Das letzte Buch der Bibel. ("The Last Book of the Bible.") Berlin: Im Furche-Verlag, 15.

8. Ibid., 16.
9. Keller, T. (2008). The Reason For God. New York: Penguin Group, 209.
10. Lewis, C. S. (1998). Narnia. Ueberreuter, 427.
11. Willard, T. No other source information available.
12. https://www.endlichlebendig.de/zitate-mutter-teresa (accessed April 3, 2022)

Chapter 4: Wondering as a Response to Reality

1. Mangalwadi, V. (2014). Das Buch der Mitte. (English title: The Book that Made Your World.) Basel: fontis -Brunnen, 29.

2. Ibid., 36.
3. Warren, K. (2013). Freude, die mich trägt. (English title: Choose Joy.) Gießen: Brunnen, 29.

4. Peck, M. S. (2015). The People of the Lie. Hrg. Cornerstone Digital.

Chapter 5: Doubting as Training for Reassurance

1. Lewis, C. S. (1998). Narnia. Ueberreuter, 432.
2. Kühner, A. (1992). Überlebens-Geschichten für jeden Tag. ("Survival stories for every day.") Neukirchen-Vluyn: Aussaat Verlag, 237f.
3. https://www.youtube.com/watch?v=uFgCtMFVa_U (accessed April 3, 2022)

4. Goritschewa, T. No further sources could be found.
5. https:/de.wikipedia.org/wiki/Der_Zauberlehrling (accessed April 3, 2022)
6. MacDonald, G. (1892). The Hope of the Gospel. Public Domain.
7. Habermas, G. (1990). Dealing with Doubt. http://www.garyhabermas.com/books/dealing_with_doubt/dealing_with_doubt.htm (accessed April 3, 2022)

8. Mangalwadi, V. (2014). Das Buch der Mitte. Basel: fontis -Brunnen, 75.
9. Ibid., 76.
10. https://www.newslichter.de/2020/04/gibt-es-ein-leben-nach-der-geburt (accessed April 1, 2022)
11. Lennox was speaker at the 2015 autumn conference of the German branch of InterVarsity Fellowship.
12. Nearly identical with my handwritten note: https://www.reformiert-potsdam.de/Mitteilungen-Texte%20Links%20Buecher%202.%20Gebot%20Leo%20Lew%20Tolstoi.htm (accessed April 3, 2022)

13. Quoted by Habermas, G. https://www.garyhabermas.com/books/dealing_with_doubt/dealing_with_doubt.htm, Chapter.1.

14. Op. Cit., Habermas, Chapter .8.

15. Klepper, J. (1976). Unter dem Schatten deiner Flügel. ("Under the shadow of Your Wings.") München: dtv, 264.

16. Lütz, M. (2009). Gott. München: Knaur, 287.

17. Yancey, P. (2003). Sehnsucht nach dem Unsichtbaren. Asslar: Gerth Medien, 38.

18. Ibid., 95

19. Ibid., 226

20. Ibid., 304

21. Ibid., 99

22. Vitale, V. (January 12, 2017). A Slice of Infinity: Science Has Disproved God. https://us5.campaign-archive.com/?u=45b75085e6ab57e339ea89d67&id=6e438e2d77&e=d265000399 (accessed April 3, 2022)

23. Lewis, C. S. (2014). Christian Reflections. Grand Rapids, Michigan, USA: Eerdmans, 52–53.

24. Lewis, C. S. (1995). Die letzte Nacht der Welt. (English title: The World's Last Night.) Gießen: Brunnen, 30f.

25. Yancey, P. (2003). Sehnsucht nach dem Unsichtbaren. Asslar: Gerth Medien, 49.

26. Haugen, G. A. mit G.Hunter (2009). Freiheit für Linh. (English title: Terrify No More.) Gießen: Brunnen-Verlag, 259.

27. Metaxas, E. (2013, 5.Auflage). Bonhoeffer. Holzgerlingen: SCM Haenssler, 196.

28. https://www.nordkirche.de/nachrichten/nachrichten-detail/nachricht/protestanten-debattieren-ueber-judenmission-europa-und-rechtspopulisten (accessed March 2022)

Chapter 6: Teaming Up to Believe, Hope and Love Together

1 .Chambers, O. No further source information available.

2. https://www.godreports.com/2013/07/corrie-ten-booms-chocolate-sermon-sweetened-hearers-to-the-gospel/ (accessed March 29, 2022)

3. Niles, D. T. in: Bailey, K. E. (2008). Jesus through Mediterranean Eyes. Downers Grove, IL: InterVarsity Press, 203.

4. Ibid., 204.

5. Ibid., 204.

6. Engelhardt, M., in: Rundbrief des Evangelischen Pfarrvereins Nr. 1, Juni 2015, S.8f. Engelhardt is city dean in Freiburg.

7. Eareckson, J. (1994). Secret Strength: For Those Who Search. Oregon: Multnomah Books, 61.

8. Keller, T. (2008). The Reason For God. New York: Penguin Group, 251.

9. Stahl, M. https://www.youtube.com/watch?v=8VMgMRddYRA (accessed April 4, 2022)

10. Cunningham, L. and Hamilton, D. J. with Rogers, J. (2000). Why Not Women? Seattle: Youth With A Mission, 138.
11. Buchanan, M. (2001). Your God Is Too Safe. Multnomah Books, 132.
12. Ibid., 108.
13. Bürki, H. (1983). Der Brief an Titus. Wuppertaler Studienbibel. Wuppertal: R. Brockhaus Verlag, 156f.
14. Witt, W. G. (2020). Icons of Christ. Waco, Texas 76798: Baylor University Press eBook, 77f.
15. Smith, M. B., Kern, I. (Hrg.) (2000) Ohne Unterschied? ("Without Difference?") Gießen: Brunnen, 124.

Chapter 7: Trusting as Guidance on Tough Roads

1. v.Kempen, T. (1950) Das Buch von der Nachfolge Christi. ("The Book of Following Jesus.") Hrg. Von W.Kröber. Stuttgart: Philipp Reclam Jun., 46
2. Yancey, P. (1990). Von Gott enttäuscht. (English title: Disappointment with God.) Metzingen: Ernst Franz Verlag, 179.
3. Burns, L. No further source information is available.
4. Pascal, B. https://www.zitate.eu/autor/blaise-pascal-zitate/280225 (accessed April 4, 2022)
5. MacDonald, G. (1989). Keep Climbing. Wheaton, Illinois: Tyndale House Publishers, 214.
6. Ibid., 214.
7. Ibid., 216.
8. Ibid., 218.
9. Ibid., 219.
10. Ibid., 221.
11. Ibid., 16.
12. Chambers, O. No further source information is available
13. Callaway, P. (2011). Was macht das Stinktier im Kofferraum? (English title: Laughing Matters) Moers: Brendow, 43.
14 Elliot, E. (2003). Im Schatten des Allmächtigen. (English title: Shadow of the Almighty.) R. Brockhaus, 100.
15. Naegeli, S. (1987). Die Nacht ist voller Sterne. 11.Aufl. Freiburg: Herder-Verlag, 44f.
16. Lilje, H. (1940). Das letzte Buch der Bibel. Berlin: Im Furche-Verlag, 166f.
17. Ortberg, J. (2002). The Life You've Always Wanted. Grand Rapids, MI: Zondervan, 212.
18. Peck, M. S. (2015). The People of the Lie. Hrg. Cornerstone Digital, 41.
19. Lewis, C. S. (1978). Pardon ich bin Christ. "(English title: Mere Christianity.
20. Quote comes from correspondence with an American friend.
21. Op. Cit., Peck, 123.
22. https://www.n-tv.de/politik/Wie-gefaehrlich-ist-der-Schoenheitswahn-

article21291363.html (accessed April 4, 2022)
23. Royer, H.-P., https://www.youtube.com/watch?v=z2g_F4Y_Bvo
24. Schlatter, A. (1953, 3.Auflage), Hülfe in Bibelnot. Gladbeck: Freizeiten-Verlag, 89f.
25. Schlatter, A. (1953, 3.Auflage), Hülfe in Bibelnot. ("Help in Bible Distress.") Gladbeck: Freizeiten-Verlag, 19.
26. Grünewald, S., https://www.n-tv.de/panorama/Langzeitfolgen-von-Krisen-Psychologe-spricht-ueber-Schockstarre-und-Aussichtslosigkeit-article23213540.html (accessed March 22, 2022)

ABOUT THE AUTHOR

Susanne Folkers grew up in Bünde/Westf. After high school she studied theology in Bielefeld, Heidelberg, Edinburgh and Göttingen and was ordained 1985 in Oldenburg. Then she worked in congregations alongside her husband, first within the Evangelical Lutheran Church of Oldenburg, then within the Evangelical Church of North Rhine-Westphalia. The couple has four adult married children and four grandchildren. Since retiring in 2018, they live in Schaumburg/Lower Saxony.

www.ingramcontent.com/pod-product-compliance
Lightning Source LLC
Chambersburg PA
CBHW071219080526
44587CB00013BA/1426